FINDING
YOUR OWN
NORTH STAR

FINDING
YOUR OWN
NORTH STAR

HOW TO CLAIM
THE LIFE YOU WERE
MEANT TO LIVE

MARTHA BECK

PIATKUS

Copyright © 2001 by Martha Beck

First published in the UK in 2001 by
Judy Piatkus (Publishers) Limited
5 Windmill Street
London W1T 2JA

Reprinted in 2002

e-mail: info@piatkus.co.uk

First published in the USA in 2001 by
Crown Publishers of Random House

The moral right of the author has been asserted

A catalogue record for this book is
available from the British Library

ISBN 0 7499 2257 5

This book has been printed on paper manufactured
with respect for the environment using wood from
managed sustainable resources

Printed and bound in Great Britain by
Butler & Tanner Ltd, Frome and London

Karen, this one's for you.

AUTHOR'S NOTE

Throughout this book, I have drawn heavily on examples from the clients in my Life Design program and workshops. However, to protect their privacy and ensure confidentiality, I have changed their names, descriptions, and other identifying characteristics. I am profoundly grateful to them for their example and trust in me; in helping them find their own North Stars, they have helped me find mine.

I have not disguised the names of any members of my family, my friends, or my sainted beagle, Cookie.

ACKNOWLEDGMENTS

This book owes a great deal to my students at the American Graduate School of International Management (Thunderbird), who put up with my unorthodox teaching style, forgave me for my mistakes, shared their life and career histories, and urged me to explore my interest in "life design." In particular, I'd like to thank Jessica Walters and Susan Bagdadhi for their insight, energy, and sensitivity. I'd also like to thank the individuals who allowed me to interview them, in an undisguised attempt to steal the secrets of their success.

The ideas for this book began to take shape while I was working as a research assistant for Dr. John Kotter, of Harvard Business School. I thank him for hiring me despite my total lack of experience or ability, and for being patient while I developed a little of each.

I'm also deeply grateful to Dr. John Beck, of Andersen Consulting's Institute for Strategic Change (no, the name is *not* a coincidence). Many of the ideas in this book came from John, and all of them were run through his brain at least three or four times as we debated over our morning lattes.

Aristotle believed that a physician had to experience a disease before trying to cure it. I've definitely been through the process of losing and regaining my own North Star, and without certain people as guides, I would never have found my way back. It's impossible to name all these people, but some of them are (in the order they showed up) Rebecca Nibley, Robert Bennion, Will Reimann, Sibyl Johnston, Ruth Killpack and the gang at Aspen, Lydia and Sylvia Nibley, Dawn Swanson, Annette Rogers, and all my brave, wonderful clients.

My incredible editor, Betsy Rapoport, has been not only a friend and North Star guide, but a midwife to this book and my writing in general. I can't thank her enough for her brilliance, kindness, wit, and sheer endurance. My agent Beth Vesel and her assistant Emilie Stewart have also been stalwart supporters. My magazine editors, including Jeanie Pyun, Lisa Benenson, Marcia Menter, Carol Kramer (and all the other folks at *Real Simple*), encouraged me to push "life design" ideas further and put them in readable form. It has been a privilege having them as teachers.

Finally my love and thanks to the population of my Stella Polaris: John, Kevin, Kat, Adam, Liz, Cookie the Intrepid, and especially Karen. Their presence in my life is daily proof that even impossible dreams come true.

CONTENTS

INTRODUCTION

"Right in the middle of my life, I realized that I wasn't where I wanted to be. It was like I'd wandered off the right path into a very, *very* bad neighborhood. I don't even want to remember how scary that space was—makes me feel like I'm gonna die or something. I'm only telling you about it because a lot of good came of it in the long run. So anyway, I don't even know how I ended up so far off course. I felt like I'd been sleepwalking."—*Dan, age 41*

This story could have come from any one of the hundreds of people I've met in my office, classes, and seminars, but it didn't. As a matter of fact, "Dan" is short for Dante, as in Dante Alighieri. The paragraph above is my own exceedingly loose rendition of the first twelve lines of *The Divine Comedy,* written in 1307. Sometimes I tell clients about it, because it helps them believe they aren't the first people who've ever snapped awake at midlife, only to find themselves dazed, unhappy, and way off course. It's been happening at least since the Middle Ages, and not only to the middle-aged.

I see a lot of folks like Dan in my line of work. I offer a service called "life design." It isn't therapy, although I do tend to talk a lot with my clients about their feelings and personal histories. It isn't career counseling, although I've helped many people spiff up their résumés, prep for job interviews, and refine business plans. Life design, at least the way I practice it, is the process of helping people find what Dante called *"la verace via,"* the true path. Not that there's only one true path, you understand. There are as many paths as there are people, and the only one I can chart is my own. I have no idea, for example, where your true path may lie. But you do.

In *The Divine Comedy,* the poet Virgil shows up out of nowhere— poof!—to guide Dante out of the Dark Wood of Error. I certainly hope this happens for you, too, but I wouldn't hold my breath. And God knows, I'm no Virgil. What I am is a coach who can help you recognize your true path, find your way back to it, and stay on course. After reading thousands of helpful books, getting lost in my own Dark Wood of Error several million times, and helping hundreds of people create lives where their souls can thrive, I've developed concepts and tools for facilitating the process. This book contains the best advice I can give.

Though each person's life path is different, I believe that the human journey, writ large, has some universal aspects. All cultures, in every geographic region and historical period, have idealized the qualities of truth, love, and joy. I've never had a client who wasn't in search of these things, who didn't feel that a blend of these components is both our real home and the best version of our inner nature. When Dante went off looking for a situation where he could experience the ultimate realization of these qualities, he called the goal Paradise. You can call it Heaven, Nirvana, the Garden of Allah, Enlightenment, a condition resulting from high levels of serotonin in the brain, or Disneyland—I don't really care, so long as we have some shorthand label for the ultimate manifestation of our potential for good and happiness. I think of this condition as the North Star.

According to my dictionary, the North Star, known to its friends as Stella Polaris, is "situated close to the north pole of the heavens." Because of its location, the North Star doesn't appear to move around in the sky as the other stars do; it is a "fixed point" that can always be used to figure out which way you're headed. Explorers and mariners can depend on Polaris when there are no other landmarks in sight. The same relationship exists between you and your right life, the ultimate realization of your potential for happiness. I believe that a knowledge of that perfect life sits inside you just as the North Star sits in its unalterable spot. You may think you're utterly lost, that you're going to die a bewildered death in the Dark Wood of Error. But brush away the leaves, wait for the clouds to clear, and you'll see your destiny shining as brightly as ever: the fixed point in the constantly changing constellations of your life.

I've been privileged to watch many people discover their own North Stars—and it always is a discovery, an "uncovering," rather than a creation ex nihilo. Even people who have never experienced much happiness, who have been plagued since birth by confusion, injustice, and pain, know exactly what set of conditions will allow them to fulfill their potential while creating the greatest positive impact on the world. I guarantee that you have a similar image inside you.

Once you've found your own North Star, keeping it in view is a fine way to stay on course—as long as the sky remains clear. But what about the cloudy nights, the dark tunnels, the moments when you realize that your soul is acutely nearsighted and you've lost your glasses? In situations where you feel utterly befogged, you may need some help figuring out where your North Star lies. This is what compasses are for. Whichever direction you turn, the needle of a compass remains pointed at Polaris.

In moments when you can't see your destiny, or can't believe that it's really guiding you, it helps to know that you have several different "compasses" built into your brain and body. In Chapters 1 through 8, you'll learn how to read your internal "compasses" to guide you in the search for your true path. If your life is cloudy and you're far, far off course, you may have to go on faith for a while, but eventually you'll learn that every time you trust your internal navigation system, you end up closer to your right life. By reading these compasses, you can continue the journey toward your own North Star even during the times (and there will be many) when you feel blind and lost.

Knowing what your own North Star looks like and understanding the built-in compasses that guide you toward it are necessary but insufficient conditions for actually reaching the life you were meant to live.

You also need vehicles to carry you forward. Fortunately, you have them. Your energy, ingenuity, relationships, and resources are all vehicles that move you through your life. Most people, however, don't drive all that well. Their lives often feel out of control, as if they're being steered by some hostile power whose single-minded goal is to keep them away from their right lives. If this is how you feel, you'll find some helpful driver's education tips in Chapters 9 through 11. They will help you regain control and steer your life in the direction of your North Star.

The last thing this book will do is draw you a map of the terrain you'll have to cover once your life starts to change—because, if you follow the advice in the first two sections, it will. If you've lost your true path, you'll have to make changes in order to find your way back to it. Once you're on course, you'll discover that change, in the form of growth and forward progress, is an intrinsic and unalterable component of a fulfilling existence. As any good Buddhist will tell you, the only way to find permanent joy is by embracing the fact that nothing is permanent. Chapters 12 through 15 will discuss the "patterned disorder" that organizes the chaos of change, so that even on a road no one has traveled before, you'll have some idea what dangers you face, and how to conquer them.

I'm not going to tell you that all this is going to be painless, but I can assure you that it will be wonderful. Take it from Dan. You may recall that in his case, the way back to *la verace via* lay directly through Hell. Dante's journey took him as low as a human being could sink, through his worst fears and most bitter truths, down to the very center of the earth. And then, by continuing straight "downward" *through* the center and beyond, he was suddenly headed up. Before him he could see "the beautiful things that Heaven bears," things like purpose, fulfillment, excitement, compassion, and delight. He was still tired and scared, but he wasn't sleepwalking, and he wasn't lost. There was still a long road ahead of him, but it was the right road. And so, Dante wrote, "we came forth, and once more saw the stars." Once you get that far, you're on your way to Paradise.

Finding Your Own

NORTH
STAR

THE
DISCONNECTED SELF

Melvin worked as a middle manager at IBM, and a miserable middle manager Melvin made. If clinical depression had a phone voice, it would sound just like Melvin's did the morning he called me to see if I could take him on as a client. He'd been feeling sort of flat and listless for a while, he said—no big deal, just the past couple of decades. Lately, things had reached the point where Melvin's work performance and marriage were both showing signs of strain. He thought the problem might be his job, and for the past month or two he'd been surreptitiously checking upscale want ads and sending his résumé to friends at other companies. He'd gotten a few nibbles, but nothing that really interested him. Melvin said all this in dull but fluent Executese, rich in words like *incentivize* and *satisfice*.

I decided to give Melvin the little verbal phone quiz I sometimes use to evaluate potential clients before they spend time and money in my office. I asked him his age (forty-five), his marital status (separated, no children), and job history (a Big Blue man since the day he left college). Then we got to the questions that really interest me.

"So, Melvin," I said. "When you were a little kid, did you have an imaginary friend?"

"Excuse me?" said Melvin.

I repeated the question.

"I really don't remember," said Melvin, stiffly.

"Okay," I said. "Is there anything you do regularly that makes you forget what time it is?"

"Time?" Melvin echoed.

"Yes," I said, "do you ever look up from something you're doing to find that hours and hours have gone by without your noticing?"

"Wait," said Melvin. "I have to write this down."

"No, no," I said, "you really don't. Do you laugh more in some situations than in others?"

"Listen," said Melvin tensely, "I didn't know I was going to have to answer these kinds of questions. I thought you could tell me a little about midcareer job changes, that's all. I've had no time to prepare."

I had a mental picture of Melvin calling in the marketing department to measure his laughter rates and interview family members about his favorite childhood fantasies. "Melvin," I said, "relax. I don't grade on a curve. Just tell me everything you can remember about the best meal you ever had in your life."

There was a very long silence. Then he said, "I'm sorry, but I'll have to put together some data and get back to you on these questions. Will next week be soon enough?"

I never heard from Melvin again.

Actually, I never heard from Melvin in the first place—at least not all of him. As a matter of fact, I don't think *Melvin* had ever heard from all of Melvin. The conversation I had was with Melvin's "social self," the part of him that had learned to value the things that were valued by the people around him. This "social self" couldn't tell me what Melvin loved, enjoyed, or wanted, because it literally didn't know. Those facts did not fall in its area of experience, let alone expertise. It didn't remember Melvin's preferences or his childhood, because it had spent years telling him to ignore what he preferred and stop acting like a child.

There was, of course, a part of Melvin that knew the answer to every question I'd asked him. I call this the "essential self." Melvin's essential self was born a curious, fascinated, playful little creature, like every healthy baby. After forty-five years, it still contained powerful urges toward individuality, exploration, spontaneity, and joy. But by repressing these urges for years and years, Melvin's social self had lost access to them. It was inevitable that Melvin would also lose his true path, because *while his social self was the vehicle carrying him through life, it was cut off from his essential self, which had all the navigational equipment that pointed toward his North Star.*

Melvin was like a ship that had lost its compass or charts. It wasn't just the wrong job that made him feel so aimless and uninspired; it was the loss of his life's purpose. If Melvin had become a client, I would have advised him to stay put at IBM until he had learned to consciously reconnect with his essential self. Then he would have regained the capacity to steer his own course toward happiness, whether that lay in his present job and marriage or in a completely different life.

NAVIGATIONAL BREAKDOWN

I base all my counseling on the premise that each of us has these two sides: the essential self and the social self. The essential self contains several sophisticated compasses that continuously point toward your North Star. The social self is the set of skills that actually carry you toward this goal. Your essential self wants passionately to become a doctor; the social self struggles through organic chemistry and applies to medical school. Your essential self yearns for the freedom of nature; your social self buys the right backpacking equipment. Your essential self falls in love; your social self watches to make sure the feeling is reciprocal before allowing you to stand underneath your beloved's window singing serenades.

This system functions beautifully as long as the social and essential selves are communicating freely with each other and working in perfect synchrony. However, not many people are lucky enough to experience such inner harmony. For reasons we'll discuss in a moment, the vast majority of us put other people in charge of charting our course through life. We never even consult our own navigational equipment; instead, we steer our lives according to the instructions of people who have no idea how to find our North Stars. Naturally, they end up sending us off course.

If your feelings about life in general are fraught with discontent, anxiety, frustration, anger, boredom, numbness, or despair, your social and essential selves are not in sync. Life design is the process of reconnecting them. We'll start this process by clearly articulating the differences between the two selves, and understanding how communication between them broke down.

GETTING TO KNOW YOUR SELVES

Your essential self formed before you were born, and it will remain until you've shuffled off your mortal coil. It's the personality you got from your genes: your characteristic desires, preferences, emotional reactions, and involuntary physiological responses, bound together by an overall sense of identity. It would be the same whether you'd been raised in France, China, or Brazil, by beggars or millionaires. It's the basic you, stripped of options and special features. It is "essential" in two ways: first, it is the essence of your personality, and second, you absolutely need it to find your North Star.

The social self, on the other hand, is the part of you that developed in response to pressures from the people around you, including everyone from your family to your first love to the pope. As the most socially dependent of mammals, human babies are born knowing that their very survival depends on the goodwill of the grown-ups around them. Because of this, we're all literally designed to please others. Your essential self was the part of you that cracked your first baby smile; your social self noticed how much Mommy loved that smile, and later reproduced it at exactly the right moment to convince her to lend you the down payment on a condo. You still have both responses. Sometimes you smile involuntarily, out of amusement or silliness or joy, but many of your smiles are based purely on social convention.

Between birth and this moment, your social self has picked up a huge variety of skills. It learned to talk, read, dress, dance, drive, juggle, merge, acquire, cook, yodel, wait in line, share bananas, restrain the urge to bite—anything that won social approval. Unlike your essential self, which is the same regardless of culture, your social self was shaped by cultural norms and expectations. If you happen to have been born into a mafioso family, your social self is probably wary, street-smart, and ruthless. If you were raised by nuns in the local orphanage, it may be saintly and self-sacrificing. Whatever you learned to be, you're still learning. Your social self is hard at work, right this minute, struggling to make sure you're honest and loyal, or sweet and sexy, or tough and macho, or any other combination of things you believe makes you socially acceptable.

The social self is based on principles that often run contrary to our core desires. Its job is to know when those desires will upset other people, and to help us override natural inclinations that aren't socially acceptable. Here are some of the contradictory operational features that, mixed together, comprise the You we know and love:

YOUR TWO SELVES: BASIS OF OPERATIONS

Behaviors of the Social Self Are:	Behaviors of the Essential Self Are:
Avoidance-based	Attraction-based
Conforming	Unique
Imitative	Inventive
Predictable	Surprising
Planned	Spontaneous
Hardworking	Playful

As you can see, you are definitely an odd couple. Only in very lucky or wise people do the social and essential selves always agree that they're playing for the same team. For the rest of us, internal conflict is a way of life. Our two selves do battle against each other, in ways small and large, every single day.

Let's make up some details about the life of Melvin the Middle Manager, to serve as a hypothetical example. When his alarm clock rings at six A.M., Melvin's essential self tells him that he needs at least two more hours of sleep; he's been getting less than his body requires each night for the last several years, and he's chronically exhausted. His social self, however, reminds him that he's been late to work three times this month, and that the boss is starting to notice. Melvin gets up.

He eats breakfast alone. This floods his essential self with loneliness for his wife, who moved out last week. For just a minute, Melvin thinks about calling her, but his social self immediately nixes that idea. For one thing, it's six-thirty in the morning. For another thing, Melvin's wife is sleeping at her boyfriend's apartment. Melvin barely even notices his essential self's suggestion that he go after the boyfriend with a baseball bat, because his social self knows how wrong and futile that would be. Instead, Melvin goes to work.

At the office, Melvin's social self sits quietly through a meeting that bores his essential self almost to death. The guy next to him is a smarmy twenty-eight-year-old with an MBA from MIT who was recently pro-moted right past Melvin. Just looking at this guy makes Melvin's teeth clench. His essential self wants to squirt ink from his fountain pen onto the little twerp's oxford shirt, but his social self bars the way yet again. Instead, Melvin's essential self writes a nasty limerick about the MIT MBA in the margin of his notebook. Then his social self scribbles it out, lest it fall into the Hands of the Enemy.

And so it goes, hour after hour, day after day, week after week. After mediating this constant struggle for decades, Melvin's inner life is hol-low and numb. If you ask him what he's feeling, he won't have an answer; his social self doesn't know, and it is the *only* part of Melvin that is allowed to speak to others. Melvin's social self has kept him in his job, his marriage, and his life—but only by sending him off his true path. Now everything is falling apart. His sacrifices seem to have been for nothing. The problem isn't that Melvin's social self is a bad per-son—in fact, it's a very good person. It has the horsepower to get Melvin all the way to his North Star. But only his essential self can tell him where that is.

THE DISCONNECTED SELF

Most of my clients are like Melvin: responsible citizens who have muzzled their essential selves in order to do what they believe is the "right thing." There are, of course, people who fail—or refuse—to develop a social self. They live completely in essential-self world, never accommodating society in any way that runs contrary to their desires. But I very rarely see anyone like this in my practice. You, for example, are not one of them.

How do I know? Because if you were totally dominated by your essential self, you wouldn't be reading this. You'd avoid taking advice from any book, even if it happened to be the only thing available in the prison library. That's where you'd probably have to read it, because people without social selves generally end up in cages. If we all ignored our social selves, every neck of the human woods would be another variation on *Lord of the Flies;* people would be stabbing each other with forks, looting rest homes, having sexual relations with twenty-one-year-old interns in the Oval Office, and God knows what else.

So I'd lay heavy odds that you, personally, are heavily identified with your social self. You're reading this because you're the kind of person who seeks input from other people, people like life-design counselors and book authors. You're trying to make yourself a better person, and you're pretty darn good at it. Congratulations. Having a strong social self is a terrific asset. It's allowed you to sustain relationships, finish school, hold down jobs, and meet a lot of other goals. But if, in spite of all these achievements, you're feeling like Melvin—discontented and unfulfilled—I can tell you with a fair degree of certainty that your internal wiring is disconnected. You need to re-establish contact with your essential self.

Paradoxically, if you want to do a really good job at this, you're going to have to stop thinking about doing a really good job. *To find your North Star, you must teach your social self to relax and back off.*

LEARNING TO NOT-DO

I say these things from hard experience. For many years, I was so over-identified with my social self that I had to be practically beaten to death before I'd let it relax. Like anyone else, I based my social self on the values I'd learned from the people who raised me. In some ways, this was wonderful; in others, a bit frightening. My father, a university professor, was deeply committed to the culture of intellectual achievement. He and my mother raised their eight children without access to television, popular music, or any of the other brain candy of modern culture. Instead, we listened while my father read Homer to us in the original Greek, translating line by line. He taught me to read English at age four, French at eight. My parents would wake us up on especially clear summer nights to go outside and memorize the constellations. I remember lying in bed the night before my fifth birthday, paralyzed with anxiety because I hadn't accomplished nearly enough for a person of my advancing years.

The results of this enriched environment became obvious as soon as I started school: I got beat up more than any other girl in the history of Joaquin Elementary. Years later, I would spend hundreds of hours watching reruns of *Gilligan's Island* and *Star Trek* in a last-ditch effort to overcome terminal geekiness. But that was after I reached adulthood. Through adolescence, my social self remained obsessively committed to intellectual achievement. In college, I became a Chinese major, not because I liked it but because I'd heard it was really, really hard. My social self was convinced that if I could conquer this subject, I would win the Intellectual Olympics.

My essential self, which had been locked in a very cold, very small dungeon near the basement of my soul, *hated* being a Chinese major. I had to work like a maniac just to become a mediocre student, memorizing thousands of those impossibly intricate little characters, forgetting them with almost magical rapidity. I still think that the Chinese have a secret phonetic alphabet, one my professors spitefully decided to keep hidden from me. I pictured them assigning another couple of hundred characters for me to memorize, then locking their office doors and shrieking with laughter until they got the hiccups and had to lie down.

All of this is just to say that if you push far enough toward any extreme, you eventually reach its opposite. As I struggled my way through the foothills of Oriental scholarship, I began to stumble across bits and pieces of Asian philosophy. Right in the middle of my fourteen wretched daily study hours, I'd read something like this passage:

In the pursuit of knowledge,
every day something is added.
In the practice of the Way,
every day something is dropped.
Less and less do you need to force things,
until finally you arrive at non-action.
When nothing is done,
nothing is left undone.

The first time I read these lines, from the Chinese philosopher Lao-tzu, they hit me like an explosion. I had no idea what they meant, but I found myself crying like a baby. In retrospect, I can see that it was one of the first times my essential self felt welcome in my own mind. My social self, on the other hand, was deeply unnerved. Every day something is dropped, until you arrive at non-action? What kind of pinko heresy was this?

I'm sure this knee-jerk skepticism was exactly what Melvin the Middle Manager felt when I started asking him about his favorite meal. A lot of my clients react this way during our first few sessions. They come dressed for success, sit at attention, and write down everything I say. When I tell them to put away their notebooks, take off their shoes, and *stop doing anything,* they look as though they've just discovered I'm on the wrong medication entirely. Whether they say it out loud or not, I know what they're thinking: You don't get ahead in this life by "non-action." You get ahead *working,* by *pushing,* by making a gosh-darned *effort.*

What these people haven't yet experienced—what I had not yet experienced during my college years—is the feeling of "doing without doing." There's an old Taoist story about a group of Confucian intellectuals who, while strolling past a huge waterfall, glimpse a human body in the churning, roaring froth. Horrified, they gather by the banks, trying to figure out how to fish out the body and give it a decent funeral. The discussion comes to an abrupt end when an old man pops out of the water at their feet, dries himself off, and walks away.

Once the scholars have stopped gaping in astonishment, they run after the old man. "How did you do that?" they demand. "No one could swim in that water without being killed."

"Oh, no, it's really very easy," the old man tells them. "You just go up when the water goes up, and down when the water goes down."

The idea here is that when you relax the thinking mind, the rule-bound, anxiety-ridden social self, you are not simply stopping everything. Taoists believe that there is an immense benevolent force flowing through all reality, and that each of us—at least our essences—are a part of that force. Once you're aligned with this force (the Tao, or "Way"), you're like a surfer on the perfect wave; you move forward with tremendous power, but the only thing you have to do is go up when the water goes up, and down when the water goes down.

The way to do this is to turn off the rules you've learned from culture, and allow your essential self to come out and run the show. While the social self is rigid and fixed, the essential self is relaxed and responsive. In any situation, it can give you instructions about how to "not-do" in a way that carries you closer to your North Star.

I learned a lot about this while recovering from minor surgery. I'd been given a phone number I could call to contact a kindly nurse, who would answer any post-op questions I might have. A few days after the operation I found myself feeling rotten. I was in a lot of pain and very frustrated that I was required to rest until the pain went away. I finally picked up the phone and dialed the hotline, hoping the nurse would write me a prescription for a potent drug, one with both anesthetic and recreational properties. Instead, she gave me some of the best advice I've ever heard. "Listen," she said, "you're supposed to avoid stress and get lots of rest. *But if your soul wants to dance, staying in bed is stressful, and dancing is restful.*" I got up and went for a walk, and I started feeling better immediately. For me, that day, "non-action" meant getting up, not lying down.

Over years of personal experience and helping clients find their North Stars, I've come to believe very deeply in "doing without doing." I have a framed copy of the phrase, written in Chinese characters, hanging on my office wall. I've spent whole hours looking at it. However, I could no more write the characters from memory than I could remove my own appendix. Why not? Because, although Chinese is a great and majestic language, being a Chinese scholar is not part of my North Star. I truly believe that if it were, I'd have picked up the writing system without much effort. That's the wonderful thing about heading toward your North Star—compared to a strictly social-self existence, it's *fun and easy*. It's like falling in love or breathing. Not-doing can involve intense activity, but that activity will feel better by far than doing nothing.

MAKING BEAUCOUP BUCKS THROUGH NON-ACTION

"Fine," your social self might be saying right now. "This is all very sweet, this stuff about essences and reconnection and the Force. Thanks for sharing, Yoda, but I have a real life. I have to pay my rent. I have a cat to feed." Well, let me assure you, I started recommending that people resort to non-action only when I realized that *in today's economic climate, your essential self is a much more reliable moneymaker than your social self.*

I began to suspect this when I was a research assistant at Harvard Business School. I became firmly convinced of it while teaching at the American Graduate School of International Management, the top-ranked international business school in the United States. The more I focused on the realities of economic life, the more I came to see that the obedient, conformist behavior of the social self is no longer the key to high income and job security. The best way to make your fortune in today's economic climate is to master the spontaneous, creative "not-doing" of the essential self.

This wasn't always true. The generations that preceded us learned that the most dependable path to financial security was to do what Melvin did: earn a business degree, put on a gray wool suit, get a job with a big firm, and march in step all the way to the corner office. The better you followed the social rules, the greater your success. Listening to the beat of a different drummer was career suicide. Thoreau was thinking of the modern workplace when he wrote, "The majority of men lead lives of quiet desperation."

Now, however, business is undergoing a great sea change. (When I say "business," I mean the way you make your living, whether you're a banker or a street musician. As Robert Louis Stevenson pointed out, "everybody lives by selling something," and in this broad sense, we are all businesspeople.) There are thousands of books about this change, which I encourage you to read only if your essential self finds them interesting. Mine does, so I'll tell you what they say.

For one thing, a job with a large organization is no longer the bastion of stability it once was. Today, plodding methodically through bureaucratic structures and routines doesn't equal economic competitiveness—not for companies, not for you as an individual. Technological development, globalization, trends toward downsizing and outsourcing, the whole massive switch from an industrial to an information economy—all of these things mean that you need a whole new set of skills to be successful in business. Here's how the most marketable skills of yesteryear compare with those that will bring you success today.

MAKING MONEY: THEN AND NOW

What Used to Succeed in Business	What Succeeds in Business These Days
Consistency	Flexibility
Routinization	Innovation
Enormous size	Lean structure
Hierarchically controlled information	Open communication
Insistence on rational logic	Tolerance for incongruity
Reliance on tried-and-true methods	Openness to new ideas
Cultural conformity	Cultural diversity

Compare this chart with the one on page 5, the one that shows the qualities of the social and essential selves. As you can see, we are in the process of moving from a social-self environment to one where the essential self is much better equipped to succeed. This transformation is not yet complete, but it's accelerating all the time.

I've worked with many Melvins, guys who made the "responsible" choice by burying their essential selves and becoming Company Men, only to have quiet desperation overtake them at midlife. (These clients are almost always male, by the way. God knows we women face our own problems and injustices when it comes to getting ahead in business, but at least we're not under the illusion that we can match the perfect image of the Company Man, so we rarely try.) Today, the Melvins of the world are being downsized out of the very careers for which they sacrificed their essential selves.

By finding what you love best, by taking your true path to your own North Star, you put yourself in harmony with today's increasingly changeable economic environment and add value to every job in ways that are absolutely unique. Your skills and passions will stay with you when corporate loyalty fades, or technology makes your job obsolete, or an opportunity that never existed before suddenly crosses your path. The stolid, predictable social self doesn't have a clue about what to do in situations like these—but the creative and unorthodox essential self does. In an economy where it's getting harder and harder to find organizations that will chart a lifetime course for your career, finding your inner navigational system is not only personally gratifying—it's the best chance you have of achieving financial security.

EXERCISE: CONNECTION QUESTIONS

Whether you picked up this book hoping for an antidote to your existential angst or whether you just want to make a lot of money, I hope you've begun to see that establishing a clear connection with your essential self is a good idea. If you're not sure whether your two selves are working in tandem, grab a pencil and take the quiz below.

QUESTIONS FOR TESTING YOUR
SOCIAL-ESSENTIAL SELF CONNECTION

Please circle the most accurate response to each statement.

1. My life feels like a great adventure:

    often   sometimes   rarely   never

2. I feel sure I can solve any problem I encounter:

    often   sometimes   rarely   never

3. I have fun:

    often   sometimes   rarely   never

4. I laugh out loud:

    often   sometimes   rarely   never

5. I feel overwhelmed by gratitude:

    often   sometimes   rarely   never

6. I spend time in comfortable solitude:

    often   sometimes   rarely   never

7. I am fascinated by things I'm learning:

    often   sometimes   rarely   never

8. I feel deeply understood:

    often   sometimes   rarely   never

9. Things just seem to work out for me:

    often   sometimes   rarely   never

10. I get so involved in projects I forget to stop:

    often   sometimes   rarely   never

11. I use my imagination:

    often   sometimes   rarely   never

12. I do things I loved when I was a kid:

    often   sometimes   rarely   never

13. People seem to enjoy being around me:

    often   sometimes   rarely   never

14. I play:

    often   sometimes   rarely   never

15. I feel perfectly safe:

    often   sometimes   rarely   never

16. I get excited when it's time to go to work:

    often   sometimes   rarely   never

17. I feel mentally sharp and alert:
    often   sometimes   rarely   never

18. I have really cool ideas:
    often   sometimes   rarely   never

19. I love my body:
    often   sometimes   rarely   never

20. I'm flooded with love for other people:
    often   sometimes   rarely   never

21. I do new things, or old things in new ways:
    often   sometimes   rarely   never

22. I do what I want to, even if it's scary:
    often   sometimes   rarely   never

23. I'm completely relaxed with other people:
    often   sometimes   rarely   never

24. I feel intense physical pleasure:
    often   sometimes   rarely   never

25. I am very pleased with myself in general:
    often   sometimes   rarely   never

SCORING

The scoring for the Connection Questions test is very simple: **If you didn't answer "often" to *every one* of the questions, you could stand to be in closer contact with your essential self.**

My new clients usually find this scoring system insulting, even dangerous. Solidly ensconced in their social selves, they judge many of the experiences listed above to be *silly, selfish, unrealistic,* and *morally suspect.* Bob, for example, was shocked and angry when I told him how to score his quiz. "Don't put that in your book," he told me. "It's wrong. You'll just get people's hopes up—they're not supposed to feel all those things often." Andrea concurred. "I think anyone who felt all these things *often* would be a pretty irresponsible person," she told me primly.

When I ask people like Bob and Andrea to pick out the items that are particularly wicked and destructive, the ones that we *shouldn't* experience "often," they never do it. They just get furious and stomp off in a huff, the way Melvin did when he ended our sadly brief acquaintanceship. Just thinking about the questions was enough to make his social self run for the hills—directly away from his North Star.

Of course, not everyone responds this way. I have encountered a total of one client (I'll call her Lori) who answered "often" to every one of the Connection Questions during her very first appointment. After five minutes, I shook Lori's hand, told her there was nothing I could do for her that she wasn't already doing for herself, and wished her luck in the future—not that she needed it. I was not at all surprised when I started seeing articles in business magazines about Lori's wildly successful career. I'll bet her personal life is going beautifully, too.

If you happen to be a Lori, someone who's already homed in on your North Star, you might as well stop reading this book and get on with your fabulous life. The rest of us—we who spend whole weekends alternately checking for new gray hairs and wondering what we want to be when we grow up—are very happy for you. Really. The occasional surges of rage and despair we experience as we watch you sail by are just hormonal aberrations. But if you can't imagine feeling like Lori—if answering the Connection Questions quiz merely stirred up frustrations, disappointments, and regrets that have bedeviled you for years—read on. Things are going to get a whole lot better.

RECONNECTING: HOW YOUR ESSENTIAL SELF SAYS "NO"

Anne's job search was not going well. When I met her, she'd just blown big corporate interviews, not with one company but with several. It was same thing every time: Anne would go into the interview process smiling and gracious, like a Miss America contestant, and pass the first screening with flying colors. As she moved on to the next round of interviews, Anne would start feeling a bit irritable. This grumpiness got worse and worse until, in each of her top-level interviews, Anne found herself barking inappropriate answers to the simplest questions.

"In my last interview," she told me, "this vice president asked me why I wanted to be in banking, and I said, 'I don't.' Just like that—'*I don't!*' It sort of popped out, like a burp. Have you ever heard anything so stupid in your entire life?"

"Depends," I said. "Do you want to work for a bank?"

Anne recoiled visibly, as though I'd tossed her a snake. "Of course not," she said. "But it's good money."

In other words, Anne's social self (with lots of input from the "three P's": peers, parents, and professors) had decided that she should go into a field her essential self loathed. She told me she was "sabotaging" herself, and indeed she was—not by flunking her interviews, but by trying to get a job in a bank. Every time she came close to sealing this pact with Satan, her essential self managed to struggle out of its restraints and save the day. It was sabotaging her interviews, *but it wasn't sabotaging Anne.*

This is the dynamic at work in most of the people who tell me they're chronic self-saboteurs. James said he was ruining his life by "flaking out" every time he got his career on track and straightened out his relationship with his parents. His pattern was to start showing up late—or worse, forgetting to show up at all—for office meetings or social events with his family. Dorrie's problem was that her mind "froze" whenever she had to give presentations, an important part of her job. Kurt had a little anger-management problem: He'd ruined any number of personal and professional relationships by starting shouting matches over trivial issues.

As these people examined their lives, they all found that their "self-sabotage" was actually in harmony with their essential desires. James's parents were extremely controlling and had persuaded him to pursue a career that didn't interest him much. Dorrie didn't want the position she'd occupied since her most recent promotion; she preferred more solitary, analytical work. Kurt's anger had its roots in the prejudice he'd encountered growing up Turkish in Germany. The path to his North Star was to step back from his daily life, follow the anger until he could identify its source, embrace his ethnic identity, and learn to feel like a worthy person.

As they set out on paths chosen by their social selves, these clients' essential selves set up barriers, closed down operations, blew up bridges, and generally made it as difficult as possible to proceed down those errant roads. In this chapter, you'll learn the most basic navigational tool that will help you find your own North Star: the ability to recognize warning messages from your own essential self. By itself, this skill can't get you on your true path. What it will do, however, is help you change course before you end up in a catastrophically "self-sabotaging" situation.

One of the reasons the essential self has to resort to such extreme measures in order to communicate is that it can't talk. Not in the usual way, at any rate. The language center of your brain, the part that processes, analyzes, and communicates verbally, is overwhelmingly dominated by the social self.

This is not to say that the essential self never uses words. It does. But when it speaks, you—that is, your social self—are usually surprised by what it says. Creative writers and others who express their essential selves through language often describe the process as occurring in a kind of dream state, during which they're not fully conscious of the words they're about to use. The social self does its best to interfere with this process. It peers over the poet's shoulder, making comments like "Not exactly Shakespeare, are we?" or "What will your mother think?" or " 'Darkness visible'? What the hell does *that* mean, 'darkness visible'?" This is why so many writers drink.

Even for nonpoets, the essential self will occasionally verbalize its opinions. The classic Freudian slip is a good example: The speaker says what he means without even realizing it. (A friend of mine recently bought an antique at an Internet auction, only to find it was a fake. She complained to the seller, who wrote her an unctuous apology, urging her to return the object "at your earliest connivance.") Other verbal cues are more direct, like the comment that "popped out like a burp" during Anne's interview. Something similar happened to Joe, with much happier results. After a comfortable but unspectacular first date, Joe gave his companion a chaste peck on the cheek, then heard himself say, "Good-bye, Clare. I love you." He was absolutely horrified. "I thought I would explode like the *Hindenburg* from sheer embarrassment," he told me. "I barely knew her!" Apparently, Joe's essential self was on the right track, because at this writing, he and Clare have been happily married for five years.

The fascinating thing about these incidents is that although the conscious, verbal self is completely blindsided, the words that come out of nowhere are true in the deepest sense. Pay attention if your own words begin to surprise you. You probably don't have brain damage or multiple-personality disorder; on the contrary, you're getting crucial information to take you toward your North Star.

Most essential-self guidance, however, isn't so obvious. Because it takes enormous energy to shove the social self out of its command center in the rational, verbal part of your brain, the essential self usually "speaks" through parts of your being that aren't under conscious control. These are commanded by the deeper, more primitive layers of the brain, the parts that manage your emotional responses and basic body-maintenance functions like respiration, sleep and waking, and sexual desire.

When you leave your true path and start heading away from your North Star, your essential self will use any or all of its skills and tools to stop you. If your social self won't pay attention to mild warnings, the essential self has to get more and more dramatic. As a last resort, your core self will simply hijack the controls you use to direct your own behavior. You may be blithely oblivious to your own discontent until the very moment you find yourself weeping at a business luncheon, or punching your son's first-grade teacher. Fortunately, you can avoid such unpleasant situations if you learn just one "word" in your essential self's nonverbal lexicon: NO.

THE WAY YOU SAY "NO"

You probably don't remember it, but "no" was one of the most fabulous discoveries of your childhood. Two-year-olds go absolutely crazy over this word. They use it constantly, loudly, fervently. We call this behavioral stage the "terrible twos" because our job is to socialize children, and socialization does not work well when individuals run around screaming "no" all the time. In fact, socialization basically consists of learning to say "yes" to all cultural demands, whether you want to or not. The more conformist the culture, the more taboo "no" becomes. (For example, the Japanese word for "no" is *iie,* but the *sensei* who taught me this told me very firmly that I must never use it. She seemed to feel about *iie* the way my mother felt about the f-word.)

Speaking of mothers, every family and organization has its own unwritten rules about whether and when its members can say "no." Generally speaking, men are allowed to say it much more often than women, except in situations involving the risk of physical injury or death, where males must always say "yes." From the social self's perspective, letting yourself be used as cannon fodder is infinitely preferable to being ostracized by those around you.

Take your age and subtract two. That's the number of years you've spent forcing yourself to say "yes" when your essential self wanted to say "no." If you grew up in a social environment that met your real needs, with people who cared what you were feeling and wanted to facilitate your happiness, this occurred relatively rarely (but it still happened). However, if your environment was hostile to your true desires, you were forced to say "yes" when you meant "no" time after time after time, until you stopped even feeling your inner resistance. Your social self no longer knows what you want; it's fully focused on forcing you to fit in. But your essential self *cannot be corrupted*. It knows from "no," honey, and it will fight you like a trapped tiger—or a trapped two-year-old—every time you make a decision that takes you farther from your North Star.

Teaching your social self to pay attention when your essential self says "no" is the most basic way to reconnect the two sides of your personality. By doing this, you begin to rewire the navigational devices that lead you toward your right life. Without putting too fine a point on it, you'll know when you're headed "not north." Below are some of the most common ways I've noticed people's essential selves signaling "no." As you read through them, I ask that you remember times when you had these "symptoms," and write them down. Grab a pencil and give it a try—we'll be using this very valuable information throughout the book.

1. Energy Crisis

Over and over again, my clients tell me that they feel drained and exhausted on their way to jobs, classes, medical appointments, or social functions they think they *must* attend. The nearer they get to the dreaded event, in both time and space, the more they feel their strength ebbing away. If your whole life is dominated by rigid social-self requirements, you may feel enervated and listless all the time. If the negative activity is more limited (you hate your job, but you really, truly leave it at the office), you may notice that your energy level varies wildly, depending on what you're doing at the moment.

There was a time in my life when I was pretty sure I was dying from an unknown disease, probably related to bipolar disorder, which caused my energy to rise and fall like some berserk form of tidal surge. One day I'd feel great, full of vigor and enthusiasm. The next day I'd wake up so exhausted that my only ambition was to find a nice sepulchre, lie down in it, and wait for the end.

Just when I was getting ready to sign the psychiatric commitment documents, I noticed that my exhausted days were always the ones I spent doing academic work at the university where I was teaching, while my zippy times correlated perfectly with staying off-campus. Shortly after making this discovery, I quit my job. My social self was filled with trepidation—after all, I was now unemployed—but the effect on my energy level was incredible. I had a physical sensation of unburdening, as though I had just shed a suit of heavy metal armor. My posture straightened up, I walked faster, I felt more clearheaded and alert. I've seen the same kind of thing happen to dozens of clients. When your essential self knows you're headed away from your North Star, it can make itself very heavy.

EXERCISE

Try to remember three different events or types of events (dental appointments, jobs, classes, social functions, etc.) where you *had to* show up but felt reluctant and low-energy.

Event No. 1: _____

_____

Event No. 2: _____

_____

Event No. 3: _____

_____

Now please circle the response that has the *most negative* associations for you.

2. Sick, Sick, Sick

A doctor for a university health clinic once told me that his staff prepared for minor epidemics during every exam period. "I'm not talking about faking illness to get out of a test," he said. "These students are really sick." The abundant medical evidence on the relationship between stress and immune response includes plenty of studies showing this "exam effect" on college students. Bottom line: Stress decreases your immune response, leaving you vulnerable to all sorts of interesting diseases.

A lot of people with overly developed social selves experience this kind of stress, sometimes for years, without even realizing it. They never consciously articulate the thought that they hate their lives—or at least parts of their lives—but the essential self is very clear about it, and the effect on the immune system is disastrous. You may remember a time in your own life when you picked up every little flu bug within a twenty-mile radius, or couldn't shake a virus that everyone else kicked within a few hours. If so, you were probably headed away from your North Star.

I've had a handful of clients who made dramatic life changes after they were diagnosed with cancer. Although there are many causes for cancer, most of them strictly biological, all of these clients seemed to feel that their disease was abetted by the stress of trying to force themselves to be happy in a life that didn't really fit them. Carol told me she was certain her cancer would return if she didn't get out of a difficult relationship. "It may sound crazy," Carol said, "but I know how I felt the first time I got sick, and that's how I feel now." Given this conviction, it was amazing to see how difficult it was for Carol to make life changes. Like most social-self types, she was incredibly conscientious and reluctant to hurt her boyfriend's feelings. Her essential self had to bring out some huge guns to make change more attractive than tenacious persistence.

EXERCISE

Try to remember three times when your health was below par. What was going on in your life during each of these three time periods? Please list each situation, along with the physical symptoms you suffered. Don't worry if these situations are the same ones that came up in the last section, or if all three caused the same symptoms. Repetition is welcome in this game.

Situation No. 1: _____ Symptoms: _____

_____

Situation No. 2: _____ Symptoms: _____

_____

Situation No. 3: _____ Symptoms: _____

_____

Circle the *worst* symptom.

3. Forgetting

When my daughter Katie was three, she came home from visiting a neighbor, whom she called "the nice old fat lady across the street." I tried to tell her that I knew the person she meant but that, thenceforth, she should always refer to the nice old fat lady as "Mrs. Stephens."

Katie looked pensive. "What if I forget?" she asked.

"Well, honey, I'll remind you."

She nodded slowly, then said, "What if I refuse?"

The answer, of course, was that there wasn't a damn thing I could do to make Katie use polite forms of address if she simply balked. The essential self operates on this principle all the time. You can drag it away from your North Star, but you can't make it think. It will conveniently forget things that help you go in a direction it doesn't like, and when your social self tries to remember what you're doing, your brain will simply refuse to recall the information.

This is what happened to me when I was learning—or trying to learn—Chinese characters. You've probably had similar experiences. At some point in your education, you may have spent hours in fierce concentration, memorizing the stylistic quirks of French novelists, the details of the Magna Carta, or any number of useful calculus formulas. You probably remember a lot of things you learned in the courses you enjoyed. But do you remember *anything* from your least favorite high school class? Of course you do. You remember that the teacher, Mr. Spackle, had three long black hairs growing straight out of the bridge of his nose. *And that's all.*

It isn't just that you have a lousy memory. You remember the entire plot of *Star Wars*—including the weird alien names, 'droid model numbers, and several verbatim quotations, even if you saw the movie twenty long years ago and made no attempt to memorize anything. Of course, this is true only if your essential self liked *Star Wars*. If it didn't, you don't know what the hell I'm talking about.

Your essential self doesn't limit its control to long-term memory. For example, if you're headed for an appointment you dread, one that is antithetical to your North Star, you may reach a truly spectacular level of forgetfulness. You'll forget when the appointment is supposed to take place, where you put the car keys, how to drive, the person you're supposed to meet, and your own name.

My friend Mark, a workaholic business consultant, fell apart when he was assigned to a large corporate client. Every time he set out to meet with this client, he'd forget his airplane tickets, his passport, his briefcase, the presentations he'd spent hours preparing. It got so bad that Mark finally resigned from the case—something he'd never done in twenty years of consulting. A few months later, that corporation became the target of an FBI investigation. Most of the people Mark had encountered during his time with the company were indicted for ethical violations and fraud. Once again, an apparent "sabotage" by the essential self turned out to be a smart move.

Write down three types of information that you find difficult to remember (for example, "people's names," "my kids' school schedules," "where I put important papers").

Info-type No. 1: _____

_____

Info-type No. 2: _____

_____

Info-type No. 3: _____

_____

Circle the type of information that you forget most often.

4. Bundles o' Blunders

Here in Wild West Phoenix, where real men still have obscene tattoos and keep rattlesnakes as pets, we recently experienced a rash of brazen burglaries. The thieves entered empty houses to steal any jewelry, silverware, and electronic equipment they could find. In one home, their loot included an expensive camera. The thieves sold the goods at a swap meet later the same week, leaving no clues to their identity—except that they'd taken several pictures of one another burglarizing the house, then left the film in the camera when they fenced it. The police had lots of nice photographic evidence to help them find and convict the whole gang.

Many criminals do incredibly stupid things like this, because they're actually very conflicted about breaking the law. It's a rare thing to find a burglar who thinks it's dandy if other people steal his stuff; when it comes right down to it, his deepest self believes that stealing is immoral. Your essential self will fight you by committing "stupid" blunders whenever you violate your own values. It's as likely to happen when you try to be too virtuous as when you break the law. Do you think it's an accident that every time your mother-in-law arrives to take you to her Bible study group, she finds you naked in your backyard hot tub, singing the blues and drinking Kahlúa through a straw? I think not.

What looks to you like inordinate stupidity is probably your essential self trying to steer you toward your North Star.

Write down three stupid mistakes you remember making.

Mistake No. 1: _____

_____

Mistake No. 2: _____

_____

Mistake No. 3: _____

_____

Circle the most disastrous mistake.

5. Social Suicide

Have you ever met someone around whom you regularly behave like a lobotomized chimpanzee? Have you noticed that in certain situations, you just can't pull off the suave, clever, graceful image to which you so desperately aspire? Don't blame fate; blame your essential self. When you're in circumstances that poison your core, all the subtle mechanisms that make for smooth social behavior get gummed up. You stutter, trip, and tell ill-timed jokes that make you look like a narcissistic half-wit. Then you try to talk yourself to a safe haven and end up so deeply embarrassed that certain people will cross the street to avoid you for the rest of your life.

I had a client I'll call Gretta who, for reasons I could never pin down, made me feel incredibly uneasy. I routinely forgot Gretta's appointments, and when she showed up I was usually painting my office or hosting an impromptu party, just so it would be absolutely clear to her how badly I'd screwed up. Gretta was extremely European, and she always wanted to kiss me on both cheeks when she entered or left the office. I wasn't comfortable with this, and I should have told her so, but I didn't. Instead, Gretta and I would go into a strange greeting-and-departure dance, which consisted of her lunging at my head while

I tried to simultaneously pull back and deliver a polite air kiss. My hands, which usually seem to take care of themselves, would start flapping around awkwardly, like a deranged waterfowl doing a courtship display. Once I even fell down. God, how I wish I was kidding.

From the perspective of the social self, this kind of thing is the Torment of the Damned. But the essential self creates it quite deliberately. It doesn't want you to be equally comfortable around just anybody. Life is short, and far too many people in it would like a chunk of your time. If certain situations or people routinely trigger spasms of hideously awkward social behavior, you can be sure that your essential self is not happy with them. Human social dynamics are far too subtle for the linear, logical social self. The essential self is really the only part of you that can do it well, and it, not you, decides when that will happen.

EXERCISE

Name three people who bring out your very worst social behavior. It might help to review your life's most embarrassing moments; the two are often linked.

Person No. 1: _____

Person No. 2: _____

Person No. 3: _____

Please circle *all three* of these names.

6. Fight or Flight

I'm sure you know all about the fight-or-flight mechanism. It's one of the most powerful instruments under the essential self's command. When your North Star progress is halted or reversed, your body reacts like the threatened bipedal mammal it is. It prepares your body for battle or escape by flooding you with adrenaline, speeding your heart rate, making your breath come in explosive little gasps, and revving your engines in a number of other ways.

When the fight-or-flight mechanism has been triggered, our social selves have to muster all their powers to force a calm facade. If you've ever endured a full-blown panic attack, you know that the impulse to run and hide can be truly overwhelming. So can the desire to lash out in a rage at anyone and anything. Keeping all that energy inside instead of acting on it, trying to go along in a Socially Appropriate manner, is like standing naked in a gale-force wind. It messes up your waking life, and completely trashes your sleep.

Whenever you feel trapped in a situation that your essential self knows is keeping you from your North Star, you may either lie awake night after night, churning with anger and anxiety, or sleep fifteen hours a day without ever feeling rested. We'll talk about how to deal with this kind of thing in later chapters. For now, suffice it to say that fight or flight is one of the many tools wielded, with fearsome power, by your essential self.

EXERCISE

List times when you couldn't sleep, slept very poorly, or slept so much you felt groggy and squalid. What was the problem in your life that caused the sleep disturbance?

Problem No. 1: _____

_____

Problem No. 2: _____

_____

Problem No. 3: _____

_____

Circle the issue that most disrupted your sleep.

7. Addiction

Whenever you're headed away from your North Star, your essential self feels a constant sense of yearning emptiness. If you stumble across a substance or activity that dulls this feeling (like eating, sex, drugs, shopping, or gambling), your essential self may mistake the mood-altering device for your North Star. The result is often addictive behavior. Once you're hooked, the essential self emerges uncontrollably, like good old Mr. Hyde shoving Dr. Jekyll into the background, and sets out on habit-forming rampages that may ruin your life.

Years ago, when I was doing research on addiction, I found as many addicts among hyper-responsible, perfectionistic folks as among rebellious, irresponsible criminals. Both types talked about their "Dr. Jekyll–Mr. Hyde" personalities. All of them were trying to stop their compulsive behavior by controlling or eradicating their essential selves. This was the most counterproductive thing they could have done. There's nothing to love about addiction, *but it will not loosen its grip until addicts learn to act lovingly toward their essential selves.* The true self becomes destructive only when it can't endure what's happening; when it's being starved, tortured, and dragged away from your North Star. Aligning your life with your deepest sense of purpose is one of the most important steps in recovery.

For example, Allen was a classic overachiever who came across as squeaky-clean, like Ron Howard in *Happy Days,* but that was only Dr. Jekyll. Every few weeks, Allen embarked on a major alcoholic binge. He'd generally wake up after one of his drinking episodes in a brand-new location, with a brand-new woman. He was tremendously ashamed of this and spent a lot of time despising himself.

Sometime before we started working together, Allen started attending A.A. meetings. His sponsor refused to excuse or encourage the part of Allen that turned to booze and sex—but he also refused to insult it. "You're not evil," this sponsor would say when Allen began another tirade of self-loathing. "You're just in pain." Slowly, Allen stopped flagellating himself with ineffective guilt and started paying more considerate attention to his inner experience. This meant that Allen's essential self no longer had to hijack his behavior to make itself feel better; Allen could figure out what it really wanted and treat it kindly. His compulsions became less compulsive as soon as Allen's essential self was satisfied that his social side was listening to it.

Of course, this meant that Allen began to rethink his role in his family, where his social self had been trained to ignore all personal needs and longings. His mother and siblings threw fits when Allen changed this pattern. He also began reconsidering his career path in ways that upset his mentors and coworkers. By the time he came to see me, it looked from the outside as though all hell had broken loose in Allen's life. But on the inside, Allen had ended a miserable, internecine war. His social and essential selves were finally on the same path, his true path, and the pain that had driven him to drink was gradually disappearing.

EXERCISE

Name a bad habit or obsessive thought pattern you've been unable to eliminate: _____ .

Now remember what happened to trigger that bad habit the last three times you fell off the wagon. (For example, "I'd had an argument with my mom," "I'd been working day and night for a month," "I was facing a performance review.")

Habit trigger No. 1: _____

_____

Habit trigger No. 2: _____

_____

Habit trigger No. 3: _____

_____

Circle the "trigger" that is most likely to make you turn to your addiction or habit.

8. Moody Blues

Mood control is another of the essential self's many skills. It's one thing to feel sad at a funeral or happy at a wedding; that makes sense to the social self. But what about the times you suddenly break down in tears halfway through an ordinary workday, burst out laughing during a Serious Staff Meeting, go ballistic with rage in light traffic, or slog your way through a surprise party feeling nothing but hollow ennui?

If you're experiencing moods you can't explain, or think your emotional reactions are "inappropriate," you can be sure that your social and essential selves are seriously disconnected. (*Appropriate* and *inappropriate,* by the way, are the social self's all-time favorite words.) Instead of fighting your unexplained bad moods, pay special attention to them. They are a clear sign that you've lost your North Star, and that your essential self is trying to tell you where to find it.

Michelle, a twenty-eight-year-old newlywed, felt lifeless, dull, and completely asexual. She and her husband tried to rekindle their romance with elaborate dates, dinners, and vacations, but the more Michelle knew she was supposed to be carried away with rapture, the more she felt like Edgar Allan Poe on a bad day. She was terrified to really hear the messages she sensed were coming from her essential self, afraid she'd discover her marriage was defunct. Eventually, though, things got so bad that she consented to work with me on figuring out what her essential self was trying to tell her.

The results were gratifyingly anticlimactic. It turned out that Michelle's beliefs about marriage were the problem, not her feelings for her husband. Michelle's social self had been taught that women are supposed to become silent, spineless domestic servants the moment they say "I do." Her essential self wasn't going there—no way, no how—and it turned off all her positive moods and sexual responses until she agreed to rethink her socialized beliefs.

EXERCISE

List the last three times you experienced a very bad mood or a mood that seemed inexplicable, unjustifiable, or extreme. Again, note what was happening in your life at the time this occurred.

Bad-mood setting No. 1: _____

_____

Bad-mood setting No. 2: _____

_____

Bad-mood setting No. 3: _____

_____

Circle the situation that brought out your worst mood.

SUMMARY: GETTING TO "NO"

I'm hoping that this chapter has stirred up some very unpleasant memories for you. Every person's essential self says "no" in its own unique way, but most people's negative reactions involve at least some of the symptoms I've just discussed. Now we're going to play around with your responses, in order to create a clear image of the unique "no" response that occurs when *you* are moving away from your North Star. This exercise is fairly involved, but it's well worth the time.

Step 1

To get your essential self to "speak" to you, we first need to assemble all the things you hate most. In the spaces below, list the answers you circled on all the exercises in this chapter. Flip back to see your responses if you need to.

List your:

A. Lowest-energy situation: _____

_____

B. Three people who bring out your worst social behavior:

1. _____
2. _____
3. _____

C. Worst medical symptom: _____

_____

D. Most forgettable information type: _____

_____

E. Stupidest mistake: _____

_____

F. Problem that most disturbed your sleep: _____

_____

G. Worst bad-habit "trigger": _____

_____

H. Setting for your worst mood: _____

_____

Step 2

Now we're going to create a little scenario together—a scenario that should set your teeth on edge. Using the items you've written on the list in Step One, fill in the blanks in the following story. For example, if you wrote "dental appointments" next to the letter "A" in Step One, you'll write "dental appointments" in the blank labeled "A" below.

YOUR OWN WORST-CASE SCENARIO

Imagine for a moment that you are in (A: your lowest-energy situation)

_____

_____ .

You are surrounded by (B: *all three* names on your list)

_____

_____

_____ .

You're not feeling your best; in fact, your (C: worst medical symptom)

_____

is bothering you more than ever before.
You've been given a lifetime assignment that involves working with (D: most forgettable information)

_____

_____

_____ .

All the people in the room are authorized to watch you constantly, criticize your performance, and punish you if you make any mistakes.
   Speaking of mistakes, you've just done (E: stupidest mistake)

_____

_____

_____ ,

a fact that is being noted by your three supervisors. Your life in general is pretty difficult right now; that whole thing with (F: most sleep-disturbing problem)

_____

_____

is happening all over again. You're also trying to deal with (G: worst bad-habit trigger)

_____

_____ .

To top it off, (H: your bad-mood situation)

_____

is more intense than ever before.

Just when things are at their worst, (B-1: the person who makes you most uncomfortable)

_____

walks up. He or she orders you to sit up politely, smile in a way that is both humble and worshipful, and say to the entire assembly, "I admire you so much. Thank you, thank you for letting me be here. You are such a terrific person, and this is just what I deserve. I want to live this way for the rest of my life."

Step 3

Read over this scenario, once you've filled in the blanks. Really put yourself into it. Then pay attention to your own reaction. How do you feel? Rotten, I hope. If you vividly imagine this horrible situation, you'll experience your own particular blend of anger, despair, illness, and anxiety. This should reach a peak when you imagine facing the person you hate most and turning over all your power to change anything. *Whatever you feel in that moment is the sensation of your essential self saying, "NO!"*

Don't run away from this feeling just yet. Focus on and wallow around in it. Explore its particular shape, texture, and size. Notice how it differs from other negative feelings. Your true path will take you through frightening challenges, saddening departures, angry resistance, and a number of other profoundly unpleasant experiences. But the pain you experience en route to your North Star feels clean, necessary, and right to the essential self. It is very different from the intense aversion you would feel in the scenario we've just created. *You're not supposed to feel that way, ever.*

That feeling of choked hostility, or numb depression, or nauseated helplessness is a sure sign you're steering away from your North Star, toward a life you were *not* meant to live. *When you feel it, you must change course.* You must say to the people around you what your essential self is saying inside: "Nope. Not going there. Not doing that. Sorry, but the answer is no."

Most of my clients reject this theory at first. "You can't just obey your essential self," they say. "You can't just say 'no' every time something unpleasant comes along. People have to do what they have to do." This, of course, is the battle cry of the social self. It has learned to say "yes" in aversive situations because it believes there is no way out. It learned this from people around you, people who, for whatever reason, wanted you to do things that were inimical to your essential nature. If you stop obeying the "no"s that come from the people around you, and start listening to the "no"s that come from within you, a lot of these folks—possibly including the ones you love most—are going to be startled and resistant. Chances are you're going to sustain some losses.

If this seems like a reason to turn back, to abandon the quest for your own North Star, consider the losses you'd guarantee by spending your life in situations that resemble your worst-case scenario. As Jesus put it, "What profiteth it a man if he should gain the whole world and lose his own soul?" You've just had a taste of that. If you want to stick with a situation that makes your essential self scream *"No!"* that's your prerogative. If, on the other hand, you'd like to regain your own soul— quite possibly at the cost of losing what looks like the whole world— read on. Now that you know the feeling of "not north," we're going to find out how your essential self tells you that you're headed in the *right* direction.

GETTING TO YES

I was sitting in a bookstore three blocks from my freshman dorm, trying to decide on my college major. It had been a tough year—the most
stressful of my life so far—and I felt too tired to make the most trivial
decision, let alone one that might have a serious impact on my future.
Glumly, I leafed through the *Fields of Concentration* booklet I'd received
from the registrar. Should I concentrate on English literature? Well,
maybe; I liked to read. Philosophy? No—too pretentious. History?
That was a possibility. Visual art?

As this thought occurred to me, a most peculiar sensation swept
through my body. It felt as though my cells had suddenly become buoyant. For a dizzy moment, I almost believed that I was rising up into the
air. A panorama of memories rushed through my brain: the thousands
of hours I'd spent drawing as an art-obsessed child and adolescent; the
gorgeous smell of crayons, paper, paint, and turpentine; the wordless
enchantment I experienced whenever I made pictures. The feeling was
so surprising and lovely that I burst out laughing.

I cannot tell you how atypical this was. For several scared, bewildered, and lonely months, I hadn't so much as smiled for an I.D. photo.

Now I felt as though I'd discovered the canary in the coal mine of my soul, still singing away under tons of bedrock. Emily Dickinson's line "Hope is the thing with feathers" popped into my mind, and for the first time, I knew what she meant. I also understood something else Emily once said: that when she read great poetry, she felt as if the top of her head were coming off. I'd always thought this was a sad commentary on how desperate the recluse poet was for entertainment, but now I realized Emily must have been talking about something similar to the strange lightness I felt when I considered majoring in art.

I'll bet you've had this feeling too, or a sensation close to it. Everyone experiences this a little differently, but in each individual it tends to be very consistent over time. It's the feeling of your essential self saying, *"Yes! This way to your North Star!"*

Of course, when this happened to me in the bookstore, I didn't listen. Within thirty seconds, my social self had launched a full frontal attack. It dredged up a conversation I'd overheard in the freshman dining hall several weeks earlier. A group of my peers had spent half an hour mocking visual-arts majors, whom they saw as a bunch of wannabe-European airheads with dim minds and even dimmer futures. A degree in art, my friends had all agreed, was worse than useless. So much for *that* idea. My body seemed to crash back into the chair, and my mood into its inky funk.

For the next ten years, as I charted my course to a "secure" career in academia, I occasionally pondered that experience in the bookstore. I thought about it as I slogged my way through one Chinese class after another, feeling as though the subject and I had mutually repellent force fields. I thought about it when I toted up all the income I'd earned working my way through college and graduate school, and realized that I'd made more money teaching and selling art than by any other means. I thought about it the day I quit my academic job, finally acknowledging that I simply wasn't cut out to be a sociology professor, no matter how fail-safe such a career might seem.

I'll never know what would have happened if I'd listened to my essential self when it tried to choose my major for me. I don't think I'd be a professional artist; my sense is that studying the subject was my truest path, but not a final destination. I do believe that if I'd chosen art as my major, the next few years would have been more enjoyable, more fulfilling, and easier. I think I might have lived the breadth of those years, as well as their length. I'm basing this conjecture on experiences I've had since: both the times that I ignored my essential self shouting *"Yes!"* and the times I listened to it. I also have lots of corroborating data from people who habitually listen to their essential selves, and have extraordinarily rich lives to show for it. I hope that after reading this chapter, you'll want to become one of them.

HOW THE ESSENTIAL SELF SAYS "YES"

If you ever want to see a roomful of people wilt like dehydrated begonias, try running a seminar group through the "worst-case scenario" from the last chapter. By the time I finish this exercise, the participants are all sitting slumped or rigid, their faces wan with misery, their breathing shallow and reluctant, like marine mammals waiting to be rescued from an oil spill. Then we get to the second part—the material we're going to cover in this chapter. It's like magic: Within five minutes, most of the participants become visibly brighter and cheerier. They've moved from a set of memories that poison their essential selves to memories that nourish them. Just about everyone starts smiling, telling jokes, making friends. There's a good chance that reading this chapter will alter your mood this way, by focusing your attention on positive memories. (But a caveat, see opposite, is in order here.)

HAPPY TALK:
HOW THE ESSENTIAL SELF SAYS "YES"

We've already discussed the way the essential self communicates. The mechanisms it uses to shut down or sabotage your social self whenever you're headed away from your North Star are the same ones it uses to say *"Yes!"* We're going to go through a list of "symptoms" similar in type (but opposite in content) to the ones discussed in the last chapter. Try to remember times when you've experienced the following phenomena, and note them in the spaces provided.

CAVEAT

Though every client I've ever had can come up with a "worst-case scenario," about one in twenty can't or won't do the "best-case scenario" exercises in this chapter. These exercises require you to look back on experiences where your essential self said *"Yes!"* Some people literally can't remember any such experiences. Others can, but don't want to. Why not? Because thinking about joy when you're not particularly joyful can make you feel like an impoverished orphan staring through the window of F. A. O. Schwarz. It rubs salt in the wounds created by a life that's less than ideal.

If you find it painful to do the following exercises, you are almost certainly in the wrong life. Eventually, you will either have to give up on happiness or start reconnecting with the experience of joy, but *don't push yourself.* Read this chapter as purely hypothetical; just allow it to create space for the possibility that you may one day experience the happiness that comes naturally to people who've found their North Stars. Let it introduce you to the thing with feathers.

1. Nuclear Energy

David was an attorney with a tax-law firm. It was a good job; the only problem was that David had no energy for it. When I met him, he was so oomph-impaired that he was finishing only about a third of the work assigned to him, and spending most of his nonworking time stretched out on the couch, watching television. David had basically decided to end his law career—I think he came to me mainly for permission to quit—but I was hard-pressed to come up with any ideas about what he might do instead. I was trying to think of a career that would allow him to spend almost all his time napping, perhaps as a subject in an extended study of chronic fatigue syndrome.

But what did David do, the very day he finally resigned from his job? He started jogging, hiking, rock climbing, river rafting, and generally rushing around like a maniac. I'd known for a long time that David had a thirst for outdoor adventures, but I'd thought it was a passion he'd have to pursue through books, movies, and magazines. I had no idea how his energy would skyrocket when he got out of the law office and into the wild.

One day, David told me about an experience that convinced him he'd have plenty of energy to do whatever his right life demanded of him. The previous weekend, he'd been hiking with his friend Ben when a massive thunderstorm rolled in, trapping them near the top of a mountain peak. The red rock around them contained so much iron that it drew lightning like a radio tower; this particular area records more lightning strikes than any other region in the United States. Violent, deafening blasts began striking so near David and Ben that they could smell the electrical heat. The rocks became slippery with rain, the temperature dropped drastically, and the probability that the two hikers would fall down the steep mountainside, die from hypothermia, or get flash-fried started to look uncomfortably high. Although David knew they were in serious danger, he found the scene so wild and beautiful that he wasn't afraid.

"I felt something shift inside me," David said. "It was as though every part of me lined up perfectly. All of a sudden, I noticed that I was moving incredibly fast. I wasn't aware of any effort; it felt like I was gliding over the rocks. Ben is a much stronger hiker than I am, but he fell way back while I found the best route down the cliff. I felt absolutely calm. I knew I couldn't make a wrong step, and that I could keep moving at that pace without getting tired. I've never felt anything like it."

David's hiking experience was a particularly dramatic example of what happens when you and your true self are headed in the same direction. It wasn't just the adrenaline of fear that got him moving, it was also the joy of being in his favorite place, with a good friend, doing something he loved. David had been in tight spots before, but he'd never felt as though everything "lined up" inside him. Now that he is more responsive to his essential self, the effortless high energy of "doing without doing" is more and more available to David, in more and more situations.

I've learned to expect astonishing energy surges in clients who've had the courage to end miserable situations. You may experience this, in small ways, every day. By four o'clock, you're so trashed you can hardly sit up at your desk, but when you make the decision to head home early, your energy leaps like a ballet dancer on crack. You're numbingly tired talking to your best friend about her latest health crisis; then she mentions the person you've secretly fallen in love with, and suddenly you're at full attention. You go into a near coma chatting with your in-laws after dinner, only to stay up half the night avidly reading a new murder mystery.

What kinds of activities increase your energy levels? Does being with certain people seem to pep you up? What about places—do you feel perky and energetic near the ocean, at the movies, walking through the mall? Look back over your history, both recent and long-term, to see if you can recall times of notable peppiness.

EXERCISE
List three things that can always get you moving. (Examples: "The family New Year's party," "Playing pickup basketball," "Going to the mountains.")

Energy-inducing person, place, or thing No. 1: _____

_____

Energy-inducer No. 2: _____

_____

Energy-inducer No. 3: _____

_____

Look over the list and circle the response that makes you feel *most enthusiastic*.

2. To Your Health

Remember, your essential self exercises a lot of control over your immune system and may lower your resistance to disease when it isn't happy. On the other hand, I believe that it actually *strengthens* your immune response when you're headed directly for your North Star.

Katherine had spent many years playing by the social rules. She'd endured a hollow marriage to a cold, hypercritical man, who'd divorced her after she'd raised their children. Katherine had been stoic and long-suffering through the whole lonely time. Not long after her divorce, Katherine was diagnosed with ovarian cancer. It was a particularly lethal type of malignancy, and Katherine's case was already very advanced. Surgeons removed a twenty-pound tumor from her abdomen. The malignancy was virtually everywhere. She overheard her doctor, who didn't know she was in earshot, telling another physician, "She's a dead woman." Despite the surgery, chemotherapy, and radiation, Katherine knew the medical experts expected to be reading her obituary any minute.

Figuring that she had very little to lose and perhaps not much time to experience the things she'd always dreamed about, Katherine abruptly changed her whole life. She sold, trashed, or gave away everything except a few treasured possessions and moved from New York City to a small town in northern California. She chose this location simply because she found the landscape stunningly beautiful and "something about the place just felt right." At first it didn't occur to Katherine that she'd end up getting a job and making close friends; the chances that her cancer would recur were so high that she didn't really expect to be around that long. She was a little surprised when she began connecting with people who, like the town, "felt right" to her core self.

That was ten years ago. Today, Katherine is a beautiful, vital, and healthy woman. The only reminder of her bout with cancer is numbness in her toes, stemming from damage to her spinal cord caused by radiation therapy. Of course, we can't tell what would have happened if Katherine had stayed in New York, near her ex-husband, in the life she'd been living when her disease took root. But the fact that immune response and stress are so closely linked might explain why this "dead woman" is so healthy today. Practically every decision Katherine has made since her bout with cancer has been guided by the sense of "rightness" that took her to California, the feeling of her essential self saying *"Yes!"*

You may not even know that you don't like something until you drop it and suddenly see your health getting better. I've had many clients who clung to the very thing—a job, a relationship, a lifestyle—that was draining their physical stamina. Lenny, for example, was convinced that his position at the top of his small company was the only thing that gave meaning and value to his life. When the company was acquired by a larger firm, erasing Lenny's job, he thought the world had come to an end. Lenny was amazed when his chronically bad health, including asthma, severe allergies, and constant respiratory infections, suddenly cleared up. "I guess I was so obsessed with what other people were thinking that I didn't notice the job wasn't letting me breathe," he said.

If you're already a healthy specimen, you may not notice that great a difference between times when your essential self is saying "yes" and times when it says "no." However, you may be able to think of situations where you were able to push yourself very hard without falling ill (for example, working around the clock on a political campaign), when you were more resistant to pain (barely noticing a gash sustained in a rugby match), or when you were unaffected by a virus that mowed down everyone else in your office. List three such times below.

EXERCISE

Try to remember three times when your health seemed better than usual. What was going on in your life at the time?

Situation No. 1: _____

_____

Situation No. 2: _____

_____

Situation No. 3: _____

_____

Circle the situation that has the *most positive* associations for you right now.

3. Memories, Light the Corners of My Mind . . .

The essential self that blocks memory when you're headed away from your North Star is capable of incredibly mnemonic feats when you correct course. I've found that every one of my clients has a passionate essential-self interest in at least one category of information. You may regularly forget your phone number, your mother's birthday, and everything you ever learned in school, but in this one area, you're a memory genius.

I think of this as the Rosie O'Donnell syndrome, because of Rosie's famous ability to remember every popular song she hears, from advertising jingles to Broadway musicals. It's sort of fun to get together with a bunch of friends and figure out where their O'Donnell tendencies lie. Here are some of my friends' supermemory categories: Sadie remembers the caloric and fat-gram content of every edible substance on earth; Bill can glance at any airplane in the sky over his hometown and tell you the plane's model, airline, city of origin, and destination; Mary knows the name of every actor on every television show, along with the names of the actors' spouses, children, and tropical fish. My son, Adam, who has Down's syndrome and isn't supposed to remember much of anything, has an encyclopedic knowledge of Bugs Bunny cartoons. From the age of three, he's been able to act out every role from every feature with flawless accuracy.

This supermemory phenomenon isn't just about categories of learning. Something your essential self forgets in one setting may be the very thing it slurps up in another. When I was teaching a course called Multinational Business Management, I had a terrible time remembering the material and never did pick up on my students' names. But, when I designed a course on career development, I was stunned to find that after hearing each of my eighty-five students' names just once, I remembered all of them without any conscious effort. Moral: Life coaching is one thing my essential self loves, and it allows me free memory access whenever I'm doing it.

I've noticed that most people aren't impressed with their own supermemories. Because a topic is easy for them to learn, they decide it isn't impressive or useful. Mary was actually embarrassed about her ability to remember everything about celebrities and their exploits—she admitted it with a red face and downcast eyes. She didn't realize how useful her skills could be in areas like publicity, marketing, and entertainment. I'm convinced that every supermemory can be put to use in some productive endeavor. Now, if I can just figure out how Adam can parlay his Bugs Bunny fixation into a career . . .

EXERCISE

Where's your supermemory? If you can't think of anything, you're probably overlooking the obvious. Ask some friends and loved ones what they've noticed about your ability to pick up certain categories of information. List these categories below.

Info type No. 1: _____

_____

Info type No. 2: _____

_____

Info type No. 3: _____

_____

Circle the type of information that interests you most. Be honest; nothing you really enjoy is stupid or trivial.

4. Time Warp

My first client is due to show up in half an hour. I have three different alarm systems to remind me of this: the internal clock on my computer, my watch (which is lying across the top of my keyboard so that I won't forget about it), and the timer on my oven, which is set to go off five minutes before the appointment time. I need these redundant systems because when I write, hours disappear with bizarre, almost alarming speed. I can't tell you how many times I have checked my daily schedule, sat down to write for just a couple of minutes, and suddenly realized that the day is over. My children, bless them, have learned that when Mom's in "writing world," they have to remind me to take them to music lessons and play dates every five or ten minutes.

Mind you, this happens only when I'm genuinely interested in my topic. When I was writing my Ph.D. dissertation, for example, the minutes flew by like months. It was all I could do to stay focused for half an hour. I could feel myself withering into premature senility as I forced myself to write that endless document, which my essential self found boring, frightening, and generally hideous.

Think how differently time flowed for you when something wonderful was happening in your life. During your childhood, did you ever settle in to play a game and forget the time until your mother called you for dinner? Have you ever become engrossed in conversation with someone who seemed to be a kindred spirit, and suddenly realized that hours had passed without your noticing them? Is there anything you do now that swallows your sense of time, allowing you to simply experience the present? If so, list it below.

EXERCISE

Write down three types of activities that make you forget what time it is.

Activity No. 1: _____

_____

Activity No. 2: _____

_____

Activity No. 3: _____

_____

Circle the activity you find most absorbing.

5. Emotional Intelligence

Not only can your essential self shut down your social skills in order to get you out of bad relationships; it may also enhance those skills when you're headed in the right direction. When you meet someone who is part of your true path, you may be surprised and gratified at how well the whole social-interaction game unfolds. You'll say just the right things, at just the right times. Your jokes will be genuinely funny; in fact, even if they're not, people will seem to think they are. You'll feel waves of positive attention gravitating toward you. Your social self won't have a clue about why things are clicking so beautifully; it will just ride along in amazed delight as the essential self taps into the interpersonal energy and feeds back to it.

Two sure signs that your essential self likes the person you're with are *relaxation* and *empathy.* You not only feel very comfortable in your own skin but also find yourself forgetting to worry about that, and stepping into the other person's shoes. You understand the person you're with and feel understood in return. Though you may barely have met, you may feel as though the two of you have known each other forever.

Tamara is a beautiful and intelligent woman whose natural caution reached near-phobic levels after she was date-raped. It took years for her to have the courage to go out with a man again, and when she did, the conversation was always stilted and tense. Tamara knew when she met Ron that he was a kind, honest person. She liked him a lot. To her conscious mind, her social self, he seemed similar to most of the other guys she'd dated. But on her fourth date with Ron, the first time she invited him into her apartment, Tamara's essential self did something astonishing. She kissed Ron, let him put his arms around her, and promptly fell into a peaceful sleep.

"I know that may not sound like a good thing," Tamara told me. "But for me, it was fantastic. I'd had trouble sleeping at all since the rape, and I was terribly nervous about being alone with a man. But some part of me seemed to trust Ron completely. It was like this damaged part of me was finally home and safe."

The fact that Ron understood this, instead of feeling insulted by Tamara's less-than-passionate response, is a testament to the fact that he empathized with her. There was never a sense of awkwardness or unease between them; they responded to each other like perfectly partnered dancers. Ron and Tamara eventually moved in together, and three years later they're still a happy couple.

Name three people who make you feel socially adept and confident, people who seem to understand you and enjoy spending time with you.

Person No. 1: _____

Person No. 2: _____

Person No. 3: _____

Please circle the name of the person who makes you feel most comfortable and relaxed.

6. Magnetic Attraction

I've found that clients who report the happiest romantic relationships are grounded in the kind of mellow mutual relaxation Tamara and Ron feel around each other. This is quite different from another response the essential self may create when it wants you to move closer to your North Star. I call this feeling the Urge to Merge. It's an intense, almost chemical reaction that comes out of nowhere and makes some person, place, or thing so attractive to you that for a while, you can't think about much else.

I think of the Urge to Merge as the physiological opposite of the fight-or-flight response. Like the fight-or-flight reaction, it creates a whole array of physical conditions that aren't under our conscious control. For example, when you're looking at something you find intensely appealing, your pupils dilate and your rate of blinking drops, as though your eyes are trying to take in more of what you're seeing. Your pulse rate may quicken, but instead of panic you'll feel a flood of euphoria and desire. I'm sure you already know how your body responds to flat-out lust, which is one of the strongest manifestations of the Urge to Merge.

Of course, this is the feeling most movies and Harlequin Romances describe as "falling in love." The Urge to Merge may indeed be the initial impulse that draws two lovers together. But this feeling isn't the same as a real relationship. It burns very bright and very hot, but it doesn't last. It will pull you toward someone who can help you get on your true path, then disappear, leaving you to do the much less intoxicating work of long-term human interaction. It may also be directed at people you've barely met, who would be totally unsuitable as romantic partners.

Malcolm, for example, was an office-supply salesman who began to volunteer as a firefighter during his recovery from a long depression. He was horrified when, during his first week as a fireman, he found himself longing to tag around after the fire chief like a worshipful toddler. Was he psychologically warped? Obsessive-compulsive? Gay? Answer: none of the above. Malcolm was just resurrecting the part of himself he'd buried when he decided to follow his bland, unambitious dad into retail. Now he'd found a new father figure, one who could mentor the adventurous hero in him. Malcolm's fascination with the fire chief disappeared as he reincorporated this part of his personality, but the two remain good friends to this day.

Another thing that differentiates the Urge to Merge from romantic love is the fact that it isn't always about another person. I've had clients suddenly become obsessed with collecting butterflies, playing the piano, learning geology, making cameras, inventing water-delivery systems, and supplying venture capital, to name just a few activities. I myself often feel the Urge to Merge in regard to (this is true) interior house paint. My essential self has bizarrely powerful reactions to color, and when I look over a bunch of paint strips, picking out the right shade for this or that wall, I can feel my eyeballs start to twirl like a dazzled cartoon character's. When I actually paint a room in my house, which I do far more often than is strictly necessary, anyone who tries to talk to me becomes convinced I'm on drugs. I get distracted, subverbal, and deeply, deeply content, even when the room is well ventilated.

Like attractions to people, Urge to Merge reactions to activities come and go on their own mysterious timetable. You're more likely to experience these sensations when you're at a change point. Crisis, loss, transformation, and growth all tend to weaken the grip of the social self, and demand some quick decision making on the part of the essential self. Since it can't explain itself logically, the essential self may just throw out a grappling hook and latch on to something or someone that might pull you toward your true path.

When have you "gone crazy" over a person or activity? Did you turn into a snowboard fanatic after your first day on the slopes? Have you ever become utterly fascinated by a movie or TV show? How about developing an embarrassing crush that turned out to be completely transitory? Jot down any Urge to Merge memories below.

EXERCISE

List times when you felt strangely drawn to a person, place, or thing. You may have temporarily become unable to concentrate on anything else. What was the object of your desire?

Urge to Merge item No. 1: _____

_____

Item No. 2: _____

_____

Item No. 3: _____

_____

Circle the one that brings up the most positive feelings.

7. A Natural High

When you're following a direct course to your North Star, you'll inevitably make decisions that should, by the social self's reckoning, be scary and depressing. You may be surprised when you don't feel the fear or sadness that seems warranted by the situation. Instead, you'll bounce around like Ebenezer Scrooge after the ghosts finished with him: smiling at strangers, finding infinite patience for children and the mentally ill, slowing down traffic to let cats and turtles make their way across the street. Bitter, unhappy people will want to slap you, but you'll love them anyway.

This maddeningly good mood often comes over people who have found a part of their true path, or let go of burdens that were holding them back from their North Stars. Since most people seek out career counseling at about the same time they resign from their jobs, I see a lot of job quitting, and you'll have to look a long way before you find an activity that can put people in a better mood. I've come to think of resigning as a mood-altering behavior at least as powerful as smoking peyote.

Celia was an uptight, spinsterish little woman who showed up at my office in a starched, high-collared business suit and an incredibly bad mood. For almost an hour, I didn't say much of anything; Celia took up every moment venting her spleen about her horrible workplace. She spoke with such venom that my deeply codependent beagle, Cookie, decided it must be his fault and started shedding all over the carpet.

At the end of our fifty-minute session, Celia finally stopped ranting long enough for me to put in my two cents. I said something deep and profound, like, "Wow. Ever thought of quitting?" Celia shot me a glare from one gimlet eye and stomped out the door, never to return. It took Cookie and me several minutes to pull ourselves together.

Six months later, I was signing books at a Barnes & Noble, half a continent away from my office. A lovely woman dressed in bright purple-and-blue silk floated up to me like Glinda the Good, her face transformed by a beatific smile. "Martha!" she shouted, wrapping me in a bear hug. "How *are* you?"

"Uh, hello," I said, wondering who on earth she was.

"I took your advice," she said. "I quit my job. I've started my own business."

"My advice?" I said lamely.

"It's a lot of work, but things are *so* much better than they were in my old company," said the woman. "God, I hated that place." She shivered and grimaced—and in that moment I saw the sour-faced, nasty creature who had scared my dog half to death six months before. Celia was truly a different person when she was headed toward her North Star. At her old job, with her essential self in full retreat, her mood had been so dark it was all she could do not to kick people. The joy of freedom—even the hard work of becoming free—had put her in such a good mood that now she buoys up everyone she meets.

Of course, your mood may respond just as well to getting a job as it does to quitting—if the job happens to be the way to your North Star.

You may also find yourself unaccountably cheerful about adopting a stray cat, moving to a new living space, joining a dirt-biking club, or eating cherries. Nothing is too large or too small to affect your progress toward your North Star. By noticing these good moods and pursuing the activities that produce them, you reconnect yourself with the navigational instruments that lead to your true path.

EXERCISE

List the last three times you experienced a wonderful mood, particularly if your good mood came at a strange time or from an action other people may have criticized.

Good-mood setting No. 1: _____

_____

Good-mood setting No. 2: _____

_____

Good-mood setting No. 3: _____

_____

Circle the situation that makes you feel happiest.

SUMMARY

After going through the checklist above, most of my clients are in what Californians call "a really good space." Just the fact that your social self is paying some attention to the things your essential self loves is enough to increase your sense of wholeness.

On the other hand, you may be feeling incredibly dejected or angry right now. When I ask people to remember the happy times in their lives, they often get downright confrontational. "Are you telling me to quit my job?" they'll demand, or "Are you telling me I'm in the wrong relationship?" I haven't told them anything of the kind—I usually go through these memory drills when I'm first getting to know a client. But as soon as these people reconnect with genuinely positive feelings, their essential selves begin to suggest major life remodeling. This can be mighty frightening. If it happens to you, please don't get your knickers in a knot. *You don't have to do one single thing right now except reconnect your social and essential selves.* The revolution will not begin until you give the go-ahead, and you'll do that when you're damn good and ready.

If you feel hopeless or angry when you try to remember good times, be gentle with yourself. Don't try to force anything. Just let go and experience your rage or despair; trust me, you've earned them. You might want to skim or skip the last part of this chapter, where we'll try to get a really clear *"Yes!"* from your essential self. Go straight to Chapter 4, which deals directly with the factors that may be causing your social self to freak out or crack down, delivering yet another painful blow to your most sensitive psychological regions. But if you were able to dredge up some happy memories to fill in the blanks above, let's move on to create the same kind of scenario we did in Chapter 2.

Step 1

In the spaces below, list the answers you circled on the exercises in this chapter, flipping back through the previous pages whenever necessary.

List your:

A. Most high-energy activity: _____

_____

B. Person who makes you feel most relaxed: _____

_____

C. Best-health situation: _____

_____

D. Information you remember most easily: _____

_____

E. Activity most likely to make you forget the time: _____

_____

F. Item that created the strongest Urge to Merge: _____

_____

G. Best-mood setting: _____

_____

Step 2

Fill in the blanks with the appropriate response.

YOUR OWN BEST-CASE SCENARIO

It's an incredibly beautiful day. The air is clear, the scenery dazzling, and you're setting out to do (A: your most high-energy activity)

_____

with (B: your favorite person)

_____.

You've got no other responsibilities, no immediate deadlines, and no major problems weighing you down. You feel great, even better than you did back when you were (C: your best-health situation)

_____.

In fact, you're in the best physical shape of your life: strong, lean, robust, and full of energy.

You're having a great conversation about (D: the information you remember most easily)

_____

when a message arrives for you. It's a letter from the president, saying that you have been chosen to receive a lifetime of financial support for doing (E: the activity that makes you forget time)

_____.

This will require you to spend a lot of time with (F: the person or situation that creates the Urge to Merge)

_____.

happened, only more so. Lie back for a minute, take in the scenery, and enjoy knowing that this is basically how you're going to spend the rest of your life.

Step 3

As you did with the "worst-case scenario," read over your "best-case" story carefully. Picture the images as vividly as you can, and *notice how you feel*. There's considerable evidence that just visualizing this scene greatly increases the likelihood that you'll experience something like it at some point in the future. In fact, no matter how impossibly wonderful it may appear, the scenario above is only a pale shadow of the splendid realities you'll find on the path to your own North Star.

What does it feel like to you, this sense of your essential self saying *"Yes! Due north!"*? How would you describe the sensation—or is it a sensation at all? Many people experience their true path not as something that happens to them but as the simultaneous loss of self and complete connection with the universe. When the essential self is really in its element, you may be so involved with the work at hand, the people around you, and the things you're learning that you won't be aware of yourself as separate from them. This state is the goal of many mystical practices, both in Western religious tradition and in the East. It's been described by psychologist Mihaly Csikszentmihalyi as "flow," by anthropologist Joseph Campbell as "following your bliss." What do you call it?

When I was a little kid, I called it "turning on my eyes." It happened whenever I drew; the world would suddenly seem stunningly beautiful, and I would feel connected to it through my vision. This probably would have happened throughout my college career if I'd believed in myself enough to major in art, as my essential self suggested. I was far too disconnected to follow my inner compass, but I did have that amazing thirty seconds in the bookstore, when I felt as though I'd suddenly learned to fly. Brief as it was, that moment has helped me grope my way back to my true path many, many times.

Et tu? Have you always listened when your essential self said *"Yes!"* or were you taught to muffle it with cynicism, doubt, fear, righteous wrath, or despair? Even if it's nothing but an alluring tickle, push the objections aside and move into this feeling of *"Yes!"* Believe it or not, this sensation—not pain, not self-sacrifice, not stoic numbness—is the surest indicator that you're on the path that will lead you to fulfilling relationships, a productive career, and the best possible effect you can have on the world. Keep turning toward it as best you can, and eventually you'll find yourself headed due north.

JUST BECAUSE YOU'RE PARANOID DOESN'T MEAN EVERYBODY ISN'T OUT TO GET YOU

Don't look now, but a lot of very powerful people are trying to stop you from reaching your North Star. Unless we deal with them, you might as well call off the whole trip. The conspirators marshaled against you are the very people who exiled your essential self in the first place, the ones who put your overgrown social self in complete command of your life. Right this minute, they are rallying to keep you from making positive changes. Who are they? *Everybody,* that's who. *People in general. Society at large.* The whole six-billion-member kit and kaboodle we call *the human race.*

You think I sound a teensy bit paranoid? Hey, I didn't come up with this on my own. I have many, many informed sources. My clients have a very firm grasp of what Everybody thinks, and they share the information with me almost every day. They say things like:

"If I quit my job / have a baby / marry my secretary, *everyone* will lose respect for me."

"I can't live in a small apartment / geodesic dome / marble mansion! *People* will think all the wrong things!"

"*Society* just doesn't accept people like me, who have artistic

inclinations / old-fashioned values / forward-thinking philosoph-
ical ideals."

"I have to wear a Rolex watch / Birkenstocks / enormous pants
that start below crotch level and drag on the ground when I walk
or *everybody* will think I'm pathetic."

Ah, yes. Everybody seems to know what Everybody thinks. It's fascinating to get a bunch of people together to ask about Everybody,
because, though each individual is convinced that he or she has a finger
on the pulse of some universal Zeitgeist, each of their Everybodies
turns out to be a very small slice of the human pie. Your view of
Everybody is completely different from my view of Everybody, which
is completely different from, say, Saddam Hussein's view of Everybody.

THE GENERALIZED OTHER

In fact, everybody's Everybody is composed of just a few key people.
Our social nature makes us long to fit in with a larger group, but it's difficult to hold the tastes and opinions of more than five or six individuals in your mind. So the resourceful social self creates a kind of
shorthand: it picks up on a few people's attitudes, emblazons them on
your brain, and extrapolates this image until it covers the entire known
universe. The vague compilation of folks you call Everybody is what
psychologists term "the generalized other."

No matter how deeply your essential self longs to find the real love,
the real mission, the real meaning of your life, your social self *will not* let
you embrace these things as long as Everybody disapproves. The social
self isn't opposed to your reaching your North Star, per se; it just won't
allow you to proceed toward it until you get Everybody's permission.
Actually, the social self would prefer that you don't do anything, anything at all, until Everybody kneels down and *begs* you to do it.

When my clients go through the exercises in the last two chapters,
reestablishing the connection between their social and essential selves,
the most common reaction is not joyful reunion but fear and resistance.
If you've done the exercises, you might be experiencing something
similar yourself. The social self wigs out when you begin to listen to

the essential self, because the latter immediately begins to suggest that you do things your Everybody might not like.

ESSENTIAL SELF: I hate this job.

SOCIAL SELF: Don't you dare quit! Do you know how that will look on your résumé? Everybody will think you're a complete failure!

ESSENTIAL SELF: I was much happier in San Diego.

SOCIAL SELF: So, you're going to slink back to San Diego with your tail between your legs, huh? Going to let everybody see what a big ol' mess you are? Over my dead body!

ESSENTIAL SELF: Ooh, I love those purple socks!

SOCIAL SELF: Sure. Right. Walk around in those, and you'll never date a sighted person again.

Remember, your social self is just trying to keep you from getting hurt. Everything it says may be partially true. Some people may indeed think you're a failure if you quit your job and move back to San Diego wearing purple socks. What your social self doesn't know is that 1) very few people actually feel this way; 2) these people are not likely to be the best source of information about your ideal life; and 3) there may be a whole bunch of other people who would actually praise and accept you for doing exactly what feels best to your essential self. By installing a hypercritical social group as your definition of Everybody, your social self may well be keeping you from the Everybody who will applaud and support your quest for your North Star.

The way to solve this problem isn't to reject or condemn your social self; it's just doing its well-meaning best. No, we're going to give the social self exactly what it wants—Everybody's approval—while also allowing you to take directions from your essential self. This is the only way to find your North Star, but you may not like how we have to go about it. See, you want the Everybody you have now, the people whose influence landed you in your present life, to approve of your essential self. This will happen right after Hell becomes the official Olympic ice-dancing venue, and you may have that kind of time, but I don't. I'd rather take the quick approach by *exchanging* your present generalized other for a whole new Everybody.

This process is fairly simple, considering how much it can transform your life. Since we know that human psychology will always create a subconscious generalized other that has very little to do with objective reality, we're simply going to make sure your particular set of delusions is consciously chosen, rather than randomly acquired, and helpful, rather than hurtful. This chapter will help you figure out who your Everybody really is, and whether it's encouraging you to find your own North Star. This will set the stage for you to disassemble your Everybody, keeping its useful elements and discarding those that are damaging you. Finally, you'll learn how to install an Everybody that will support your quest and protect you from whatever destructive elements have knocked you off your true path.

MEETING YOUR EVERYBODY

It never fails to surprise me how limited our Everybodies really are. One of the first things I learned when I was being trained as a sociologist was to avoid false generalizations, yet I still do it almost every day. Whenever I'm presented with a choice, I reflexively test the potential outcomes against my idea of what "people" will think. When I stop and try to pin down who these "people" are, I rarely come up with more than three individuals. Often, this little group differs wildly from the statistical majority in our culture, but despite years of sociological training, that doesn't matter to my social self.

Speaking of sociology, I once wrote a book about women's issues, which was based on some of the theories I'd used in my Ph.D. dissertation. At the time, I belonged to a small writing group; three other hopeful writers and I would get together every other week, hand out the new pages we'd written, and then critique one another's recent work. My writing group's reaction to the first chapters of my book was less than glowing. "What's with all the five-dollar words?" one of my friends asked. "Why can't you just write like you talk?" The others agreed completely, telling me to lose the social-science jargon, cut the academic "literature review," and stop footnoting everything.

Well, I freaked like a Chihuahua on bad acid. If I did what my writing group wanted—made my book reader-friendly and accessible—I was sure that my crucified body would be found on the nearest telephone pole by dawn on publication day. People would *destroy* me. By "people," of course, I meant the sociology professors in my alma mater. Several of these scholars had criticized my work very harshly—that, after all, was their job. As I scampered to meet their demands, I'd sworn a mighty (though subconscious) oath that no matter what I wrote, I would always use the pseudo-omniscient, sesquipedalian style that characterizes academic journals. One reason this sank in so thoroughly was that my father was a well-known academician whose views underlay the Everybody I'd built from other teachers. It took me a long, long time to realize that not Everybody is a college professor.

This is a pretty typical story; yours is probably a variation on the same theme. Most people have an Everybody made up of the people who raised them, plus a few individuals who became very important to them at crucial developmental stages in their lives. Celia's Everybody boils down to her parents, her oldest sister, and three friends she met at a Buddhist retreat. Don thinks Everybody holds the same views as his mom, his mentor at work, and Howard Stern. Jane goes to her memories of her parents, her coworkers at the company where she works, a former lover, and her husband. To formally make the acquaintance of your own subconscious Everybody, try the following exercise.

EVERYBODY ON DECK

Step 1: Finish the following sentences by writing down whatever comes from your gut, no matter how silly it may sound to your brain.

1. People judge me because _____

   _____

2. Everyone loves it when I _____

   _____

3. When I do well, people feel _____

   _____

4. Nobody will let me _____

   _____

5. Everybody always tells me to _____

   _____

6. People just can't accept the fact that I _____

   _____

7. When I fail, everyone thinks _____

   _____

8. Nobody cares when I _____

   _____

9. Society keeps telling me I have to _____

   _____

10. Everyone expects me to _____

    _____

Step 2: For each statement above, write the names of six people you know who *actually, verifiably* hold the opinions you've ascribed to Everybody. You can use the same names for every question if that's what pops up.

	Person 1	Person 2	Person 3	Person 4	Person 5	Person 6
1.						
2.						
3.						
4.						
5.						
6.						
7.						

8. _____

9. _____

10. _____

If you're like most people, you'll find that it's hard to come up with the names of six individuals who really, truly hold the various expectations and judgments you feel coming from Everybody. Most of my clients can point to a few solid representatives of their Everybodies, but usually only two or three. To get six, they usually have to start generalizing or naming people they don't know all that well, like "everyone at work," or "the Republican Party." Even when they can actually name individuals, a lot of the people they list don't actually hold the opinions my clients ascribe to them.

Whenever Leo started talking about what "people" thought of him, you could be sure he was thinking of his three older brothers. They had teased Leo unmercifully throughout his childhood, telling him that he was a pathetic baby who couldn't play in their games and would never amount to much. Leo's one objective in life was to prove his value to Everybody by equaling or exceeding his brothers in the career game. He'd gone into investment banking, just like all of them, even though it didn't interest him. Not surprisingly, he wasn't doing well. Leo virtually frothed with anger and anxiety: Everybody was looking down on him, and Everybody was *right!*

Leo hit a major turning point when he began actually talking to his brothers about the way they had shaped his life. None of them had any idea how much their adolescent teasing had influenced him. As one of them succinctly put it, "Why would you pay any attention to us? We were total idiots." Leo's Everybody consisted not of his real brothers but of three pubescent figments of his memory and imagination.

An important point about your Everybody list is that it's probably made up partly of loved ones *and partly of hated ones.* Yes, it's true: Every single day, you hand over control of your life to the very people you most dislike. This irony is almost universal. Especially when you're striking out in a new direction, feeling a bit scared and vulnerable, the voice of Everybody begins to sound just like the most demanding, rigid, narrow-minded, and, frankly, stupid people you know. Why? Because the social self is programmed to *avoid danger,* and nasty people are far more dangerous than the loving, accepting folks in your universe. If you're sitting in a room full of ten darling, harmless little puppies and one big, deadly king cobra, you're not going to ignore the snake and just lose yourself in frolicking with the puppies, right?

Right. And so you fill the few chairs in your Everybody committee with the most insecure, vindictive jerks who have ever hurt your feelings. In fact, your social self is so devoted to this merry band of lowlifes that it tries to pre-empt an emotional thrashing by *imagining* how they would respond to your choices before you even make them.

This is a useful, even wise response when you are completely surrounded by hostile people. I see a lot of clients who were raised in emotionally (and sometimes physically) dangerous situations, where large, powerful adults repeatedly blasted any attempt they made to find their North Stars. As children, they accurately assessed the situation, then shut down their essential selves to keep them from getting damaged any further. That's a healthy defense mechanism. It becomes unhealthy when people leave a dangerous environment but continue to believe that Everybody is an extension of those who hurt them. A really scarred-and-scared social self will set your view of Everybody in cement, refusing to even perceive objective information about people who differ from your expectations. This, in turn, makes you react in ways that actually elicit all the negative behaviors you've come to expect, which reinforces your expectations, and so on, and so on. Before long, you're riding along on a vicious cycle with a crushed-glass seat.

Pam was raised by two of the meanest drunks I've ever met. She went to Catholic school even though she was Jewish (long story, you don't want to hear it), and was therefore a sitting duck for judgment from both her peers and her teachers. Later, Pam married a compulsive gambler who became violently angry every time she questioned his behavior in any way. He eventually squandered the couple's life savings, then took off to parts unknown. By the time she'd reached her mid-thirties, Pam had quilted together a truly horrendous Everybody. Her generalized other was a hideous patchwork of cruel, deceitful addicts and the kind of nuns who whacked small children with rulers as their major form of aerobic exercise.

When her husband left and she had to enter the workforce, Pam acted exactly as any healthy person would in a world where Everybody fit this profile. She felt suspicious, besieged, and persecuted, and her behavior alternated between cowering obedience and confrontational rage. Most importantly, *Pam picked out information about people that reinforced her view of Everybody, while going blind to people and situations that operated on kindness, tolerance, and understanding.* Her fear of a few people in her past literally screened out the goodness and approval coming from many more people around her, stranding Pam in a world populated exclusively by fiends and sadists.

Naturally, Pam's interaction style didn't win her any Miss Congeniality awards. People found her very unpleasant to work with, and she lost many jobs for reasons that were never made really clear, reinforcing her belief that Everyone was out to get her. It wasn't until Pam courageously examined her view of Everybody, took the huge risk of believing that not Everybody hated her, and began to notice when other people were well-meaning, that her delightful essential-self personality began to emerge.

Though your story is probably less horrific than Pam's, I'd bet my purple socks that your Everybody is not really representative of the human species. I'd also bet that you are creating many of the reactions you expect to see in the people around you. If so, then looking closely at your Everybody (tearing it into little bits, if necessary) is the first step toward breaking destructive patterns and finding support and encouragement in your quest for your own North Star.

GROUP EVERYBODIES

As a kid, did you ever laugh along with a group of bullies who were tormenting someone else, simply because you didn't want the group to turn its aggression on you? Have you done anything similar in the past year, say, at a cocktail party? The structure of human psychology makes this kind of "agreeing" behavior very hard to resist. Psychological experiments show that when a group of people expresses a strong, united opinion, an individual thrown in with that group will change his or her own perceptions—literally see and hear differently—in order to match the rest of the gang. At the very least, we tend to remain silent when we think people might disagree with our opinions.

This means that most groups end up with a few very vocal members and a large silent majority. We tend to assume that such silence means agreement, that the group is totally united and monolithic in its beliefs. We're usually wrong. I made this mistake recently, during a radio interview. I tossed off a remark about Catholicism being more restrictive than mystical Eastern religions, only to have the interviewer gently inform me that he is a mystical Catholic with a wildly unorthodox worldview, and that I might want to think twice before I lump all Catholics together.

Now, I should know this. I've met Chinese Communists who talked and acted more capitalistic than Donald Trump, U.S. Marines who were absolutely committed to nonviolence, and devout Mormons who were also lobbyists for gay rights. Of course, they weren't the rule, but they are exceptions I would never have dreamed possible if I'd taken the group's opinions at face value. One important step in reaching your North Star is to rethink your assumption that everyone in a certain group or category is united against you. Another is simply to learn which groups most commonly factor into people's Everybodies, so that you'll realize you're following predictable—and, more important, changeable—patterns. Here are the four most common groups from which people draw their Everybodies.

1. Family

I can't tell you how many of my clients are convinced that Everybody is exactly like their families of origin. The weirder and more unusual their families actually are, the more firmly they believe this. Dale grew up on his family's organic farm in Wyoming, where he was taught that banking is an unstable and essentially evil way to deal with money. To this day, Dale worries that Everybody looks down on him for having a savings account. Alice, raised by a staunchly feminist single mom, was convinced that decorating her apartment—something she longed to do—would make Everybody sneer at her for becoming a "simpering homemaker." Zack's otherwise typical suburban parents often came to the family dinner table buck naked. Zack thought that Everybody (including me) would condemn him as prudish if he admitted that he really didn't want to uphold this family tradition.

In some ways, having a wildly dysfunctional family can help shake you free of the tendency to see them as Everybody. I had one client whose parents were actually arrested for child abuse. This event made it very clear to her that her family was abnormal, and that she could expect to find a much more supportive atmosphere outside her home. Sad as this was, having the law tear down her family's Everybody-ness allowed her to start building a more benevolent generalized other, and create a happy and fulfilling life.

Conversely, even the most "functional" and best-intentioned families can still create a damaging Everybody. Though they may adore you, the people who raised you from a larva never quite shake the image of you drooling into a rubber bib, or getting your head stuck in the slats of the picket fence trying to kiss the neighbors' dachshund. As a result, they have trouble really believing that you can make it in journalism, or marry well, or manage a business empire. They feel you'd do better in a supervised group home. If only in an attempt to protect you, your family is likely to suck the wind right out of your essential self's ambitious sails. Do any of these phrases sound familiar?

"Honey, we're glad you like cooking / politics / historical fiction, but don't you think you should spend your time on something that will make some money?"

"Don't you go getting above yourself, young man / lady. I've made a damn good living teaching driver's ed / writing advertising copy / selling rectal thermometers, and what's good enough for me is good enough for you."

"And just what makes you think you can create your own Web site / be a Navy Seal / date a TV anchorperson? You wet the bed until you were twelve."

Listen carefully: *Your family of origin does not know how to get you to your North Star. They didn't when you were little, they don't now, and they never will. It isn't their job.*

This is hard to accept, whether your family treated you well or badly. People whose families were accepting and supportive have to face the fact that familial love can't take them all the way to their right lives. And if your family members did atrocious things to you, things that knocked your essential self into Siberia, they cannot bring you back to your true path. Only you can do that. I know this isn't fair, but it's true. If your parents deliberately ran over you in their Land Cruiser, they are definitely culpable and wrong. But you will still have to do the physical therapy to get your bones and muscles to work again. The same thing is true of psychological wounds.

If, upon impartial inspection, you decide to continue thinking of your family as Everybody in the Entire Universe, that's fine. Personally, I wouldn't advise it. Your family is the generalized other thrust upon you by fate, without any decision making on your part. If you're planning to wait for them to locate your true path, draw you a careful map, pack you a lunch, and drive you to your North Star, you might want to take up needlework. I hear it passes the time.

2. Media Culture

Media sources are incredibly powerful members of the Everybody committee, because they deliberately pose as representatives of whole cultures. Each time you go past the magazines at the supermarket checkout counter, or sit down for an evening to watch television, or glance at a billboard ad, you get a powerful dose of how Everybody thinks you should act, think, dress, talk, and look.

If you don't have high cheekbones, large eyes, a strong jaw, perfect skin, and thick hair, for example, the Media Everybody will suggest that instead of trying to get a date for Saturday night, you might want to consider suicide. You must also be thin, tall, toned, and young. Once you've got these qualifications down pat, you can move on to become smart, rich, and stylish. Of course, you'll have to buy a new wardrobe every season and a new car every year. Oh, and for

God's sake (the Media Everybody will clearly imply), *please* try to be Caucasian.

I myself occasionally have lucid moments when I realize the following stunning truths: 1) The people and images I see in magazines and movies, far from being Everybody, are in fact *very unusual*. 2) Not Everybody expects me to meet the criteria established by media ideals; there have been documented incidents of people loving me even though I don't meet a single blessed one. 3) The few people who would reject me solely because I cannot achieve media-based perfection are (and I say this respectfully) shallow, soulless morons. Why should I want them to like me, when I already know that I don't like them?

Meditating upon these treasures of truth can bring me to a state of Zen-like detachment, sometimes for as long as fifteen minutes. Then I go to the doctor for my annual checkup, and there's nothing to read in the waiting room except *Vogue* or *GQ,* and the nurse insists on weighing me, and I end up asking how much it would cost to have every single part of my body replaced by a plastic surgeon. As long as the media keep pumping out images of the ideal human, my social self will continue its proud tradition of pathetic, groveling longing to please Everybody.

3. Ideological Camps

I'm always amazed at the extent to which my clients' early ideological training, whether political or religious, colors their view of what Everybody thinks. This is true even for people who long ago abandoned the moral rules taught to them in childhood. I don't want to get on the bad side of any authorities here, but I have noticed that clients who were raised with religious or political devotion to poverty, suffering, and celibacy tend to feel a lot of resistance from Everybody when they later decide they want wealth, happiness, and romance.

Evan was raised in a devout born-again Christian family. He went to church every Sunday and Wednesday and was home-schooled by his parents and other church members from kindergarten through the twelfth grade. It was a good education; Evan went on to earn several graduate degrees, including one in business. Nevertheless, he had never gotten a job offer worthy of his training. Everyone wanted to hire Evan, but no one wanted to pay him what he deserved. I gave Evan a simple assignment: He was to repeat the phrase "I make eighty thousand dollars a year" twenty-five times a day for one week.

When Evan returned a week later, he told me that he'd been doing his homework faithfully—with one little glitch. After a week of chanting his affirmation, Evan noticed that at some point he had unconsciously changed it to "I make *thirty* thousand dollars a year." After we finished marveling at this little piece of self-defeating behavior, Evan tried saying the phrase as we'd originally scripted it. He immediately developed such a severe anxiety reaction, I considered mashing a paper bag up to his face. Suddenly, he was back in church, listening to a preacher he admired deliver one of many blistering lectures on the love of money (see "root of all evil, the"). This version of Everybody loomed up in Evan's mind every time the phrase "eighty thousand dollars" passed his lips.

Now, if you're deeply religious and happy with your choices, far be it from me to dissuade you. You can gloat at me angelically when you're sitting in the lap of God and I'm down in the warmer regions shoveling sulfur. But if you were raised with beliefs you no longer consciously accept, and you're having trouble making your life work, you might want to re-examine those early lessons. Your mental version of Everybody is probably busy sewing you a new hair shirt, spray-painting "Death to Capitalists!" all over the walls of your brain, and renewing its fervent commitment that you will die a virgin.

4. School

The educational system is a very powerful Everybody. After all, every single kid has to answer to its demands to stay within the law. You spent most of your tender years in a huge, well-rooted system with crystal-clear priorities about what you should do and be. In school, you learned that being smart is the most important thing in the world. This was closely followed by working hard, being quiet, keeping your belongings tidy, and not causing any trouble. Being happy probably never made it onto the academic value chart. It's not that the school systems *wanted* you to be unhappy, but as long as you were smart, diligent, quiet, and well organized, nobody paid much attention to your emotional state.

During my years in academia, I met many, many people who had absorbed the social norms of the educational system to the exclusion of all other Everybody input. These people truly didn't realize that not everyone was impressed by the articles they published in academic journals, or by the fact that they were given "chairs" in various departments. (Doesn't every office worker have a chair?) They never looked for work in other environments, because school had dominated their social selves since they were five years old.

On the other hand, I've had lots of bright, competent clients who thought they were stupid because, at some point, their abilities hadn't lined up perfectly with academic requirements. I once gave a seminar in which two participants had dyslexia. Over the course of a few days, they became more and more open about the intense shame, self-hatred, and despair they'd felt every school day of their lives. Everyone in the seminar ended up in tears as we came to understand how hellish school can be for those who don't fit in.

5. Peers

School is also the place where we interact most closely with same-age peers, and this can be a hard-knock life for the essential self. Personal friends contribute to your Everybody in a slightly different way than the overall herd of people your own age. You may run with various different crowds at any time from babyhood to old age, but their effect tends to be strongest during adolescence and early adulthood, when people are trying to establish an identity independent of their families.

My client Christopher, who was having inordinate trouble deciding what he wanted to do with his life, traced his lack of a strong identity back to his experience in an inner-city gang. "I was afraid every day," he told me. "Ha ha! Every day!" Christopher laughed as though he found this just hilarious. It was clear that he'd learned long ago not to actually *look* scared, even when he was confessing his fears. "I never got beaten up very badly," he said, "because I learned to fit in. I'd become like the group I was with, and then fade back into the scenery. My whole life was about camouflage."

Without his savvy social self, Christopher wouldn't have learned to "disappear," and he might have lost a few crucial limbs and digits back in South-Central Los Angeles. But at thirty-five, he still didn't know how *not* to fade away. The violent peers of his youth still made up the Everybody in his mind, and his social self still refused to let his essential self out to express its unique nature.

I've met many adults who spent years trying to impress the cheerleader who wouldn't date them, the college pals who sneered at their taste in clothing, the "cool" group at work who never asked them to go to lunch. This is a great way to run your life, if you really want to be enslaved to an insecure, pack-minded Everybody who is desperately busy battling nonexistent demons.

6. Organizations

Organizations have very powerful cultures, which almost invariably become part of the members' Everybodies. Even if you view an organization as an alien force, within which you are merely an observer, any group with which you come into regular contact influences your social self. If the organizational culture comes close to your essential temperament, this will be exciting and empowering—you'll feel like Everybody loves you. If you and the organization differ, however, you're liable to abandon your essential self and conform to the majority. It's not that you're weak, it's just that group dynamics are incredibly strong.

I've had clients whose Everybodies came from Fortune 100 companies, the military, universities, sports teams, and a variety of other organizations. Long after they'd left these institutions, my clients still believed that Everybody thought along organizational lines.

Matt was a top performer in the Peace Corps, instrumental in bringing fresh water to a village in Africa. He made most of his lasting friendships while in the Corps, and years after his return, these are still the people with whom he feels most comfortable. Matt married another Peace Corps veteran, Angela, and together they set out to fight for the rights of the poor and oppressed in the United States and abroad. They earned a little money doing housecleaning and odd jobs, living simply and pouring most of their time into activism.

A serious disagreement arose between Matt and Angela when they were expecting their first child. Angela was nervous about having a baby, let alone raising one, without health insurance. She wanted to buy a house, instead of living in low-rent apartments. She wanted—Matt shuddered to hear this—a corporate job. Eventually, she went out and got one.

This was a deal breaker for Matt and Angela's relationship. In Matt's world, Everybody was passionately opposed to the "establishment," and regular work with benefits definitely came under that heading. Matt felt that Angela had shamed them both. The last I heard of them, the couple had separated.

Experiences in organizations can be as traumatic, or as healing, as one-on-one relationships. I've had clients whose hearts and spirits were broken by corporate cultures, whose time was consumed by bitter wrangling with this or that religion, whose lives were dominated by their need to fit in at the PTA. All these organizations inevitably projected an illusion of unanimity, and the power of group psychology turned them into overwhelming Everybodies in the minds of each individual member.

FACING THE TRUTH

None of the individuals you've loved or hated, and none of the organizations that have touched your life, has the ability to control your choices. What does possess this power is the part of your brain that contains your generalized other. Depending on what it thinks Everybody wants, your social self will make it either impossible or inevitable that you will reach your own North Star. To see which direction you're headed, note whether you "believe" or "don't believe" the following statements. Answer based on *what you feel in your heart*, not what your head thinks is the "right" answer. Remember, you're doing this to find your true path, not to please Everybody.

Please note whether you believe or disbelieve each of the following statements.

I do believe	I don't believe	
_____	_____	1. I'm a natural-born winner: always was, always will be.
_____	_____	2. The world is full of people who would love to be my friends.
_____	_____	3. I'll always have plenty of money.
_____	_____	4. I deserve a life full of joy and fulfillment.
_____	_____	5. I'm physically beautiful, and I always will be.
_____	_____	6. I can be wildly successful at my chosen career.
_____	_____	7. I have an amazingly capable brain.
_____	_____	8. I'm perfectly lovable exactly as I am.
_____	_____	9. I'm highly creative by nature.
_____	_____	10. My dreams are in the process of coming true.

I believe that all ten of these statements can, and should, be true for every single person on this planet, so I'll be blunt: If you marked "don't believe" on any of the self-image statements, your generalized other is lying.

Some of my clients get a little upset when I say this. I see their throats clench up, their teeth clamp tight, their backs go stiff. They don't just think I'm talking like a lobotomized Pollyanna; no, they actually feel threatened. They show every sign of being furiously angry, or overwhelmed by shame, or deeply depressed. Now, nobody has to fight that hard to reject an idea that's manifestly false. If I told clients they were Jersey dairy cows, they'd just smile nervously and leave. The reason they freak out when I give them accurate descriptions of themselves (that they are beautiful, creative, intelligent winners) is that *they once believed all these things, until somebody taught them a pack of devastating lies.*

Babies show up knowing the truth: Each of them is an utterly lovable, beautiful creature, with a unique mission in life and all the equipment necessary to fulfill that mission. If the people around them support and nourish their essential selves, their social selves never have to disengage from this reality to serve the social group. This can be true for anyone, even people who appear to have a lot going against them.

For example, I was once lucky enough to have lunch with the mother of Chris Burke, the actor who has appeared regularly on TV shows such as *Life Goes On* and *Touched By an Angel* and who happens to have Down's syndrome. As I've mentioned, I also have a son with Down's syndrome, and Chris's success has been a source of hope and happiness in my family for a long time. His mom is an absolutely lovely woman, very kind and funny. Over lunch, she told me about Chris's career: He's booked solid for speaking and acting jobs more than two years in advance, travels constantly to keep up with his engagements, and is mobbed by well-wishers and autograph seekers wherever he goes.

Naturally, hearing this made me practically effervesce with admiration. "At the moment the doctors came in and told you Chris has Down's syndrome," I asked Mrs. Burke, "would you ever have dreamed he was going to be a famous TV star?" I thought this question was rhetorical; naturally, she would have been completely unable to believe that her poor retarded baby would ever make good. But Mrs. Burke didn't bat an eye.

"Of course," she said, a bit quizzically. "Why not?"

I could tell this wasn't revisionist history. From the moment he was born, Chris Burke's family really had seen the truth of his talent and potential. I have no doubt that his generalized other is based on this limitless, optimistic, and clear-eyed love. Does this mean Chris has suffered no failures, disappointments, or humiliations? Of course not. Does it mean everybody, literally everybody, loves and admires him? No again—a lot of people while away their pathetic little lives pelting people like Chris with rocks and insults. But his benevolent Everybody does mean that Chris Burke feels, and projects, enormous faith in himself and complete acceptance of others. It means he handles criticism thoughtfully and well. And it means that he lives in a virtual ocean of positive feedback, coming from literally millions of people. He firmly believes every one of the positive statements above applies to him and that Everybody can see it's true.

One reason I can see my clients the way Mrs. Burke sees Chris is that my essential self tends to come out when I'm doing life design. As this occurs, it becomes impossible for me to see the false, social-self version of the person sitting across from me. The more you integrate your essential self, the more you will perceive both yourself and others in this way. When the curtain of social judgment pulls back, it reveals the most amazing beauty.

I first became aware of this phenomenon when I was a college art student. Every few weeks, I'd join this or that group of artists, and we'd all pitch in a few bucks to rent a studio and hire a model. Most of the people we got to pose were college students with bodies that matched the social ideal—slender, fit, perfectly proportioned. (After all, who else would risk standing naked in a roomful of strangers?) And then, one day, we got somebody really different.

She looked well over sixty, with a deeply lined face and a body that was probably fifty pounds heavier than her doctors would have liked. She'd had a few doctors, too, judging from her scars. Shining purple welts from a cesarean section and knee surgery cut deep rifts in the rippled adipose fat of her lower body. Another scar ran across one side of her chest, where her left breast had once been. When she first limped onto the dais to pose, I felt so much pity and unease that I physically flinched. But we were there to draw her, so I picked up a pencil.

The thing about drawing is that you can't do it well with your social self. You have to bring out your essential self, which doesn't know anything about social stereotypes. And so, as I began to draw this maimed old woman, the most amazing thing happened. Within five minutes, she became a person of absolutely wondrous beauty. She didn't look like a supermodel; she didn't have to. Her body, in and of itself, was as beautiful as a piece of polished driftwood, or a wind-carved rock, or a waterfall. My essential self didn't know that I was supposed to compare the woman to various movie stars, any more than it would have evaluated the Andes Mountains by judging how much they looked like an Iowa cornfield. It simply saw her as she was: an exquisite sculptural form.

When this perceptual shift happened, I was so surprised that I stopped drawing and simply stared. The model seemed to notice this, and without turning her head, looked straight into my eyes. Then I saw the ghost of a smile flicker across her face, and I realized something else: *She knew she was beautiful.* She knew it, and she knew that I'd seen it. Maybe that's why she had consented to pose nude in the first place. Knowing that a roomful of artists couldn't draw her without seeing her—I mean really *seeing* her—she may have decided to give us a gentle education about our perceptions.

If none of this is new to you; if you answered *all* the "Self-perception Exercise" questions with an unequivocal "yes" and have an Everybody who would back you up right down the line, you can skip the next chapter. On the other hand, if you feel a bit isolated or scared, and your faith in yourself isn't exactly earthquake-proof, you must learn to do what Chris Burke and my Mystery Model seemed to do naturally: replace your hypercritical, limiting, lying Everybody with an Everybody who sees you as you really are. Once again, find yourself a pencil and prepare to do a little work. You're about to learn what it feels like to search for your own North Star with Everybody on your side.

GETTING EVERYBODY
ON YOUR SIDE

For years, Linda had been lugging around a romantic torch so large, hot, and heavy that it drained almost all her energy. The object of her affection was a man named Roger, whom Linda had dated briefly some years before I met her. The relationship ended when Roger checked into a rehab center to clean up a drug problem. Apparently, Linda told me in an anguished voice, Roger had lost interest in her once he was clean and sober. Shortly after his release from rehab, he'd bid her a coldly casual farewell and gone off to graze in greener pastures.

To hear Linda tell it, Roger was such a brilliant, powerful, charismatic giant of a man that there was simply no replacing him. Even though she hadn't seen him for many months, Roger's tastes and opinions still dominated Linda's choices. She dressed in clothes she thought would appeal to him, entered a Ph.D. program she thought would impress him, even judged other men by his standards ("I don't want to get stuck with a man Roger would laugh at," she said). Roger made up an enormous proportion of Linda's internalized Everybody. You'd think she'd had a fling with Jesus.

One day, Linda and I were leaving a restaurant when she suddenly froze. She had spotted Roger on the other side of a busy street. While

Linda tried not to fall down, I stared in amazement: Her Roger turned out to be someone I'd known since I was seventeen. In college, he'd come across to me as a mildly ridiculous, bland, chubby dork who had a tendency to drink a bit much and launch into endless orations about the fiction of J. R. R. Tolkein. A dozen years later, Roger still looked like a bland, chubby dork, but with less hair. It was inconceivable to me that this completely ordinary person was the god Linda had been worshiping all these years. The only reason I could even begin to understand her fixation on Roger is that I know we all have a psychological tendency to give unwarranted power to certain individuals.

This is one of the tricks the social self uses to create a powerful generalized other. It can elevate the lowliest people to an illusory omnipotence, turning them into the deities of our inner lives. Usually, no matter how old we are, we see our Everybody representatives through the worshipful eyes of children, making them appear large, mighty, and wise. (The German psychologist Alice Miller has written convincingly about the way Adolf Hitler epitomized a certain type of militant Teutonic father. Because of this, Miller hypothesizes, Hitler's pompous mannerisms and screaming speeches won the awestruck devotion of his supporters, while to other people he came across as an unhinged little freak with bad facial hair.)

If you've lost your true path and are unsatisfied with life, it's quite probable that, like Linda, you're doing psychological obeisance to someone who really doesn't deserve it. In this chapter, we're going to break the trance that may be holding you in thrall to a less-than-desirable Everybody. Like Toto ripping the Wizard's little curtain off its runners, we're going to expose your generalized other as the posse of ordinary, uncertain, flawed human beings it is. Then you'll learn to create a new Everybody, composed of people who support your quest for your own North Star.

EXERCISE: ALTERNATE VOICES

In the last chapter, you identified some of the people on your Everybody committee. Now we're going to separate the committee members who are on your side from those who are trying, for whatever reason, to keep you off your true path. This exercise is best done with at least one other person, *provided it's someone you trust.* If possible, get a small group of honest and thoughtful friends together to help you. The reason for this is that your friends probably have a clearer perception of you than you do. Your memory will screen out evidence that goes against your beliefs, and more objective opinions can be immensely helpful.

I saw this very graphically when I test-drove the exercise below. I'd gathered a small group of friends for the occasion. One of them (I'll call her Liz) was absolutely certain that Everybody thinks she's ugly. Ugly, ugly, ugly; she just couldn't emphasize it enough. However, when it came to actually listing the names of people who'd told her she was unattractive, Liz couldn't come up with anybody. This was hardly surprising to the assembled company, since Liz looks a lot like Julia Roberts. In the end, Liz decided that her father and brothers should go on the list, not because they'd ever overtly said she was ugly but because they used to call her "Goofy" and never told her they liked her looks. Then it was time for Liz to make a list of people who had told her she was beautiful. She immediately barked, "Nobody has ever said that to me."

Liz's husband, Hank, who was sitting beside her, looked stunned. "What about me?" he protested.

Liz rolled her eyes. "You don't count," she said. "You're biased."

"What about us?" demanded all the other people in the room. "We think you're beautiful."

Liz looked flustered, but quickly came up with an explanation. "You're just being polite."

"Well," Hank said, yanking his beard in frustration, "what about your students?" He told us that at the junior college where Liz teaches, the students hold a raucous and unsanctioned yearly award ceremony, in which Liz routinely receives the award for "Sexiest Faculty Member." Individual students often develop such passionate crushes on her that she has to set strict limits on office-hour appointments. They write poetry about her, send her love letters, and eventually wander off, heartbroken, the image of Liz's beautiful face indelibly seared into their visual cortexes. After Hank related all this, Liz gave him a puzzled frown.

"But that's just sexual harassment," she said.

At this point, everyone else in the group began shouting, laughing, and tossing small objects at Liz, trying to jar loose her infuriatingly selective Everybody. It worked, as group psychology usually does. By articulating her preconceptions about her looks, instead of hiding them in shame as she customarily did, Liz got enough clear feedback, from enough people, to begin changing her internalized Everybody. The power of group dynamics began pushing some of her committee members (mostly media images) out of the chairs in her brain, filling them instead with competent people who gave her realistic feedback.

If Liz continues this kind of behavior—challenging her preconceptions, getting information from new sources—her self-image will inevitably undergo a deep transformation. Even if she fights to keep her beliefs from changing, the social self's Everybody mechanism will automatically create a more accepting attitude toward her appearance. This is the Achilles' heel of the social self: If you can convince it that Everybody approves of your true path—and remember, the social self needs only three or four opinions to draw this conclusion—it will automatically begin to disassemble the barriers that keep you from your own North Star.

COMPARE AND CONTRAST: THE OPPOSING FORCES OF YOUR EVERYBODY

In the spaces below, I'm going to repeat the self-perception statements from the last chapter. If you come to a statement you already deeply believe, simply skip over it—your Everybody doesn't need any work on that issue. For each of the statements you *don't* believe, write down the names of up to ten people who have told you that it isn't true. For example, if you don't believe the statement "I have an amazingly capable brain," list everyone who's ever called you stupid. *No generalizations are allowed; these must be specific individuals.*

Next, I want you to make another list, directly across from the first one. In this column, I want the names of up to ten individuals who have given you positive feedback on the same issue—for example, people who have told you that you have a good head on your shoulders or complimented you for quick thinking. Remember, you'll probably screen out memories that don't fit your preconceptions. Most of my clients seem to store positive experiences in a sector of memory quite separate from unhappy information. If they can think of just one instance where they succeeded or elicited praise, they tap into a whole stream of similar experiences. This is where other people's less biased memories can be very useful, so please try to get a second opinion (if possible, get several).

ALTERNATE VOICES EXERCISE

Fill in as many of the blanks as you can. You don't have to fill all of them, and it's fine if the same names come up in response to different statements. Bother only with the statements you *do not believe*, and remember: no generalizing!

1. I'm a natural-born winner: always was, always will be.

People who have told you that you *are not* a natural-born winner	People who have told you that you *are* a natural-born winner

2. The world is full of people who would love to be my friends.

People who have told you that there *aren't* a lot of people who'd love to be your friends	People who have told you that you there *are* a lot of people who would love to be your friends

_____

_____

_____

3. I'll always have plenty of money.

People who have told you that you   People who have told you that you
won't always have plenty of money   *will* always have plenty of money

_____

_____

_____

_____

4. I deserve a life of joy and fulfillment.

People who have told you that you   People who have told you that you
don't deserve a joyful life   *do deserve* a joyful life

_____

_____

_____

_____

5. I'm physically beautiful, and I always will be.

People who have told you that you   People who have told you that you
are not physically beautiful   *are* physically beautiful

_____

_____

_____

_____

_____

6. I can be wildly successful at my chosen career.

People who have told you that you
cannot be wildly successful

People who have told you that you
can be wildly successful

_____

_____

_____

_____

_____

7. I have an amazingly capable brain.

People who have told you that you
are not intellectually capable

People who have told you that you
are intellectually capable

_____

_____

_____

_____

8. I'm perfectly lovable exactly as I am.

People who have told you that you
are not perfectly lovable

People who have told you that you
are perfectly lovable

_____

_____

_____

_____

_____

9. I'm highly creative by nature.

| People who have told you that you *are not* highly creative | People who have told you that you *are* highly creative |

_____

_____

_____

_____

10. My dreams are in the process of coming true.

| People who have told you that your dreams *are not* going to come true | People who have told you that your dreams *are* coming true |

_____

_____

_____

_____

COMPARE AND CONTRAST: EVALUATING EVERYBODY

Have you completed your lists? Good. Now I'd like you to simply look over all the names you've written in the left-hand column and *notice what you feel when you think about these people.* Do you remember the "worst-case scenario" we developed in Chapter 2? I'd be willing to bet that the left-column names above evoke a similar kind of anxiety and visceral misery. Now look over the names in the right-hand column. How do *they* make you feel? Probably a lot like the "best-case scenario" in Chapter 3. Mind you, I'm not talking about your reactions to the *opinions* voiced by the folks on your list—I just want to know how the *individuals themselves* make you feel. To clarify this, answer the following questions.

EVERYBODY EVALUATION

Looking over the columns of names you've written down in the previous exercise, please answer the following questions:

1. Whom do you like more?

   People on the left   People on the right

2. Whom do you respect more?

   People on the left   People on the right

3. Which people have the happier, more fulfilling lives?

   People on the left   People on the right

4. Which people have more stable, intimate relationships?

   People on the left   People on the right

5. If you had a baby and were forced to leave your child to be raised by other people, whom would you choose?

   People on the left   People on the right

6. Which individuals most deserve to have their opinions ignored, belittled, and discounted?

   People on the left   People on the right

7. Why in the name of all that's holy would you give any credence to the people on the left?

   People on the left   People on the right

Most people find that the folks on the left are living in the grip of their own highly critical Everybodies. They're often people whose personal dreams have been dashed, or who see themselves as victims, or who are so frightened of life that they project their timidity onto everyone around them. Not infrequently, your left-hand list will include really destructive people whose essential selves have all but vanished, leaving pod beings who rarely even bother to do a reasonable imitation of actual humans.

The people on the right-hand list are usually much healthier and happier. This is because the scared, hypercritical, or condemnatory folks who undermine other people's basic sense of self-worth aren't living in accordance with their essential selves. If they were, it would be impossible for them not to see the beauty and promise in every other person, including you. You never hear about truly self-actualized people, like Buddha or Christ, telling people they're stupid losers. It goes against the nature of enlightenment. On the contrary, people who exemplify truth are always turning up in the lives of "stupid losers" and telling them that they're priceless and beloved, that their essential nature is literally divine and that they are destined for joy and fulfillment.

Of course, just knowing intellectually that the people in the left-hand column aren't your first choice as role models won't solve your Everybody problems. Many of my clients will tell me in the same breath that 1) their parents (or spouses, bosses, siblings) are completely crazy, and 2) until those crazy people understand and support them, they'll never be able to believe in themselves. Whatever the intellect says, the emotional power still lies with the hostile Everybody. If the exercises above have convinced your head that you need to revise your generalized other, it's time to convince your heart.

STRATEGIES FOR EXCHANGING YOUR EVERYBODY

When you buy a pair of shoes that don't fit, you lug them back to the store and get a pair that does. It's a pain in the neck and it takes time you'd rather spend doing something else, but if you want shoes that fit, you do it. Exchanging your Everybody is the same kind of pedestrian, pragmatic task. True, it's also laden with emotional dynamite, but if you go through the basic drudgery, it will simply happen. You'll wake up one day and discover that Everybody is on your side, and you've got a clear shot at your own North Star.

The social self will turn virtually anybody into a generalized other, given two conditions: exposure and repetition. This is how you got the Everybody you have today. At some point, you were exposed to conditions and people that sent a powerful message about you. Then this message was repeated over and over and over. Sometimes the repetition came from outside the self: Your family may have made you the scapegoat, your governess may have criticized you ad nauseam, whole classrooms full of peers may have mocked you for being different. Whether or not this happened, at some point your own social self took on the job of repeating insults and discouragement. Desperate to keep you from being hurt by Everybody, your social self developed various abusive mantras. It has spent years chanting things like, "Don't be stupid. You're so damn stupid. I can't believe how stupid you are. My God, that was stupid!" and so on, every minute of every day, year after year after year.

This repetition has worn deep ruts in your brain, so that if the entire membership of Mensa lined up to tell you how brilliant you are, their words would skitter off your consciousness and land in some obscure mental waste depository. The only way to counteract persistent lies is to wear in a different set of ruts, new tracks for your mind to follow in its unconscious meanderings.

There are a number of simple ways you can achieve this, some of which I've listed below. All these processes take time, and at first it's very hard to steer firmly along the new course you've chosen without slipping back into the old mind ruts. During this period you'll have to consciously, actively, forcefully repeat the truth. You will experience frequent setbacks, as your social self panics and tries desperately to keep you from developing the confidence that might make you forget to honor your hostile Everybody. No matter. If you keep taking the steps below, your social self will end up believing in you, and it will begin to tell you that Everybody else believes in you too. Your mind will still know that you can't please all of the people all of the time, but your heart will live in a much friendlier universe.

1. Positive Feedback

Write down any positive feedback you've ever gotten, from other people or from circumstances. Put copies of this feedback list everywhere, and read it often.

Brad was a successful businessman with a toothpaste-commercial smile, a happy family, and Major Money Issues. His Depression-era parents raised him with an overwhelming conviction that life is perpetually insecure, and that he must spend every single second earning money and hoarding it for a rainy day. Brad is a wealthy man, but until recently he lived every day in dire fear of poverty. He drove himself unmercifully to earn and save more, all the time aware that his children were growing up barely knowing their father, except as a mythical figure who paid all the family bills.

Brad's parents died within a year of each other. Strangely, this actually increased their influence over Brad's behavior. Their voices still rang in his head, telling him that he wasn't working hard enough, that he was about to lose his fortune. His wife pointed out that nothing in Brad's experience indicated that they were right. On the contrary, Brad had received countless bits of feedback about what a capable businessman he was, how much his talents would always be needed, and how well he managed the money he earned. Both the spoken comments of respected peers and every bit of evidence supported the idea that Brad would always have plenty of money.

One day, Brad decided to write down all the reasons why he shouldn't have to worry about being struck poor. He typed up every compliment he'd ever gotten from his business-school professors, various bosses, partners, clients, customers, and competitors, his accountant, his broker, his wife, and several of his friends. Once he got going, he remembered evidence of his business skill that stretched back into his early childhood. By the end of the exercise, Brad was feeling so calm that he decided to take a day off to spend with his children.

The minute he called the office to say he was staying home, Brad's parents came shrieking back from the grave like Hamlet's father, warning him that his finances and family were in dire jeopardy. He went into a violent workaholic frenzy, rushing to his office, arriving barely in time to keep panic at bay. But after a few hours, when the fit had passed, Brad had the presence of mind to get out his trusty List o' Positive Feedback and read it again. Sure enough, the parental harpies backed off. Brad left the office and spent a whole hour with his kids before he was overwhelmed by another wave of anxiety, at which point he read over his list again.

Things went on this way for some time, but Brad was persistent. By focusing on accurate feedback in written form, he was gradually able to wear new ruts in his brain. Now when the Depression Blues start playing in his head, it takes only a glance at his list to remind Brad that he doesn't have to enslave himself to his parents' fears. He eventually quit the job where he'd put in years of hundred-hour weeks. Though he's comfortably well-off simply living on his investments, he plans to start his own company once his children are a bit older. This time, he'll work for the joy of it, not for fear of his parents and their financial demons.

EXERCISE

I strongly recommend that you follow Brad's example by writing—and reading—reminders of your true nature and accomplishments. You can start by going over the list of people in the right-hand column, above, and trying to remember the positive words each of them said to you. Write it all down, every single thing anyone ever said that made your heart lift a little in your chest. When you've exhausted the spoken compliments, jot a few words about every success you've ever had. Write down every instance, no matter how small, when your value was affirmed or your hopes realized. Again, you may need a buddy to help you remember the good times.

Once you've compiled this praise-and-success record, make several copies and put them in places where you'll see them often. Slide a copy into a drawer in your desk where you can yank it out and read it quickly. Stick one to the fridge with magnets. Tape one to the phone book. Frame one and hang it on the bathroom wall, where you'll see it every time nature calls. Put those suckers *everywhere*. Remember, you have lived through years of repeated negative comments. We're just trying to right the balance. It's going to take a lot of iterations.

2. Your Fan Club

Display pictures and mementos of people who believe in you. Do not display pictures or mementos of people who attack your true self.

In my office, I have a photo-collage of people who've given me support and encouragement over the years. Some of these people are family and friends, some are old teachers who have long since forgotten me, and some are writers, philosophers, or social reformers I've never even met. Every one of them, at some point or other, has spoken directly to my heart. They've cut through the doubt and self-accusation I gleaned from my social self's Everybody, and freed my essential self to follow my true path.

Of course, my photo gallery is a highly nonrepresentative sample of the human population. I could just as easily post pictures of people who think I'm a fool, or a slob, or a sinner. Especially a sinner. In my late twenties, I realized that my beliefs didn't agree with my childhood religion and decided to officially resign—an act we call "apostasy" in the old country. I'd grown up in a very devout community and I knew my actions would appall my family and friends, but I felt pretty strongly about the whole thing, so I did it anyway. Several people told me in no uncertain terms that I was a lost soul, an evil seed with a one-way ticket to the worst part of Hell. I got a few pieces of hate mail, including one that suggested the author was planning to help me end my church membership by literally "dismembering" me—specifically, tying me to his pickup truck and dragging me until significant chunks of my body disengaged from one another.

You know, there's nothing like community outrage and anonymous death threats to convince your social self that Everybody hates you. Intellectually, I knew that very few members of my former religion had any ill intentions toward me; the vast majority of them are the salt of the earth. But emotionally, the few aggressive attacks I experienced expanded into a nightmare of antagonism. I went around feeling scared and uncertain, flinching every time someone drove by in a pickup truck. This kind of generalized anxiety is exactly what the hate-mail authors wanted me to feel, and it bothered me immensely that they'd accomplished their goal.

Around this time, a wise friend suggested that I have my husband screen my letters and simply throw away the hate mail without letting me read it. I was surprised to see that even when I knew angry letters were coming in, they didn't bother me nearly as much if I never saw them. This strategy had such a salutary effect on my mood that I started weeding out my life, putting away physical objects and pictures I associated with religious condemnation. I hadn't lost sight of the fact that many people disapproved of my choices; I just didn't post reminders of them in my immediate environment.

I still don't. Instead, I have my wall of cheerleaders. There's my friend Rebecca, a deeply compassionate physician whose family thinks she's going to burn eternally for divorcing her first husband. There are my favorite cousins, who accept me absolutely and tell hilarious stories about the often-bizarre religiosity with which we all grew up. There's the Dalai Lama, with a quotation under his picture: "My religion is kindness." When self-doubt and a sense of unworthiness overwhelm me, I glance up to see all these people, and more, smiling at me from my office wall. They crack jokes, shout encouragement, and wave their invisible pom-poms, and after a minute I start to feel as though Everybody likes me just fine.

EXERCISE

Go through your house and take down any mementos that have negative associations. Bury them. Start collecting pictures and memorabilia that remind you of people and situations that encourage your true self. Display them.

3. Storytelling

Be the hero of your autobiography—Not the victim.

Nothing ever went right for Mary. She spent her childhood in a family fraught with buried feelings and poor communication. As a result, she had a hard time establishing relationships; from adolescence onward, she had only a few real friends. Her sole serious romance was with a self-proclaimed Emotionally Disturbed young man. They broke up at a particularly vulnerable time in Mary's life, just as she was entering college.

Mary was totally unprepared for the financial responsibilities of adult life. She scraped by but never managed to put any money into savings or buy the condo she desperately wanted. When I met her, she'd just entered a very stressful graduate program. She was barely surviving from semester to semester. Her life, she told me, had been one long run of hardship and bad luck.

Lynn, on the other hand, had a pretty darn good life. Her family was comfortably well off, and her parents cared deeply about their daughter's happiness. Lynn was so bright that she intimidated her peers, but the friends she did make were fascinating people who adored her. She had a fling with an intense young poet, broke it off when she moved to a different state, and had many other suitors.

Lynn was amazingly lucky with money. She had never actually looked for a job; whenever she needed one, somebody seemed to show up and offer her interesting work. Once, when she had to buy a car, a distant relative she barely remembered kicked the bucket and left her more than enough to pay for it in cash. After college, Lynn was admitted to an elite graduate program that put her on track for a dazzling career.

Clearly, Lynn had a much better life than Mary—or she would have, except that Lynn and Mary are the same person. Mary Lynn was, in fact, one of my very first clients. During our initial session, she sobbed out the story of her miserable life with such wrenching pain that my heart ached for her. Her anxiety about money was so intense that she asked me to see her for free, until she got a better job and could pay me back. Being a bear of very little brain, I agreed.

Months passed, but nothing in Mary Lynn's life changed. Every time I saw her, she spent our whole hour together relating the bad luck she'd suffered since our last session. None of her emotional wounds ever healed. The jobs people kept giving her didn't pay well enough. The money she inherited didn't last. Her parents entered therapy, but they never managed to make Mary Lynn feel any better. She simply could not catch a break.

After a while, I started feeling a certain codependent pissiness toward Mary Lynn. My dawning realization that she was never going to pay me didn't upset me as much as the fact that she'd written all my pro bono work right out of her life story. She would not have recognized herself as the "Lynn" I've described above, yet the factual content of that story is every bit as accurate as "Mary's" depressing autobiography.

A branch of clinical psychology called "narrative therapy" holds that we all walk around, day in and day out, telling ourselves the stories of our lives. (As Ashleigh Brilliant once put it, "My life has great characters; I just haven't figured out the plot.") No storyteller can describe everything that ever happens to a hero; as autobiographers, we choose elements of what William James called "the blooming, buzzing confusion" around us, and build our stories from a very limited selection of facts. The information we choose to include or exclude determines whether we see our lives as comedy, tragedy, romance, or action-adventure. Narrative therapy teaches people to literally rewrite their life stories, so that they tell themselves the happy truth, instead of the miserable truth. My observations of clients put me firmly in the camp of narrative therapists: You're inevitably going to "spin" the story of your life, so you might as well spin it in a cheerful direction.

I'm not suggesting that you deny the pain and misfortune in your life. The important thing is to tell yourself a life story in which you, the hero, are primarily a problem solver rather than a helpless victim. This is well within your power, whatever fate might have dealt you. Imagine, for example, what a pitiful story James Bond could tell about his life. An hour doesn't go by when that man isn't attacked by snipers, crushed between some woman's viselike thighs, or confronted by men tossing deadly hats. If he decided to see himself as a victim, 007 could organize a pity party that would put your hard-luck stories to shame. Instead, people sit around having fantasies in which they take his place.

Right now, you may be reacting the way my seven-year-old daughter did when I told her I'd always wanted to hang around with Robin Hood: She raised one cynical eyebrow and said, "Mom: fiction." True enough, James Bond is a fictional character in a made-up story. *But so are we all.* To Mary Lynn, her "true" story was one of unrelenting injustice and victimization. From my perspective, that story was fictional, and the "truth" was that Mary Lynn had plenty of good luck in her life, though she rarely appreciated it. Neither story is the absolute truth; all our life narratives are based on selection and "spin."

Write a brief time line of the major events in your life. Read over it, and see whether you've written a happy story or a sad one. Now rewrite it, selecting events and recounting them in ways that show you as a helpless victim (this is just to get it out of your system). Then try still another personal history, this one designed to make your reader laugh. Finally, tell your life story as an adventure saga in which you are the resourceful hero: a modern Odysseus overcoming every obstacle on his perilous voyage, a Joan of Arc beating almost infinite odds to lead the French to victory.

Learning to look at yourself this way is an incredibly effective step toward psychological freedom, personal power, and mastery of your circumstances. Most people think they'll believe in their own potential for success when they see it; the truth is, you'll see it the very instant you decide to believe it. If you simply can't see anything but victimization in your history, I suggest that you read memoirs such as *Angela's Ashes,* by Frank McCourt, *An Unquiet Mind,* by Kathleen Redfield Jamison, the introduction to *A Brief History of Time,* by Stephen Hawking, or *The Liars' Club,* by Mary Karr. Every one of these authors was stuck in circumstances that seem utterly devastating, and each describes his or her bad luck with honesty, humor, and not a trace of victimization.

4. Media Blitz

Seek out media products (books, movies, TV shows, magazines) that support your essential self. Avoid those that don't.

When I was teaching college courses in the sociology of gender, some of my students created an experiment involving popular magazines. The students had a group of female subjects look through women's fashion magazines, the kind featuring models who stand six foot two and weigh ninety pounds (thirty-five for each breast, twenty for everything else). A group of male participants were given men's magazines full of glaring hunks with washboard abs. Control groups, both male and female, looked through *National Geographic* and *Scientific American*. After they'd spent some time with the magazines, all the participants filled out questionnaires designed to measure their confidence in their own looks.

As expected, the people who'd just flipped through glossy magazines full of dazzling beauties felt they were much less attractive than the ones who'd been reading articles like "Sea Cucumbers: Dancing Denizens of the Deep." The women who saw the fashion magazines were more likely than the men to compare themselves to the models and to become deeply depressed by that comparison. However, both men and women who read the fashion magazines came away believing that Everybody thought they were unattractive.

Avoiding media products that make you feel lousy and perusing those that make you feel good is an extension of my friend's advice not to read hate mail. Not only magazines but television, movies, books, and radio can create a powerful illusion that the world is either benevolent or malicious, comforting or threatening. I've had clients go into major neurotic spasms after listening to Dr. Laura Schlessinger, Howard Stern, or Rush Limbaugh. They spend enormous amounts of time in mental arguments with these media icons, who are on the radio in the first place because they are obnoxiously provocative and have a delusional belief that Everybody should think exactly the way they do. If you really hate such media giants, or if they thoroughly demoralize you, pay them the ultimate insult: Don't listen to them.

I know a therapist who forbids depressed patients to watch the local news. Journalists are paid to report the most sensational and frightening bits of information they can dig up—and they often have to dig deep. Think about it: For every person who goes crazy with an assault rifle, there are probably hundreds who would risk their lives to help a stranger. These people do not get equal time on the news, which is a condensation of all the worst things that ever happen. If you're already feeling a bit shaky, TV news can throw you into morbid gloom or outright terror. Skip it for a few days. Believe me, if anything really important happens, you'll hear about it.

Ignoring media products that make you miserable should free up some time for you to spend with books, magazines, movies, and television programs that support your essential self. When I'm working on a writing project, I stock my bedroom with a whole shelf full of books and articles about writers and "the writing life." A little peripatetic reading from this collection creates the illusion that I have a peer group of authors who are always happy to discuss the joys, frustrations, logistics, and strategies of writing. Though I actually know very few writers, I can convince my social self that Everybody writes for a living. It gives me lots of company and support as I embark on an essentially solitary pursuit.

I've seen this approach work for people who wanted to run marathons, make a fortune in the stock market, start their own karate studios, or succeed at any number of other esoteric activities. True, after a few months of watching, reading, and listening to people who are passionate about their particular interests, these folks start to sound a little strange. They forget that not Everybody is on their wavelength; they assume Everyone knows the names of all the great stock-car racers, or bass fishermen, or restaurateurs, or what have you. While you may want to keep a compartment of gray matter that acknowledges the diversity of people's worldviews, this is a benign sort of delusion. The Everybodies that keep us from our dreams are every bit as exaggerated as those that support us, and not nearly as useful.

5. Clean It Up

Talk to everybody about your Everybody.

When Linda and I saw the godlike Roger waddling down the street, I couldn't help blurting out what I thought about him. If I'd known that Roger had treated Linda decently, I would probably have revised my opinion—but he hadn't, so I pulled out the stops. I told her about Roger's perpetual drunkenness, his J. R. R. Tolkein diatribes, his lack of social skills. I mentioned that I had not been the only freshman classmate who found him ridiculous. I pointed out that the only things he seemed to have added to his life since college were drug addiction and male-pattern baldness. Part of Linda was shocked by my lack of reverence, but another part of her took it all in with guilty eagerness, like a dog snorking food off the dinner table.

By asking third parties what they think of the people on your Everybody panel—your parents, your boss, your lover, your Roger— you can discredit unwholesome members of the Everybody committee and put more-worthy individuals in their places. Wendy learned this after years of deifying her father, Wendell, an angry, egocentric chauvinist who took out a lot of aggression on his hapless daughter. Wendell also happened to be a very successful doctor, the physician of choice for several famous sports and entertainment stars. Wendy grew up surrounded by these very impressive people, all of whom told her that her daddy was an amazingly smart and admirable man.

When she was fourteen and chronically grumpy, Wendy ran into one of her dad's patients—a famous movie actress—in a restaurant. "Your father is such a wonderful man," gushed the star. In a fit of adolescent pique, Wendy replied, "Well, that's funny—I've always thought he was a jerk." (Actually, the word she used was considerably spicier than *jerk,* but this is a family book.)

The movie star looked taken aback, then broke into a huge smile and exclaimed, "You got that right, kid!" As it turned out, the unctuous bedside manner Wendell affected for his famous patients didn't fool much of anybody—but a lot of people *pretended* it did. Wendy was the unfortunate target of polite deception from dozens of people who assumed they were making her happy by complimenting her father. The minute she started actively seeking honest feedback, Wendell began to lose his omnipotence in the eyes of Wendy's social self.

EXERCISE

If you have someone on your Everybody committee who doesn't support your true self, start asking third parties what they really think of this person. Make sure they know you want the straight story, and don't react defensively if the feedback is negative; just take it home and think about it. Get opinions from at least three different people, or groups of people, preferably folks who have little or no interaction with one another. Try to get as many different points of view as possible.

6. Hang with Your Tribe

Spend as much time as possible with people who support your true self. Spend as little time as possible with those who don't.

Since I don't recommend that you even look at photographs of people who attack your true self, it should be obvious that I'd like you to avoid them in the flesh. This is easy for people who have been raised in supportive environments, but not for people whose lifelong Everybody is hostile or destructive. You can spend years in therapy learning to deal with your impossible lover, or your psychotic boss, or your verbally abusive mother (one psychologist uses the term "mother wallop" to describe the incredible hits your essential self can take from this closest of all relationships). By the time you're finished, you'll have a black belt in emotional intelligence, and that's cool. But in the meantime, why not surround yourself with supporters, rather than detractors?

I had one client whose parents told him at his sister's funeral that her suicide was all his fault—he simply hadn't been a good enough brother. Another client's boyfriend constantly reminded her that she was so ugly no one else would take her. Many a manager has insulted the intelligence of a much more functional subordinate. Browbeating and vilification may come at you from all sorts of significant others. My action plan in these cases is as follows: *Get away!* Hie thee to a nunnery, a shrink, a twelve-step group, a Morris dancing class—anywhere the folks are friendly.

There are two possible reasons you may find it difficult to disengage from your Everybody. One is that your daily activities bring you into frequent contact with certain people. If this happens at work, you should keep conversations to a civil, functional minimum. Many of my clients greatly improved their work relationships when they realized that not all their colleagues have to be friends. It's quite possible for people with antagonistic ideals to work harmoniously in areas where they share responsibility. (You see this in the best of politics, though, sadly, not the majority.)

If your hostile Everybody is a family member, even a spouse, learn to excuse yourself politely and seek solitude when you're feeling overwhelmed by social-self demands. In very codependent or enmeshed relationships, this may hurt the other person's feelings. However, if you continue to violate your essential self in order to avoid minor conflict, you will end up storing large amounts of anger and *really* messing up the relationship. Anyone who loves you will understand if you say you need occasional minutes or hours of solitude, and that's plenty of time to disengage from your Everybody and get back in touch with your essential self. If you feel you "can't" ask for more space, or if you're overwhelmed by guilt when you do it, you have what psychologists call "boundary issues." This comes from emotional wounding, which we'll discuss in a couple of chapters. Specifically, it means you have overactive internal rules against dealing effectively with anger. You'll find a set of quick-fix instructions for handling this on pages 198–206, but to really get through it, you can't beat therapy.

Another reason you may find yourself reluctant to back away from interacting with your Everybody representatives is that you urgently believe that these people *must* be persuaded to see things your way, condone your true path, and grant you their heartfelt blessing. While their hard-heartedness is their problem, your inability to detach is yours. It's based on a childlike desperation to control the uncontrollable. Learn to recognize this pattern when it emerges. Then gently remind your social self, over and over, that there is no way you can coerce anyone to change his or her opinions and beliefs. If your Everybody committee members aren't convinced by your initial arguments, they aren't likely to yield to repetition or escalated debate. Detaching, finding your true path, and becoming a whole, strong person will put you in a much better position from which to influence them than staying locked in a dance of futile control efforts.

Once you free up the time you're now spending with an unsupportive Everybody, you'll have space in your schedule for people who support your true self. Make a regular practice of this and you'll eventually end up finding the best of all Everybodies: your very own tribe. These are people who live according to their essential selves, share your interests, and value your uniqueness. Finding them is no pipe dream, though it does come at a cost.

When you first begin to avoid the people who attack you, the Everybody chairs in your brain may go empty for a while. Even if you hated your Everybody, not having one is just about the worst feeling in the world. You feel around in your brain for social support, and you find . . . nobody. It's terrifying, alienating, and lonely. We'll discuss it at greater length in subsequent chapters; for now, suffice it to say that the feeling is both temporary and more than worth it. After you've found your tribe, the Everybody who understands and adores your essential self, you'll be thrilled that you went through it.

CONTINUING EVERYBODY HYGIENE

As you begin to find your true path, you can expect your old, stale Everybody to rear up and shout verbal abuse on a regular basis. The techniques described in this chapter can come to your rescue any and every time you are overwhelmed by anxiety, shame, self-doubt, or exhaustion. Despite our individualistic culture's pretense that we can all build our dreams by our little lonesomes, the truth is that we must have social support to do something as audacious as finding our own North Stars. Before you head out on your journey, and all along the way, take the time to get and keep Everybody on your side. You need it, and you deserve it. Everybody thinks so.

6

HOW HOLLY GOT
HER BOD BACK

*The body is an astrolabe to calculate
the astronomy of the spirit.*
—RUMI AL-JELADDIN

Until a few years ago, I felt about my body exactly the way Captain Ahab felt about Moby Dick. I saw it as an unduly large, pale, monstrous creature that had permanently disabled me, and I hated it with a roaring passion. If I'd been wiser, less headstrong, and more acquainted with the logic of paradox, it might have occurred to me that the object of my deepest loathing was in fact the most direct way to my true path. This chapter is meant to help you learn in a few minutes of reading what it took me years and years of physical pain to figure out: How to use your body as one of the most accessible and reliable North Star locators you will ever have.

My war against the flesh began in my teens, when I started dieting severely, running several miles a day, and skipping a lot of sleep in order to earn straight A's while participating in as many extra-curricular activities as possible. If the words *eating disorder* are popping into your head at this point, I can only join those TV starlets—the ones whose spinal vertebrae are clearly visible from a full-frontal view—in decrying unfairness of snap judgments and glib labels. Jeez, every time a girl loses 30 percent of her body weight while developing delusions of obesity, an obsession with exercise, and a fixed intention to starve herself to death, all of a sudden she's "anorexic." People can be so cruel.

As I moved into my twenties, things began to deteriorate—and by "things," I mean body parts. It seemed as though I was always sick, injured, or both. I developed chronic pain that made it excruciating to stand, sit, walk, or use my hands. I was hospitalized for something or other about every six months, undergoing several emergency surgeries to patch up malfunctioning organs. Doctors diagnosed me with a number of different conditions, all of them incurable, poorly understood, and "thought to be related to immune dysfunction." My own immune system had turned against me. In hindsight, I can hardly blame it.

My reaction to all this was furious resistance. I took vengeance on my body by continuing to work it very hard, reward it very sparingly, and pledge its service to things I knew would trash me physically. For example, I had three children while negotiating a high-pressure Ph.D. program, an experience that made my teenage-anorexic lifestyle look like a picnic in the park. I got less sleep during those five years than my dog got yesterday.

As I neared my thirties, the warranty on my body finally ran out. I got so sick that I literally couldn't fight my physical needs anymore. When, at long last, I began paying considerate attention to my body, I discovered something amazing: All along, old Moby Dick had only been trying to lead me to my North Star. Moreover, my body often knew what my essential self wanted, even when my brain was muddled and confused by social-self demands. The minute I made a decision contrary to my heart's desires—before I consciously realized that I'd done so—my body would set about disabling me. If I stopped what I was doing and replaced it with something that felt right to my essential self, lo, verily, I was healed.

Within a few years, I'd become quite the whale lover. The body I'd hated so much for so long makes it literally physically impossible for me to live a life my essential self doesn't want, and I'm deeply grateful. Without incapacitating illness, I might never have dumped my academic career and found the work I do today, or made thousands of other positive changes. Today, my life is completely different from

How Holly Got Her Bod Back

anything my teenage self would have predicted, and my body—my infuriatingly fragile, obstreperous body—is astonishingly healthy.

I certainly hope that you don't have as antagonistic a relationship with your body as I used to have with mine. I hope you don't develop shooting pains and embarrassing rashes every time you step off your true path. Most people don't. For the majority of my clients, their physical reactions to life choices are much more subtle—sometimes barely noticeable. But they are most decidedly there. I believe that your body knows a lot more than your mind about the life you're supposed to live. This chapter will walk you through a number of exercises to help you access that knowledge.

YOUR HANDY HOME LIE DETECTOR

We've already dipped into your memory for examples of the way your body felt when your essential self was miserable, and how differently it responded when you entered an environment that nourished your essential self. If you were hooked up to a lie detector, the machine would record these physical responses at a very subtle level. Heart rate, perspiration, eye blinking, muscle tension, blood pressure—all of these change, for most people, every time they so much as say something untrue. Remember, your North Star is a place of absolute truth. Whenever you do *anything,* by speech or action, that takes you away from this truth, your body probably protests.

The reason I say "probably" is that certain (very rare) people can pass lie-detector tests even when they're lying. Their bodies don't seem to reflect their psychological processes at all. Other people, like yours truly, turn every little thought into a physical symptom, a process known as "somatizing." Whether you're a "high somatizer" or someone whose body barely registers your psychological processes, you can use your natural tendencies to advantage. Low somatizers are often physically hardier than high somatizers, which gives them an advantage in achieving their goals. On the other hand, if every psychological twitch makes your body jerk like a marionette, you've got yourself a hair-trigger North Star detector. True, you may suffer annoying physical symptoms, but if you learn to follow its instructions, your devoted *corpo* will take you straight to *la verace via.*

EXERCISE: TESTING THE EQUIPMENT

Here's a simple test to find out how sensitively your body reflects your psychological state. It's easiest if you get a friend to help. 1) Start by holding one arm out straight in front of you, parallel to the ground. 2) Now have your friend try to push your arm down while you do your best to keep it horizontal. 3) The next step is to have your friend again push your arm down while you say something you know isn't true, such as "I love hemorrhoids" or "Alien abduction is good, clean fun." The more viscerally you disbelieve what you're saying, the better. 4) Finally, repeat steps two and three, this time saying something you deeply believe to be true ("A thong is not my best fashion choice" or "I shot the sheriff, but I did not shoot the deputy"). If you are a high somatizer, your arm will be much, much stronger when you're telling the truth than it was when you were lying. You'll feel this, and so will your buddy. The more your strength varies, the more likely you are to express your essential self through your physical body.

You can also do this exercise alone, by jogging, riding a stationary bicycle, or holding up a barbell while you tell various lies and truths. High somatizers will find it much harder to keep up the same strength level while lying. This exercise can provide hours of jollity, as you and your friends test the truth of statements like "I just love our family reunions" or "I've never even *thought* about sleeping with anyone but my spouse" or "Yeah, I tried it once, but I didn't inhale."

HOLLY, THE BRIDE OF FRANKENSTEIN

I knew Holly was a high somatizer the moment she lurched into my office. Holly was a young, attractive woman, but she moved as though she were being driven by a committee: legs stiff, arms immobile at her sides, head turned at an odd, rigid angle.

Holly parked her awkward self on my sofa, and I asked her a few introductory questions. She answered them enthusiastically—so enthusiastically that I felt a bit nonplussed. Some clients are difficult to work with because they don't seem interested in anything. Holly presented the opposite problem: She seemed interested in *everything*. She loved every subject in school, liked to work with every kind of person, enjoyed every type of environment. At least, that's what she said. But while Holly's voice was upbeat and pleasant, her body told me a different story. It sat there cramped and brittle, head stuck at that weird angle, doing everything but semaphore to communicate distress and anxiety.

"I've got to be honest with you," I told Holly. "I'm not sure why you're here. You seem pretty happy with your life."

"Oh, I am, I am!" She nodded, stiffly. "I have a great life!"

"Then why . . . ?"

Holly's body tensed up even more. She looked like a weight lifter about to attempt a record-setting clean and jerk. "Well," she said, "I don't seem to have a lot of career motivation. I'm not doing well at work. My boyfriend thought maybe you could help me."

"All right," I said, "what kind of motivation are we talking about? What do you do for a living?"

Immediately, Holly launched into an intricate "decision tree" of employment options in her field of venture capitalism. It was an impressive speech, but I was more interested in Holly's posture. She was so tense I half-expected to hear her bones snapping.

When she finally fell silent, I asked, "So which decision feels best to you?"

"Well, I think—" she began.

"No," I interrupted as gently as I could, "I don't want to know what you think, not right now. I asked what *feels* best."

"Feels?" Holly squinted at me, perplexed. Her face lost its perky expression. She looked lost. "I'm . . . not sure I know."

"You don't know what you feel?"

"Actually," she said, "I don't really feel anything. I haven't for a long time."

Looking at her, I found it was pretty obvious that, in fact, Holly was feeling intensely. Nevertheless, I knew she was telling me the truth as she experienced it. Although she'd been processing all kinds of sensations every minute of her life, it had been a long time since she'd been *aware* of all those sensations. At some point, like many of my clients, Holly had slammed and locked the door between her conscious mind and her feelings. Now she was battling for all she was worth to keep that door closed.

This is a physical process. Holly was literally using her body to hold sensations away from her mind. She employed unconscious strategies like muscle contraction, shallow breathing, and chemical production of fight-or-flight-related hormones to keep her feelings out of her consciousness. Holly's disconnection from her body lay at the core of her emotional numbness and low motivation. To find her heart's desires, we had to reconnect her to her physical being. And to do that, we had to overcome decades of cultural conditioning.

ATTACK OF THE BODY HATERS

It's really not surprising that Holly was so detached from her body. She lives in a society that has spent millennia denigrating the physical. At least since the ancient Greeks, Western thinkers have used rivers of ink writing down all the reasons we should see our bodies as disgusting, base, out-of-control animals—like Garfield the cat, but not as clever. The thing that redeems mankind, early philosophers declared, is our capacity for reason, logic, pure thought. Denying the body's appetites was just the beginning; Enlightenment scholars like René Descartes (who thought, therefore he was) encouraged us to discount the body altogether, worshiping only the mind. One modern author writes that we still suffer from "Cartesian attacks," which convince us that "the body is nothing more than a convenience carrier for the brain." Even if Holly never read philosophy or took religious vows, simply by functioning in American society she soaked up the idea that mind must dominate matter.[1]

Exhibit No. 1, the Schools

At some point, Holly undoubtedly had an experience like my daughter Elizabeth's first day at Montessori School. Three-year-old Lizzie came out of the classroom like a West Point cadet, chin in, chest out, baby

---

[1] Vienne, Véronique, *The Art of Imperfection: Simple Ways to Make Peace with Yourself.* Clarkson Potter Publishers (New York: 1999), p. 24.

face tinged with desperation. When I asked what was wrong, she explained, "Today I learned that I have to control my body *all the time*." I thought maybe I'd sent her to Mussolini School by mistake.

Exhibit No. 2, the Malls

If Holly shops the better boutiques, she's bound to notice that they sell size zero clothing, for the female of really ideal proportions. Yes, Holly will know her diet-and-exercise plan has finally worked when her body ceases to exist.

Exhibit No. 3, the Workplace

Holly has never been in a job that acknowledged, much less accommodated, physical rhythms such as the body's sleep cycle, or the life-cycle demands of caring for children or the elderly. That's why Holly is one of the millions of Americans who suffer from sleep disorders and perpetual exhaustion. If she ever has children or decides to care for aging parents, she'll join the ranks who, in the words of sociologist Arlie Hochschild, "talk about sleep the way starving people talk about food."

So, as you see, our culture makes Holly's divorce from her body very likely, if not inevitable. Her condition is on the severe side, but it's actually the rule among my clients, not the exception.

LOOKING FOR YOUR EYESIGHT

"Tell me, Holly," I said. "What's it like to feel nothing?"

It was a trick question. To answer it, Holly had to focus her attention, however briefly, on her feelings. Her eyes suddenly filled with tears. She started to speak, but stopped when the tears threaten to spill over.

"It doesn't look like much fun," I observed.

She covered her eyes with one hand and searched in her purse for a handkerchief. "I'm sorry," she whispered. "I don't know what's happening. I'm falling apart. I don't know what I should do."

"Well," I said carefully, "what do you *want* to do?"

She cried harder. "I don't know," she repeated, anguished. Again, this was not a lie. On the other hand, it certainly wasn't true.

At some point, almost all my clients tell me they don't know what they want, and it's *never* true. Part of you—your essential self—knows your own desires at every moment of every day (even when the message is a contented "I want exactly what I have, thank you"). Anytime you *think* you don't know what you want, it's because your social self has decided you shouldn't want it. Your social self lives by what psychiatrist Alice Miller sees as the cardinal rule of all repressive social systems: "Thou shalt not be aware." In other words, reject unacceptable sensations. Cut the phone lines between desire and the knowledge of that desire. Don't know what you know, and don't feel what you feel.

Once you've learned to obey this rule, you can easily lose access to your own experience of joy and desire, loathing and revulsion. This is like losing your glasses or contact lenses: It's damn hard to find something you've lost when that item happens to be the very thing that allows you to conduct a search in the first place. Since the only way to find lost feelings is to *feel* for them, the search for your own heart is always a blind one. Instead of any clear impulse, you register only flat nothingness, a hollow, yearning ache that doesn't lead you clearly in any direction at all.

This was what Holly had been experiencing for months, maybe years. She had no idea where to find her heart, but really, the answer was obvious. It was in her body. Whatever faults your body may have, you'll have to admit that it's one of the few things you never misplace. Mine is here with me right now, and by gum, yours is there with you. Even if you're fond of astral travel, or numb like Holly, or as dissociated as the James Joyce character who "lived a short distance from his body," your mortal coil will be right under your nose until the moment you shuffle it off.

PUTTING YOUR BODY IN CHARGE

Before my eyes, Holly gradually, painfully yanked her body back under the control of her social self. She stopped crying, mopped her eyes, and cleared her throat. "I was hoping maybe you could give me some kind of test," she said. "Something that'll tell me what I should do with my career."

"You mean an aptitude test?"

She nodded. "Something like that."

"Well, I use several different aptitude tests," I said, "but giving them to you would be a waste of your money."

Holly wasn't happy with this answer, but it was true. We could have sat around analyzing her skills until doomsday, and she would have ended up just as stuck as she was when she staggered in. Analytical conclusions are never enough to satisfy the heart.

"So . . . if you aren't going to test me," Holly asked, "what am I supposed to do?"

"I'd like you to tell me about your toes."

She blinked in alarm, as though I'd just suggested that her underwear was alive. "My toes?" she repeated, cautiously.

"Humor me," I said.

This technique springs from my early exposure to Asian ways of thinking. Most Eastern belief systems reject the Western idea that the mind, unencumbered by the body, is the only trustworthy way to achieve enlightenment. In fact, they tend to see the mind as a kind of cheap gigolo, easily corrupted, willing to serve any master. The problem is that logic never operates in a vacuum; it's always couched in values and beliefs, and these come from *felt* experience, not from the rational mind. When it's based on beliefs that violate the essential self, the mind can create twisted, monstrous towers of misplaced logic. Virtually all great crimes against humanity, from the Crusades to the Holocaust, seemed perfectly "logical" to the people who committed them.

So your mind definitely has its place in your North Star quest, but as the servant of your heart, not as its master. You must quiet your busy little brain and open yourself to what you're feeling. Your toes are a great place to start.

EXERCISE: CLIMBING BACK INTO YOUR BODY

Step 1: Choose a Sober Moment

Fortunately, Holly came to my office in pretty good chemical shape. That is, she didn't have any untreated neurochemical imbalances (like bipolar disorder or schizophrenia), and she was relatively free of other mood-altering substances. Anything from high-grade heroin to mild uppers or downers, like caffeine or alcohol, can make it difficult for you to get in touch with your authentic feelings and desires. The whole point of these substances is that they fool your body into believing you're moving toward your North Star when you actually aren't. The essential self's physical signals go haywire in these situations, so if you want to find out what the "compass" of your body has to tell you, detoxify first.

Step 2: Relax the Body and Still the Mind

Once you're as clean and sober as you're likely to get, lie or sit down. Close your eyes and take a few long, deep breaths, letting your muscles relax more with each exhalation. After five or six of these unusually deep breaths, go back to breathing normally. Focus your mind on the sensation of the air passing in and out of your nose or mouth, and *keep it there.* Your mind will act like a puppy, forgetting to focus on your breath, wandering off into other thoughts every few seconds. Don't scold or abuse the puppy; remember that the mind is a feeble, impetuous little thing and doesn't know any better. Whenever you notice your attention wandering, just gently return it to your breathing.

Step 3: Notice One Toe

After a few minutes, when you're feeling a bit limp, turn your attention to your left big toe. As you breathe in, picture the air being drawn into that toe, instead of into your lungs. Shift your full awareness to the toe, and mentally describe *everything it feels.* Is it hot, cold, or just right? Does it itch? Is it tired? What is the texture of the sock, shoe, floor, or air that's touching the toe? Wiggle it around. Marvel at its capacity to send you so much information while helping you walk through life. Tell your toe that you love it, and that you want it to move in with you. You do not need to do this out loud.

Step 4: Conduct a Full-Body Search

Now conduct a slow sensation-sweep of your entire body, moving your attention to each of your other toes, each foot, each ankle, each shin, each knee. Learn what your body is feeling, part by part. *Don't think;*

just describe. Move your focus up your legs, through your tailbone and spine, into your head, down your arms to your fingers. Pay special attention to your torso, where so many organs are stored. Feel your way through it bit by bit.

Step 5: Identify Gaps of Feeling

If, like most people, you're a high-to-medium somatizer (someone who holds a lot of tension in your body), you'll probably find that some parts of your body are easy to feel while others seem numb, tight, or paralyzed. Good—now you know where your body is storing useful information that your brain doesn't know. When you've identified a "frozen" area, let your attention linger there. Breathe into the numbness. Imagine the warmth of your breath thawing it out, allowing it to relax. And with every intake of air, let yourself feel what that part of your body is feeling.

Step 6: Lean into the Sensations

Thawing out your frozen spots is a key step toward comfort and joy, but I have to warn you: Initially, it can be *way* unpleasant. The first time I tried this exercise (while studying meditation in preparation for a move to Japan) it was just awful. As my numbness dissolved, I felt an upwelling of enormous physical and emotional pain. After about ninety seconds, I opened my eyes, stood up, and stated, in a loud and convincing tone, *"I will never do that again."* (Now, of course, I do it every day, because I've come to believe that the alternative is losing my true path.)

The point is that as your mind and body come together, you're going to become aware of any discomfort you've been holding at bay. This includes physical sensations like pain, tension, hunger, and fatigue. (If you're tired, you may fall asleep. This is fine—it means that napping is the next step to your North Star.) In most cases, the message locked in your numb tissues will be more than physical. Climbing back into your body may mean feeling intense emotions: sadness, anxiety, hatred, fear. You'll find these emotions embarrassing at best, agonizing at worst. After all, if they weren't so unpleasant, you wouldn't have pushed them out of consciousness in the first place. We'll talk much more in subsequent chapters about dealing with intense emotions. For now, just keep breathing and let yourself feel them.

BODY TALK

Holly obligingly let me run her through the "climbing back into your body" exercise. She was so numb that it took her a long time to pick up any sensations from her left big toe, but once she started to feel it again, the sensation-sweep of her body proceeded quite nicely. She told me that she felt completely "locked up" from her chin down to the mid-chest region, especially in her neck—something that didn't surprise me, given the way she was holding her head.

I asked Holly to breathe deeply into the numbness, relaxing as much as she could and paying attention to what her body felt. She did this, very slowly: once, twice, three times, four. Slowly, the tension in her muscles started to give way—and then she collapsed like a miniature avalanche. Her rigid posture dissolved into a gesture of profound exhaustion. She slumped forward, resting her elbows on her knees, supporting her face with both hands.

"Oh, God," she murmured, "I feel *horrible.*"

Simple as that, the dungeon door was open. Holly's mind and heart were once again communicating freely through the medium they share: her body.

When Holly finally looked up, her face was drawn and tired.

"How's your neck doing now?" I asked.

"Awful," she croaked. "Hurts."

"Okay!" I said, like a TV reporter pursuing a gunshot victim into an ambulance. "Tell me *exactly* how it feels."

"It's tight, like I'm choking." Holly put her hand to her throat and swallowed hard. "But, you know, it's been that way for weeks. I think I may have allergies."

"I would like to ask it some questions," I told her.

Holly frowned. "It?"

"Your neck. I'm going to ask your neck some questions, and you tell me what it wants to answer."

Holly was either too polite or too tired to argue. "Whatever," she said wearily.

"Hey, Holly's neck!" I began. "Why are you hurting? What do you want?"

Holly blinked. Against all her expectations, her neck had an answer.

"It's . . . um . . . it's trying to get me to speak up," she said, with an embarrassed blush.

"Speak up how?" I said. "Speak up where?"

"I think to my boyfriend. Alex." Holly laughed nervously. "You know, I have no idea where this is coming from."

"It's coming from your neck," I reminded her. "And I want to know what your neck would say to Alex if it could talk."

Holly began to stammer, then blurted, "It would say that I'm sick of doing everything Alex wants to do, and I didn't even *want* to go to business school—that was *his* dream—and I want to live my life *my* way!" Abruptly, her face turned from salmon red to ivory white. "Oh, my God," she said, staring at me.

"Cool," I said.

THE PANTOMIME
OF THE ESSENTIAL SELF

The unconscious portion of the human mind communicates through symbolism when it creates dreams, language, and every form of art. It can also express itself symbolically by acting its messages out with the body. Not always, but often, a physical problem is a coded message from the essential self, a dramatization of needs or problems the conscious mind can't or won't articulate.

New Age gurus claim that certain injuries always have the same meaning for every sufferer: Psoriasis means something's "gotten under your skin," leg injuries are always about lack of social support, an achy-breaky elbow indicates that you don't have enough freedom, and so on. I prefer the diagnostic criteria Jung used to analyze dreams: I think every person's brain creates its own symbols. In other words, Zelda's earache may be her body's way of telling her she doesn't want to hear the truth about her life, while Herman's represents a yearning for music, and Pablo's just means he has a bacterial infection. The owner of the body is the only person who can accurately translate its symbolic symptoms.

The most dramatic example I've ever seen of someone's essential self bypassing the mind and "speaking" through the body was the case of a woman I'll call Dolores. I met her in church, back before I lost my religion. Dolores and her two children came to our congregation as refugees from a violently abusive marriage. The first time I saw her, she had a bruise the size of a cantaloupe on the side of her face and a sling on one arm, both courtesy of her ex-husband. She also had the cheeriest smile I'd ever seen. Dolores fairly bubbled with honey-sweet goodwill.

One Sunday morning, as was the custom in our congregation, Dolores stood up to introduce herself. She gave us a little background information about her troubled past, then said she wanted to tell us about a miracle that had occurred in her life. A church leader had told her that she'd know she had truly forgiven her ex-husband when she forgot all the harm he'd done her. That very day, Dolores had checked her memory and realized that this had already happened. With the bruise on her face still a faded yellow and her arm still sling-bound, Dolores told us, "I can't remember one single thing my husband ever did to hurt me. Not even when I try. God has completely removed every last bit of it from my mind."

I didn't know much psychobabble back then, but even so I remember thinking that Dolores spelled relief R-E-P-R-E-S-S-I-O-N. I think everyone else in the room had the same hunch. There was something profoundly unnerving about Dolores's cheerfulness; it felt excessive, manic, and eerie. Still, everyone lauded Dolores for her pluck, loved her for her kindness, and admired her for achieving a depth of forgiveness that bordered on total amnesia.

By the next Sunday, Dolores had developed a physical disorder that I've never heard of before or since. I don't know what it was called, but the main symptom was that her tear ducts got stuck in the "on" position. Tears flowed from Dolores's eyes nonstop, twenty-four hours a day. For the next several years, the whole time I knew her, she had to carry a tissue everywhere, dabbing at the small rivers on her cheeks in a universal gesture of grief. Her eyes and nose were always red and blotchy, as they would be if she'd broken down and cried—not that she ever did. Dolores resolutely maintained her brilliant smile and chirpy demeanor, while her body wept and wept and wept. Her social self couldn't remember everything she'd endured, but her essential self made sure that the rest of us would never forget.

EXERCISE: CHANNELING YOUR BODY

After climbing back into your body (see above), have a conversation with any part of it that feels locked up, frozen, numb, or hurt. As a solo exercise, this seems to work best on paper. For example, if your thumb hurts, take a notebook and write, "Thumb, what are you trying to tell me?" Then write down whatever response you feel coming from your thumb: "I'm longing to hitchhike again," "I wish I were a lower primate—opposable digits entail so much responsibility," "You hit me with a hammer, you idiot." Don't censor or criticize, and most of all, *don't think.* If nothing comes up, relax and focus your mind on your breathing. Unexpected responses may bubble up as soon as your brain looks the other way.

Whatever it says to you, your body will tell you the truth about getting to your North Star. You can trust it when it says that you need companionship, or that you're dying for more autonomy, or that it's time to have some fun. Time after time, my clients get messages from their bodies that they believe will knock them off course; time after time, they discover that listening to their bodies makes them more successful. Try it. It works.

By the way, if your body's responses to your inquiries are strictly physical, without any symbolic message, they're still telling you how to find your true path. Ill or injured people can't enjoy success, wealth, or recreation until they heal. Many of my clients can't figure out what they want to do with their careers until they restore themselves to physical health by resting deeply for weeks, sometimes even months. Whatever your body tells you to do, the odds are very good that it's the next step toward your North Star.

Holly's neck had just told her more about her North Star than any aptitude test ever could. Through her body, she'd regained contact with her essential self and identified the core problem in her life: She had been shaping her choices to suit her boyfriend's hopes and dreams, not her own. To her horror, Holly realized that she was deeply angry at Alex. Her social self had kept this well out of consciousness, because it was afraid that deep anger would mean the end of the relationship. (Actually, keeping the anger unconscious was the worst thing Holly could do to her relationship with Alex—but we'll talk about that later.) Right now, we had to deal with the fact that by abandoning her essential self in order to gain Alex's approval, Holly had lost touch with her North Star. She knew that she *didn't* like the life she'd been living, but she had no vision of what she *did* want. That information couldn't come from Alex, or me, or anyone but Holly's essential self. Fortunately, we knew that Holly was a very high somatizer. This meant that her body could lead her straight to her North Star. She just had to learn to follow it.

Holly wasn't nearly as rigid as she'd been when she entered my office. In fact, she was slumped down into the cushions like a lump of Silly Putty. This loosening was exactly what I want to see. In fact, to follow her body, Holly would have to loosen up even more.

"Holly, tell me more about your job," I asked. "What's the very worst thing about it?"

Holly's jaw clenched. "I hate my manager," she said. "Just going near the woman makes me crazy." As she spoke these words, her neck stiffened and she brought her hand to her throat.

"Freeze!" I exclaimed. Holly looked startled, but she held her position.

"You did that before," I told her. "You touched your throat when you were telling me how angry you are."

"Oh," said Holly. "Really?"

"Describe the feeling in your body right now."

Holly's face scrunched up even more, her eyes squeezed shut. "Choking," she said. "I feel like I'm choking."

"All right, this is the Choking Feeling," I told her. "Whenever you try to do something that isn't right for you, your body will create the Choking Feeling, and it will try to go into this position. It's a kind of dance, a way of expressing unhappiness through movement."

"Okay." Holly nodded, face still scrunched.

"Now, imagine what it would be like to never go back to your office again."

Holly opened one eye. "Are you telling me to quit my job?"

"No, no, no—I'm just telling you to *imagine* quitting your job."

"All right." Holly grinned. For the first time, her smile looked genuine. "No job," she mused, under her breath. Almost instantly, a remarkable change came over her body. Her shoulders pulled back, her head lifted, and her arms moved outward from her neck until they were spread wide, palms up, as though she were soaking up sunlight.

"Okay, *now* describe the feeling in your body."

"Peaceful," she said. "It feels incredibly peaceful."

Just like that, Holly turned her body into a working North Star-o-Meter.

EXERCISE: USING YOUR NORTH STAR-O-METER

Step 1: Identifying Gestures and Labels

To turn your body into a North Star-o-Meter, go back to the worst- and best-case scenarios you created in Chapters 2 and 3. Read over each one, letting yourself imagine that it's really happening. As you do this, close your eyes and let your body move any way it wants to. If you don't feel any urge to move, try describing what you feel out loud. Even my most dissociated clients start gesturing the minute they do this (pay attention, and you'll notice that people tend to "dance" descriptions of their physical feelings as much as speaking them). Once your body begins to use its own kinetic language, miming the sensations of your best and worst experiences, come up with a brief phrase that describes each of these sensations.

Every person has his or her own gestures of joy or despair, and each will choose different words to describe the accompanying feelings. Sam calls his negative reaction "Being Squashed." It makes him breathe shallowly and push himself backward, as though he's being pressed to death by angry Puritans. His positive reaction is "Lightening Up," and it makes him feel like punching both fists above his head and jumping into the air. Sally's body expresses her negative "Frantic Feeling" by pushing her hands away from her chest, as if she's trying to resist an attack. The opposite reaction, which she calls the "Easy Feeling," makes her lean back and rest her head on her interlaced fingers. Joe calls his negative sensation "Red Alert" and covers his head with his hands. When his essential self is happy, his body feels as though it's a "Clear Blue Day," and he pulls his fists in toward his body, like a football player celebrating a touchdown.

What gesture does your body naturally make when your essential self is miserable? _____

_____

Think of a phrase that describes the physical sensation you feel as you make this gesture. _____

_____

What gesture does your body naturally make when your essential self is thrilled? _____

_____

Think of a phrase that describes the physical sensation you feel as you make this gesture. _____

_____

Step 2: Play Hot and Cold

Do you remember playing the children's game of "Hot and Cold"? In this game, one player—let's say it was you—left the room while the others hid some object. Then you came back in and searched for the object, while the other players gave directions by shouting temperature words. When you were moving away from the object, they'd yell "Cold!"

When you turned or moved toward it, they said, "You're getting warmer." When you discovered the hiding place, you were "red-hot."

You can use your body's innate properties to play a high-stakes game of Hot and Cold. Your body knows where your North Star is, and it does its best to tell you when you're getting "cooler" or "warmer." When you face a proposition that's wrong for you, your body will try to go into the negative gesture you've identified above. When you're headed down your true path, it will want to celebrate by moving into the positive gesture. Of course, most of us—even those who haven't been to Montessori School—don't let our bodies express their feelings through movement. Instead, we fight to keep ourselves from displaying our moods with any physical cues. *Keeping the body still when it wants to recoil or rejoice creates the physical tension that locks sensation away from consciousness.* That's why Holly used to walk like the Bride of Frankenstein. She moved much more naturally after she'd begun to face her real feelings.

Step 3: Evaluate Your Life

You can use your North Star-o-Meter to determine how close you are to your ideal life, and what you need to do to come closer. To try this out, list three things you plan to do tomorrow:

Activity No. 1: _____

_____

Activity No. 2: _____

_____

Activity No. 3: _____

_____

	Strongest Negative Feeling						
Activity No. 1:	−10	−9	−8	−7	−6	−5	−4
Activity No. 2:	−10	−9	−8	−7	−6	−5	−4
Activity No. 3:	−10	−9	−8	−7	−6	−5	−4

Think about each activity, one at a time, and notice *your body's* reaction to that item. If you're relaxed, you will find your body moving into the positive and negative gestures you identified and labeled in Step 2. Depending on how much your essential self likes or dislikes an activity, the responses will range from very strong to barely detectable. Rank your body's reaction to each of the three activities. The strongest negative reaction gets a –10, while the most positive gets a +10. If your body doesn't tend toward either good or bad reactions, the activity gets a 0. See chart below.

A lot of my clients are startled to find that their bodies have negative responses to activities they thought they liked. Holly was one of these people. Even though she told me she had a "great life," her body's reaction indicated strong dislike for almost everything on her schedule. Nothing produced the feeling of "Peacefulness" that her body used to tell her it was happy. In other words, Holly was very "cold" in her search for her North Star. To find it, she had to move toward people, places, and things that would make her feel "warmer."

PROFILING YOUR LIFESTYLE

At the end of our first session, I gave Holly some charts to fill out (you'll find your own copies on pages 124–35). By completing these charts, she created a profile of her life, which helped her measure how far she was from her North Star and figure out which aspects of her life needed to change most. Over the next few months, Holly used this information to test the many changes she made in her business and personal life.

	Neutral Response								Strongest Positive Feeling				
–3	–2	–1	0	+1	+2	+3	+4	+5	+6	+7	+8	+9	+10
–3	–2	–1	0	+1	+2	+3	+4	+5	+6	+7	+8	+9	+10
–3	–2	–1	0	+1	+2	+3	+4	+5	+6	+7	+8	+9	+10

THE BIG PICTURE:
HOW CLOSE IS YOUR NORTH STAR?

In the spaces below, write the labels you've created for the most positive and most negative reactions you've seen in your own body (for example, "Trapped" or "Free," "Panicky" or "Calm," "Knotted up" or "Loose"). Then go

---

Strongest Negative Feeling

Relationships: How does your body react to:

Mother: −10 −9 −8 −7 −6 −5 −4
Father: −10 −9 −8 −7 −6 −5 −4

Siblings (write the names of your siblings in the blanks):

_____   −10 −9 −8 −7 −6 −5 −4
_____   −10 −9 −8 −7 −6 −5 −4
_____   −10 −9 −8 −7 −6 −5 −4
_____   −10 −9 −8 −7 −6 −5 −4
_____   −10 −9 −8 −7 −6 −5 −4
_____   −10 −9 −8 −7 −6 −5 −4
_____   −10 −9 −8 −7 −6 −5 −4

Other relatives (list by name):

_____   −10 −9 −8 −7 −6 −5 −4
_____   −10 −9 −8 −7 −6 −5 −4
_____   −10 −9 −8 −7 −6 −5 −4
_____   −10 −9 −8 −7 −6 −5 −4
_____   −10 −9 −8 −7 −6 −5 −4
_____   −10 −9 −8 −7 −6 −5 −4
_____   −10 −9 −8 −7 −6 −5 −4

Romantic partner: −10 −9 −8 −7 −6 −5 −4

through the list of people and activities and record *your body's* response to each item. Remember, no judging or editing is allowed—just observation of a physical reaction.

	Neutral Response								Strongest Positive Feeling				

–3	–2	–1	0	+1	+2	+3	+4	+5	+6	+7	+8	+9	+10
–3	–2	–1	0	+1	+2	+3	+4	+5	+6	+7	+8	+9	+10
–3	–2	–1	0	+1	+2	+3	+4	+5	+6	+7	+8	+9	+10
–3	–2	–1	0	+1	+2	+3	+4	+5	+6	+7	+8	+9	+10
–3	–2	–1	0	+1	+2	+3	+4	+5	+6	+7	+8	+9	+10
–3	–2	–1	0	+1	+2	+3	+4	+5	+6	+7	+8	+9	+10
–3	–2	–1	0	+1	+2	+3	+4	+5	+6	+7	+8	+9	+10
–3	–2	–1	0	+1	+2	+3	+4	+5	+6	+7	+8	+9	+10
–3	–2	–1	0	+1	+2	+3	+4	+5	+6	+7	+8	+9	+10
–3	–2	–1	0	+1	+2	+3	+4	+5	+6	+7	+8	+9	+10
–3	–2	–1	0	+1	+2	+3	+4	+5	+6	+7	+8	+9	+10
–3	–2	–1	0	+1	+2	+3	+4	+5	+6	+7	+8	+9	+10
–3	–2	–1	0	+1	+2	+3	+4	+5	+6	+7	+8	+9	+10
–3	–2	–1	0	+1	+2	+3	+4	+5	+6	+7	+8	+9	+10
–3	–2	–1	0	+1	+2	+3	+4	+5	+6	+7	+8	+9	+10
–3	–2	–1	0	+1	+2	+3	+4	+5	+6	+7	+8	+9	+10

Children (list by name):

_____	−10	−9	−8	−7	−6	−5	−4
_____	−10	−9	−8	−7	−6	−5	−4
_____	−10	−9	−8	−7	−6	−5	−4
_____	−10	−9	−8	−7	−6	−5	−4
_____	−10	−9	−8	−7	−6	−5	−4
_____	−10	−9	−8	−7	−6	−5	−4
_____	−10	−9	−8	−7	−6	−5	−4

Friends (list by name):

_____	−10	−9	−8	−7	−6	−5	−4
_____	−10	−9	−8	−7	−6	−5	−4
_____	−10	−9	−8	−7	−6	−5	−4
_____	−10	−9	−8	−7	−6	−5	−4
_____	−10	−9	−8	−7	−6	−5	−4
_____	−10	−9	−8	−7	−6	−5	−4
_____	−10	−9	−8	−7	−6	−5	−4

Pets (don't smirk: pet relationships can be very significant):

_____	−10	−9	−8	−7	−6	−5	−4
_____	−10	−9	−8	−7	−6	−5	−4
_____	−10	−9	−8	−7	−6	−5	−4
_____	−10	−9	−8	−7	−6	−5	−4

Boss: −10 −9 −8 −7 −6 −5 −4

Coworkers (list by name or title):

_____	−10	−9	−8	−7	−6	−5	−4
_____	−10	−9	−8	−7	−6	−5	−4
_____	−10	−9	−8	−7	−6	−5	−4
_____	−10	−9	−8	−7	−6	−5	−4
_____	−10	−9	−8	−7	−6	−5	−4
_____	−10	−9	−8	−7	−6	−5	−4
_____	−10	−9	−8	−7	−6	−5	−4

−3	−2	−1	0	+1	+2	+3	+4	+5	+6	+7	+8	+9	+10
−3	−2	−1	0	+1	+2	+3	+4	+5	+6	+7	+8	+9	+10
−3	−2	−1	0	+1	+2	+3	+4	+5	+6	+7	+8	+9	+10
−3	−2	−1	0	+1	+2	+3	+4	+5	+6	+7	+8	+9	+10
−3	−2	−1	0	+1	+2	+3	+4	+5	+6	+7	+8	+9	+10
−3	−2	−1	0	+1	+2	+3	+4	+5	+6	+7	+8	+9	+10
−3	−2	−1	0	+1	+2	+3	+4	+5	+6	+7	+8	+9	+10

−3	−2	−1	0	+1	+2	+3	+4	+5	+6	+7	+8	+9	+10
−3	−2	−1	0	+1	+2	+3	+4	+5	+6	+7	+8	+9	+10
−3	−2	−1	0	+1	+2	+3	+4	+5	+6	+7	+8	+9	+10
−3	−2	−1	0	+1	+2	+3	+4	+5	+6	+7	+8	+9	+10
−3	−2	−1	0	+1	+2	+3	+4	+5	+6	+7	+8	+9	+10
−3	−2	−1	0	+1	+2	+3	+4	+5	+6	+7	+8	+9	+10
−3	−2	−1	0	+1	+2	+3	+4	+5	+6	+7	+8	+9	+10

−3	−2	−1	0	+1	+2	+3	+4	+5	+6	+7	+8	+9	+10
−3	−2	−1	0	+1	+2	+3	+4	+5	+6	+7	+8	+9	+10
−3	−2	−1	0	+1	+2	+3	+4	+5	+6	+7	+8	+9	+10
−3	−2	−1	0	+1	+2	+3	+4	+5	+6	+7	+8	+9	+10

−3	−2	−1	0	+1	+2	+3	+4	+5	+6	+7	+8	+9	+10

−3	−2	−1	0	+1	+2	+3	+4	+5	+6	+7	+8	+9	+10
−3	−2	−1	0	+1	+2	+3	+4	+5	+6	+7	+8	+9	+10
−3	−2	−1	0	+1	+2	+3	+4	+5	+6	+7	+8	+9	+10
−3	−2	−1	0	+1	+2	+3	+4	+5	+6	+7	+8	+9	+10
−3	−2	−1	0	+1	+2	+3	+4	+5	+6	+7	+8	+9	+10
−3	−2	−1	0	+1	+2	+3	+4	+5	+6	+7	+8	+9	+10
−3	−2	−1	0	+1	+2	+3	+4	+5	+6	+7	+8	+9	+10

How Holly Got Her Bod Back

Subordinates (list by name or title):

_____	−10	−9	−8	−7	−6	−5	−4
_____	−10	−9	−8	−7	−6	−5	−4
_____	−10	−9	−8	−7	−6	−5	−4
_____	−10	−9	−8	−7	−6	−5	−4
_____	−10	−9	−8	−7	−6	−5	−4
_____	−10	−9	−8	−7	−6	−5	−4
_____	−10	−9	−8	−7	−6	−5	−4

Anyone else with whom you interact on a regular basis:

_____	−10	−9	−8	−7	−6	−5	−4
_____	−10	−9	−8	−7	−6	−5	−4
_____	−10	−9	−8	−7	−6	−5	−4
_____	−10	−9	−8	−7	−6	−5	−4
_____	−10	−9	−8	−7	−6	−5	−4
_____	−10	−9	−8	−7	−6	−5	−4
_____	−10	−9	−8	−7	−6	−5	−4

Situations and activities: How does your body react to:

Your income:	−10	−9	−8	−7	−6	−5	−4
Amount of time you spend working:	−10	−9	−8	−7	−6	−5	−4

Your religious or spiritual practices (churchgoing,
meditation, communion with nature, etc.):

_____	−10	−9	−8	−7	−6	−5	−4
_____	−10	−9	−8	−7	−6	−5	−4
_____	−10	−9	−8	−7	−6	−5	−4
_____	−10	−9	−8	−7	−6	−5	−4
_____	−10	−9	−8	−7	−6	−5	−4

-3	-2	-1	0	+1	+2	+3	+4	+5	+6	+7	+8	+9	+10
-3	-2	-1	0	+1	+2	+3	+4	+5	+6	+7	+8	+9	+10
-3	-2	-1	0	+1	+2	+3	+4	+5	+6	+7	+8	+9	+10
-3	-2	-1	0	+1	+2	+3	+4	+5	+6	+7	+8	+9	+10
-3	-2	-1	0	+1	+2	+3	+4	+5	+6	+7	+8	+9	+10
-3	-2	-1	0	+1	+2	+3	+4	+5	+6	+7	+8	+9	+10
-3	-2	-1	0	+1	+2	+3	+4	+5	+6	+7	+8	+9	+10
-3	-2	-1	0	+1	+2	+3	+4	+5	+6	+7	+8	+9	+10

-3	-2	-1	0	+1	+2	+3	+4	+5	+6	+7	+8	+9	+10
-3	-2	-1	0	+1	+2	+3	+4	+5	+6	+7	+8	+9	+10
-3	-2	-1	0	+1	+2	+3	+4	+5	+6	+7	+8	+9	+10
-3	-2	-1	0	+1	+2	+3	+4	+5	+6	+7	+8	+9	+10
-3	-2	-1	0	+1	+2	+3	+4	+5	+6	+7	+8	+9	+10
-3	-2	-1	0	+1	+2	+3	+4	+5	+6	+7	+8	+9	+10
-3	-2	-1	0	+1	+2	+3	+4	+5	+6	+7	+8	+9	+10

-3	-2	-1	0	+1	+2	+3	+4	+5	+6	+7	+8	+9	+10
-3	-2	-1	0	+1	+2	+3	+4	+5	+6	+7	+8	+9	+10

-3	-2	-1	0	+1	+2	+3	+4	+5	+6	+7	+8	+9	+10
-3	-2	-1	0	+1	+2	+3	+4	+5	+6	+7	+8	+9	+10
-3	-2	-1	0	+1	+2	+3	+4	+5	+6	+7	+8	+9	+10
-3	-2	-1	0	+1	+2	+3	+4	+5	+6	+7	+8	+9	+10
-3	-2	-1	0	+1	+2	+3	+4	+5	+6	+7	+8	+9	+10

Various aspects of your job description (creative work, administration, meetings, filing papers, making presentations, traveling, etc.):

_____	–10	–9	–8	–7	–6	–5	–4
_____	–10	–9	–8	–7	–6	–5	–4
_____	–10	–9	–8	–7	–6	–5	–4
_____	–10	–9	–8	–7	–6	–5	–4
_____	–10	–9	–8	–7	–6	–5	–4
_____	–10	–9	–8	–7	–6	–5	–4
_____	–10	–9	–8	–7	–6	–5	–4

Various aspects of your domestic life
(child care, laundry, yard work, paying bills, etc.):

_____	–10	–9	–8	–7	–6	–5	–4
_____	–10	–9	–8	–7	–6	–5	–4
_____	–10	–9	–8	–7	–6	–5	–4
_____	–10	–9	–8	–7	–6	–5	–4
_____	–10	–9	–8	–7	–6	–5	–4
_____	–10	–9	–8	–7	–6	–5	–4
_____	–10	–9	–8	–7	–6	–5	–4

Leisure-time activities (watching TV, dancing, reading, exercising, making love, etc.)

_____	–10	–9	–8	–7	–6	–5	–4
_____	–10	–9	–8	–7	–6	–5	–4
_____	–10	–9	–8	–7	–6	–5	–4
_____	–10	–9	–8	–7	–6	–5	–4
_____	–10	–9	–8	–7	–6	–5	–4
_____	–10	–9	–8	–7	–6	–5	–4
_____	–10	–9	–8	–7	–6	–5	–4

−3	−2	−1	0	+1	+2	+3	+4	+5	+6	+7	+8	+9	+10
−3	−2	−1	0	+1	+2	+3	+4	+5	+6	+7	+8	+9	+10
−3	−2	−1	0	+1	+2	+3	+4	+5	+6	+7	+8	+9	+10
−3	−2	−1	0	+1	+2	+3	+4	+5	+6	+7	+8	+9	+10
−3	−2	−1	0	+1	+2	+3	+4	+5	+6	+7	+8	+9	+10
−3	−2	−1	0	+1	+2	+3	+4	+5	+6	+7	+8	+9	+10
−3	−2	−1	0	+1	+2	+3	+4	+5	+6	+7	+8	+9	+10

−3	−2	−1	0	+1	+2	+3	+4	+5	+6	+7	+8	+9	+10
−3	−2	−1	0	+1	+2	+3	+4	+5	+6	+7	+8	+9	+10
−3	−2	−1	0	+1	+2	+3	+4	+5	+6	+7	+8	+9	+10
−3	−2	−1	0	+1	+2	+3	+4	+5	+6	+7	+8	+9	+10
−3	−2	−1	0	+1	+2	+3	+4	+5	+6	+7	+8	+9	+10
−3	−2	−1	0	+1	+2	+3	+4	+5	+6	+7	+8	+9	+10
−3	−2	−1	0	+1	+2	+3	+4	+5	+6	+7	+8	+9	+10

−3	−2	−1	0	+1	+2	+3	+4	+5	+6	+7	+8	+9	+10
−3	−2	−1	0	+1	+2	+3	+4	+5	+6	+7	+8	+9	+10
−3	−2	−1	0	+1	+2	+3	+4	+5	+6	+7	+8	+9	+10
−3	−2	−1	0	+1	+2	+3	+4	+5	+6	+7	+8	+9	+10
−3	−2	−1	0	+1	+2	+3	+4	+5	+6	+7	+8	+9	+10
−3	−2	−1	0	+1	+2	+3	+4	+5	+6	+7	+8	+9	+10
−3	−2	−1	0	+1	+2	+3	+4	+5	+6	+7	+8	+9	+10

Environment (Note: a lot of people take their environment for granted. Actually, being happy with the places where you spend time is one of the strongest determiners of life satisfaction.) **How does your body react to:**

The geographic region where you live:	−10	−9	−8	−7	−6	−5	−4
Your city:	−10	−9	−8	−7	−6	−5	−4
Neighborhood:	−10	−9	−8	−7	−6	−5	−4
House or apartment:	−10	−9	−8	−7	−6	−5	−4
Workplace:	−10	−9	−8	−7	−6	−5	−4

Living logistics (getting places, running errands, etc.):

_____	−10	−9	−8	−7	−6	−5	−4
_____	−10	−9	−8	−7	−6	−5	−4
_____	−10	−9	−8	−7	−6	−5	−4
_____	−10	−9	−8	−7	−6	−5	−4
_____	−10	−9	−8	−7	−6	−5	−4
_____	−10	−9	−8	−7	−6	−5	−4
_____	−10	−9	−8	−7	−6	−5	−4

-3	-2	-1	0	+1	+2	+3	+4	+5	+6	+7	+8	+9	+10
-3	-2	-1	0	+1	+2	+3	+4	+5	+6	+7	+8	+9	+10
-3	-2	-1	0	+1	+2	+3	+4	+5	+6	+7	+8	+9	+10
-3	-2	-1	0	+1	+2	+3	+4	+5	+6	+7	+8	+9	+10
-3	-2	-1	0	+1	+2	+3	+4	+5	+6	+7	+8	+9	+10
-3	-2	-1	0	+1	+2	+3	+4	+5	+6	+7	+8	+9	+10

-3	-2	-1	0	+1	+2	+3	+4	+5	+6	+7	+8	+9	+10
-3	-2	-1	0	+1	+2	+3	+4	+5	+6	+7	+8	+9	+10
-3	-2	-1	0	+1	+2	+3	+4	+5	+6	+7	+8	+9	+10
-3	-2	-1	0	+1	+2	+3	+4	+5	+6	+7	+8	+9	+10
-3	-2	-1	0	+1	+2	+3	+4	+5	+6	+7	+8	+9	+10
-3	-2	-1	0	+1	+2	+3	+4	+5	+6	+7	+8	+9	+10
-3	-2	-1	0	+1	+2	+3	+4	+5	+6	+7	+8	+9	+10

THE SMALL PICTURE:
RATING TOMORROW

Again, fill in the labels for your strongest positive and negative *physical* reactions. Next, go through the hourly time slots and note all the activities you plan to

	Strongest Negative Feeling						
5–6 A.M.	–10	–9	–8	–7	–6	–5	–4
6–7 A.M.	–10	–9	–8	–7	–6	–5	–4
7–8 A.M.	–10	–9	–8	–7	–6	–5	–4
8–9 A.M.	–10	–9	–8	–7	–6	–5	–4
9–10 A.M.	–10	–9	–8	–7	–6	–5	–4
10–11 A.M.	–10	–9	–8	–7	–6	–5	–4
11 A.M.–noon	–10	–9	–8	–7	–6	–5	–4
noon–1 P.M.	–10	–9	–8	–7	–6	–5	–4
1–2 P.M.	–10	–9	–8	–7	–6	–5	–4
2–3 P.M.	–10	–9	–8	–7	–6	–5	–4
3–4 P.M.	–10	–9	–8	–7	–6	–5	–4
4–5 P.M.	–10	–9	–8	–7	–6	–5	–4
5–6 P.M.	–10	–9	–8	–7	–6	–5	–4
6–7 P.M.	–10	–9	–8	–7	–6	–5	–4
7–8 P.M.	–10	–9	–8	–7	–6	–5	–4
8–9 P.M.	–10	–9	–8	–7	–6	–5	–4
9–10 P.M.	–10	–9	–8	–7	–6	–5	–4
10–11 P.M.	–10	–9	–8	–7	–6	–5	–4
11 P.M.–12	–10	–9	–8	–7	–6	–5	–4
12–1 A.M.	–10	–9	–8	–7	–6	–5	–4
1–2 A.M.	–10	–9	–8	–7	–6	–5	–4
2–3 A.M.	–10	–9	–8	–7	–6	–5	–4
3–4 A.M.	–10	–9	–8	–7	–6	–5	–4
4–5 A.M.	–10	–9	–8	–7	–6	–5	–4

do tomorrow. Let go of judgment, guilt, and anxiety; think about each activity; and note how positively or negatively *your body* reacts to each item.

	Neutral Response											Strongest Positive Feeling	
−3	−2	−1	0	+1	+2	+3	+4	+5	+6	+7	+8	+9	+10
−3	−2	−1	0	+1	+2	+3	+4	+5	+6	+7	+8	+9	+10
−3	−2	−1	0	+1	+2	+3	+4	+5	+6	+7	+8	+9	+10
−3	−2	−1	0	+1	+2	+3	+4	+5	+6	+7	+8	+9	+10
−3	−2	−1	0	+1	+2	+3	+4	+5	+6	+7	+8	+9	+10
−3	−2	−1	0	+1	+2	+3	+4	+5	+6	+7	+8	+9	+10
−3	−2	−1	0	+1	+2	+3	+4	+5	+6	+7	+8	+9	+10
−3	−2	−1	0	+1	+2	+3	+4	+5	+6	+7	+8	+9	+10
−3	−2	−1	0	+1	+2	+3	+4	+5	+6	+7	+8	+9	+10
−3	−2	−1	0	+1	+2	+3	+4	+5	+6	+7	+8	+9	+10
−3	−2	−1	0	+1	+2	+3	+4	+5	+6	+7	+8	+9	+10
−3	−2	−1	0	+1	+2	+3	+4	+5	+6	+7	+8	+9	+10
−3	−2	−1	0	+1	+2	+3	+4	+5	+6	+7	+8	+9	+10
−3	−2	−1	0	+1	+2	+3	+4	+5	+6	+7	+8	+9	+10
−3	−2	−1	0	+1	+2	+3	+4	+5	+6	+7	+8	+9	+10
−3	−2	−1	0	+1	+2	+3	+4	+5	+6	+7	+8	+9	+10
−3	−2	−1	0	+1	+2	+3	+4	+5	+6	+7	+8	+9	+10
−3	−2	−1	0	+1	+2	+3	+4	+5	+6	+7	+8	+9	+10
−3	−2	−1	0	+1	+2	+3	+4	+5	+6	+7	+8	+9	+10
−3	−2	−1	0	+1	+2	+3	+4	+5	+6	+7	+8	+9	+10
−3	−2	−1	0	+1	+2	+3	+4	+5	+6	+7	+8	+9	+10
−3	−2	−1	0	+1	+2	+3	+4	+5	+6	+7	+8	+9	+10
−3	−2	−1	0	+1	+2	+3	+4	+5	+6	+7	+8	+9	+10
−3	−2	−1	0	+1	+2	+3	+4	+5	+6	+7	+8	+9	+10

A few weeks after we started working together, Holly quit her job and began to build her own import-export business, combining her graduate school training with her rediscovered passion for international travel and exploration. She also worked to become more assertive and self-governing in her relationship with her boyfriend. I recently received an announcement of their wedding. In the enclosed picture, Holly (formerly the Bride of Frankenstein, now the Bride of Alex) looks vibrant, happy, and very, very relaxed.

The charts on pages 124–35 will help you use your body's knowledge to determine how your essential self feels about your life. One examines the Big Picture (your major relationships and lifestyle patterns), while the other looks at the Little Picture (the way you spend your time these days). Filling out these forms is a way for you to get started using your body as a navigational device—but the charts are like bicycle training wheels. Eventually, you'll learn to check in with your body whenever you make a choice, to see whether a given option will take you closer to or farther from your North Star. Then you'll be ready to use the navigational devices and the strategies for change you'll find in the rest of this book. Before you know it, you'll be a whale lover too.

7

SOUL SHRAPNEL: REPAIRING YOUR EMOTIONAL COMPASS

Every neurosis is a substitute for legitimate suffering.
—CARL JUNG

So you're climbing out of bed one morning, yawning and scratching in your underwear, when without warning, a befuddled NRA enthusiast—say, Charlton Heston—fires an accidental shot through your window. Whack! It hits you somewhere in the vicinity of your heart. Just then, there's a knock at the door. You stagger over, gripping your chest with one hand, and pull the door open. On the threshold you see none other than *moi,* your favorite life-design counselor.

"Hey, sports fan!" I say as you sag against the doorjamb, bleeding. "Let's go have some fun! What do you want to do today?"

I think it's a good bet that your answer would be "Have surgery." Not that surgery is fun, of course. But you are acutely aware that *nothing* is going to be fun—not ever—until someone takes care of that bullet wound.

Most of my clients expect that as soon as they get in touch with their essential selves, they'll discover a passion, talent, or ambition that will propel them instantly to wealth and glory. In some cases, that's exactly what happens. More often, however, the first thing the essential self manages to communicate is pain. And the first thing it cries out for is surgery.

EMOTIONAL WOUNDS

Your emotions are incredibly powerful, precise navigational tools, custom-made to help you find and reach your own North Star. However, many of us have encountered circumstances that damaged our emotional compasses. In fact, if you've managed to go through life without taking any shrapnel to the heart, you and I obviously aren't living on the same planet. Your essential self has very firm priorities: It isn't going to send you toward some socially defined "success" in work or love if you're suffering from unhealed emotional wounds. This chapter will tell you how to diagnose and treat such injuries, so that your emotional compasses will be able to direct you beyond the emotional ER and on to your own North Star.

Hemingway wrote that although life breaks us all, some of us manage to become "strong at the broken places." This happens naturally if an emotional wound has the right conditions to heal. People who are lucky enough to inhabit emotionally safe environments start mending almost as soon as their injuries occur. The rest of us don't improve so quickly. We were hurt on emotional battlefields where there wasn't even a safe place to rest, let alone anyone skilled enough to administer first aid. So we patched our wounds as best we could and battled on, still bleeding, still carrying shrapnel in our souls.

There are infinite ways for this to happen. Natasha was raised by a mother who had all the maternal tenderness of a starving crocodile. Josh had terrific parents, making it all the more difficult when he learned that he was born to someone else. Consuela moved from Brazil to Alabama when she was seven, only to discover that being a dark-skinned child in the American South is a lot like wearing a fluffy bunny suit to a carnivore convention. Owen, the only son of a mainland Chinese family, was so doted on by his parents and grandparents that he pretended he was happy all the time so as not to upset them, no matter how he really felt. Over the years, this divorce from his true self grew into an agonizing isolation.

Please note that none of these people had any mental illness, and most of them came from loving, happy families. They were psychologically normal people, having normal reactions to more or less normal emotional distress. But because their wounds went untreated, each of them ended up following their broken emotional compasses in the wrong directions. Their self-doubt, fear, and grief made them pull away from desires and opportunities that would have been perfect for them if they'd been in good emotional health.

You may have made some of the same mistakes these folks did: avoiding love because the loss of a relationship left you suspicious and gun-shy, accepting harsh treatment as an adult because you got used to it as a child, or killing off big dreams because your small ones were destroyed. Or—let's face it—you may have done much worse. Many of the walking wounded struggle along in emotional agony so long that they lose all social-self control, becoming defeated, hard-hearted, or addicted to chemicals and behaviors that anesthetize their pain. They turn their anguish into a grim Gift That Keeps on Giving, wreaking terrible damage on other people—usually those they love most. This kind of existence is as far as you can get from your own North Star.

Have I convinced you yet that stopping to clean, dress, and stitch up your emotional injuries is a key step toward attaining the life you want? If not, you may be courting failure at a very basic level. Even if you achieve things that seem outwardly fabulous, an unhealed emotional injury will make you experience them as empty and unappealing. By contrast, recovering your emotional health will suffuse even small successes with joy, long before you achieve anything obviously spectacular.

DIAGNOSING EMOTIONAL INJURIES

Ron insisted on making appointments with me for two full years, though I didn't seem to be doing him any good. His promising career as a marketing manager for a start-up technology firm had stalled completely about a month after I met him. Bored and frustrated, he'd decided to quit, but no matter how much we talked, he couldn't think of anything else he wanted to do.

One day, after I'd tried pretty much every trick in my bag, we ended up sitting in silence for several minutes. Ron seemed especially depleted that day, shrunken into himself with what he said was apathy.

I got the distinct feeling it was something stronger. Since we had nothing to lose, I decided to play my hunch.

"Ron," I said, "tell me something. Are you in despair?"

Ron looked at me wearily, without a hint of surprise. After a while, he said, "I keep thinking about my girlfriend."

I began to feel the electrical, tingling sensation around my head and shoulders that I always get when a client is making a step of monumental proportions. "I didn't even know you had a girlfriend," I told Ron.

"I don't," he said. "She died three years ago. Traffic accident."

My jaw dropped. "And you never told me?"

Ron frowned. "What does Gina's death have to do with my career?"

"Well, everything," I said. "Absolutely everything."

The story didn't take long to tell. Ron had been in the process of falling in love with Gina when she was killed. He had known her for only a few months; no one thought of them as a couple, or even knew how much Ron had come to care for Gina. This is the kind of thing that most people—especially men—find difficult to explain or express. Ron hadn't even known how to begin, so he'd kept his terrible emotional wound private.

Immediately, Ron's essential self had begun boycotting all professional and social activities, doing its level best to get him to stop working and seek healing. His social self kept showing up at the office, his weekly poker game, Sunday dinner with his parents, but his essential self was off mourning Gina. Naturally, Ron lost all pleasure in his job—but a lack of aptitude for his profession was never the problem. The problem was that marketing isn't a first-choice activity for someone who's just taken a bullet to the heart.

From the day he first mentioned her, Ron and I spent a lot of time talking about Gina. I also referred him to a good therapist, who helped him process his feelings about her death. Not long afterward, he found himself enjoying his job again. He is happily employed there to this day, and recently began dating again. He will never forget Gina, but the injury caused by her death has healed.

I believe that almost everyone who feels as stymied, aimless, or directionless as Ron is carrying an unresolved emotional wound. A lack of enthusiasm for life is always a sign that the deep self is hurt. Every person's essential self is pure productive energy, and yours will send you into a fulfilling life almost automatically if your emotional psyche is in good repair. If, despite honest effort, you can't imagine a life full of enthusiasm and delight, it's time for a little triage.

Here's a short quiz to help you determine whether you're being held back by emotional wounds. If you find that you're completely hale and hearty, skip the rest of this chapter. It'll be here if—God forbid—you ever need it. However, if this test shows clear signs of injury, if something in your deep self resonates to the idea that you might be carrying emotional shrapnel, *or if you're violently insulted by the very suggestion that you might be hiding an unhealed injury* (something psychologists call "reaction formation"), completing the exercises in the rest of this chapter is likely the next step on the road to your North Star.

TESTING ROR EMOTIONAL WOUNDS

Answer each of the following questions as honestly as possible. Please note that the "Yes" and "No" responses are not always in the same column. If you are reluctant to answer the questions, or if you feel you're being tricked into revealing something you'd rather not, the game is already up: You probably have an emotional wound.

1	2	
N	Y	Do people ever tell you that you seem arrogant, cold, aloof, or distant?
Y	N	Is there at least one person who really understands almost all your feelings?
N	Y	Is there anything you do compulsively, even though you wish you could stop?
N	Y	Do you feel exhausted and irritable after being with a group of friends for a few hours?
N	Y	Do you often seek solitude to "recover" from interactions with social groups?
Y	N	Do you feel comfortable crying in front of the person/people you love most?
Y	N	Do you talk about your feelings at least once a week to at least one other person?
N	Y	Are there any events in your life you would not be willing to talk about to anyone?

Y	N	Do you regularly engage in activities that allow you to express your feelings (writing in a journal, singing along with emotional music, acting, weeping at emotional movies, etc.)?
N	Y	Do you have strange or unexpected emotional reactions, such as feeling shame when you are praised, relief when you fail, or anxiety when you are loved?
N	Y	Do you have any "dark" secrets?
Y	N	When someone makes you angry, do you tell him or her how upset you are?
N	Y	Are you lonely even—or especially—when you are with other people?
Y	N	Are you comfortable being touched affectionately by the people you love most?
N	Y	Are you *only* comfortable being touched by a sexual partner, or does all touch seem sexual to you?
Y	N	When you get good news, are there people you'd call just to share your happiness?
N	Y	Do you pride yourself on never being upset or angry?
N	Y	Would you rather "stuff" your anger than cause conflict by standing up for yourself?
Y	N	Are you comfortable verbally expressing your love for family and friends?
N	Y	On a typical day, do you laugh—genuinely, not out of politeness—less than five times?
N	Y	Do you laugh at inappropriate times, such as when you hear bad news or when someone else is expressing anger?
N	Y	Do you often cry without knowing the reason why?

Count the number of responses in column 1 and column 2. Getting more than three column 2 responses indicates a probable emotional wound.

TREATING AN EMOTIONAL WOUND

Once it's been diagnosed, fixing the damage from emotional wounds is surprisingly simple. I said simple, not easy. The steps are pretty straight-forward, but they're guaranteed to scare you, and they may be briefly but intensely painful.

Did you happen to be watching *Oprah* the day they showed the woman with the 330-pound tumor? I don't want to be rude, but this lady looked like Jabba the Hut was her conjoined twin. The benign but enormous cyst kept her housebound and bedridden for years before she consented to have it surgically removed. This is rare in the annals of medicine, but I've seen people drag around emotional wounds almost as crippling, for the same reason: They're afraid of the removal process. Some people are so frightened by the prospect of opening their wounds that they think it best to Band-Aid their bullet holes and tough things out. This does not work. The process below, in its many variations, constitutes the only way to heal emotional injuries, remove that soul shrapnel, and get to your own North Star.

Here's how emotional surgery works: 1) First, you have to locate any damaging alien objects that may be lodged in your psyche. This is done by searching your memory for the events that caused your emotional injury. 2) To clean out your wounds, you must identify at least one person who can hear your story with compassion and empathy. The ultimate goal of this step is to learn self-love. Compassion toward the self always starts with receiving understanding and acknowledgment from someone else, but once you've mastered the art of comforting and accepting yourself, you'll be able to heal many of your emotional injuries without anyone else's assistance. 3) Whether you're talking to yourself or a confidant (and here, I'd strongly suggest getting professional help, especially at first), give this person a full account of the events that hurt you. Don't recite them like a police report; include your emotional reactions to the events, and express any emotional pain you're still feeling. 4) The equivalent of stitching up the cleaned wound happens when you get a compassionate response from your listener, allow yourself to accept that love, and begin to feel it toward yourself. 5) Even after the first four steps have been completed, you may need to rest a bit while you finish healing. Time, which only makes things worse as long as you're toting shrapnel, heals emotional wounds with surprising speed once they're cleaned and bandaged.

That's it, the whole dreaded procedure. Of course, you may need to go through the steps several times, depending on how many times, and how severely, you've been wounded. Some people get so used to doing this that it becomes a lifestyle: every relationship is another chance to recount the terrible things that have happened to them. Don't get stuck in this place. After the first few times, the healing effect of telling your story will already have taken place, and you'll feel less emotional energy with each conversation. That's the signal that it's time to move on.

Step 1: Figure Out What Hurt You

Priscilla was a short, testy young woman whose parents sent her to see me after she flunked out of junior college. She had a history of failure, despite her facile mind and quirky charm. She also had many warning signs of an untreated emotional wound: She lashed out in anger with virtually no provocation, became very anxious whenever anyone said anything nice about her, and felt perpetually lonely. I told her I thought she might have emotional issues to resolve before she could break her repetitive-failure pattern. This made Priscilla absolutely furious. When she left my office that day, I didn't really expect to see her again. She surprised me by showing up early to her next appointment.

"Okay," she snapped, almost before sitting down. "So let's say I do have this emotional problem you were talking about. What do I have to do to get over it?"

"You need to tell me—or anyway, someone—what hurt you."

Priscilla chewed on this for a while. "Nothing really bad ever happened to me."

"Terrific! I don't think I can help you." I stood up and extended my hand.

For the first time, Priscilla's customary glare turned to a look of concern. "Wait!" she exclaimed. "All right, so maybe something— some things—did hurt me. I mean, we all get hurt, right? But I'm being straight with you—I can't think of anything in my life that was all that bad. I don't know what to talk about."

"Have you ever gotten something stuck in your foot?" I said, sitting down again. "If you can't see where it is, you poke around and feel where it hurts. Then you focus your attention on the most painful spot."

Priscilla nodded.

"Well, you've got something stuck in your memory. To find out what it is, you need to poke around in there and notice what feels worst. Is there anything you really, really don't want to talk about? Something you don't even want to do *think* about?"

She rolled her eyes. "You mean, like, my childhood?"

"That'll do for starters. What's the very worst thing that happened during your childhood?"

"You don't want to know."

"No," I said, "*you* don't want to know. Actually, I'm kind of curious."

It took a while for Priscilla, tough as she pretended to be, to face the prospect of describing her childhood to me. She was terrified—scared that she'd be overwhelmed by emotional pain, or cry in front of me, or open a Pandora's box she'd never be able to close.

Now, there wasn't anything earth-shattering about the way Priscilla's emotions had been injured. Her parents, both well-meaning but controlling perfectionists, had criticized their only daughter frequently, given her little approval, and rationed her food from the moment (when she was five) they decided she was a bit chubby. None of this would make the evening news, but the shame and pain that emerged when Priscilla told me her story were as real, and as important, as the agony of a badly abused child. (A lot of my clients say they don't deserve to mope about their sad little memories while children are starving in India. I say that just because your broken arm isn't as serious as someone else's gut wound, that doesn't mean your injury isn't excruciating or doesn't require attention. If you want to help the Indian children, or make the world a better place in any other way, you have to start by becoming whole yourself.)

All Priscilla's fears about telling her story were realistic; in fact, all of them came to pass. As she recounted especially painful experiences, she did feel unbearable sadness—but to her surprise, it dissolved very quickly once it was voiced and heard. She did cry, but I didn't mind, and after a while, neither did she. And her story did open a benevolent sort of Pandora's box: Once Priscilla had experienced the profound relief of releasing her pain, she would never again hide her emotional wounds from everyone. Her feelings were open to the people she trusted, ready to be heard and healed as soon as another injury occurred.

Soul Shrapnel

If, like Priscilla, you think you have unhealed wounds but don't know what they are, poke around a little. Get out a piece of paper and write down a few topics you really, really don't want to think or talk about. Write only the names of the topics, labels like "Dog ran away," "Parents divorced," or "Grandpa choked on Oreo I gave him." *Do not go into a detailed description of the incident that wounded your emotions.* Not yet, anyway. There's a good reason your brilliant little brain shoved your pain into unconsciousness: You didn't have the necessary emotional support to deal with it on your own.

This isn't a sign of mental unfitness or cowardice. For example, the gifted, courageous author Virginia Woolf, a genius at probing her memory for painful truths, began writing down all the gory details of her childhood when she was middle-aged. Shortly after penning a description of being sexually abused by her cousin, Woolf filled her pockets with rocks and walked into the Thames, drowning herself with her sorrows. That's because she didn't—or couldn't—complete the next step in healing an emotional wound.

Step 2: Find a Sane, Sympathetic Audience

You wouldn't open up a literal, physical bullet wound just anywhere, or get just anyone to help. You'd want a sanitary operating room with all the amenities, and the best-trained surgeon available. Most people don't seem to realize that emotional wounds need to be given the same kind of respect. An effective "surgical" listener is someone who: 1) genuinely cares about you; 2) is not preoccupied by his or her own unhealed emotional wounds; 3) isn't afraid to talk about emotional issues; and 4) can understand and empathize with your pain without trying to "fix" it immediately.

How do you know whether someone possesses these qualities? As far as your social self is concerned, you don't. I strongly suggest that you rent a sympathetic ear in the form of a skilled psychotherapist. (I think we should all get therapy for the same reason we should all get massage. Even if you don't really need it, it can make you feel like God is rubbing your tummy.) If you have any friends who've been through therapy, ask them if they like their therapists, or if there's someone they'd recommend. Or you can try a technique I often use to find therapists who are particularly suited to a particular client's issues: I call psychology professors and social workers at local universities and ask them to recommend a suitable practitioner. Many insurance policies cover a few mental-health sessions, but they often limit their coverage to certain therapists. If that's true for you, your insurance company will provide a shortlist of mental-health professionals.

By the way, this doesn't mean that you have to stay with the therapist recommended by your best pal or your HMO. Just because someone has a diploma on the wall doesn't mean he or she is skilled at healing emotional wounds. A bad therapist—and sadly, they do exist—will only make things worse. The concept of shopping for shrinks strikes many people as odd, even a little sacrilegious, but that's exactly what you should do. Once, during a particularly horrendous time in my life, I went to a therapist who pitched herself like some kind of miracle carpet cleaner. She was unctuously warm and friendly and told me, "This will be quick and easy. You'll be absolutely fine in six months." At one level, this was just what I wanted to hear. At a deeper level, I simply knew that she was wrong, and that trying to speed-read my deeply troubled mind was a disastrous approach. I kept seeing her for several sessions anyway, and felt more confused and upset with every encounter. Finally, I consulted another therapist. When I told her a little about the problems I was facing, she shook her head without a trace of a smile. "This is going to be hard as hell," she said. "I'm willing to support you, but I'm sure glad I'm not in your position." I immediately switched to the second therapist, and she became one of my most steadfast and helpful mentors.

There's no error-proof way to choose an emotional-healing audience or ensure a helpful response to your story; even a master surgeon can have an off day. But I've found two remarkably effective tests for determining who should hear your tales of woe. First, choose someone who makes you *want* to open up. This may not be someone who is gushy and hypersympathetic. Like the psychologist I just mentioned, great therapists often come across as rather detached and cool, especially when you've just met them. But they also display a kind of steady, even blunt emotional honesty that you will instinctively want to trust.

Desire is a function of the essential self, not the social self, and the former's instincts are far more sophisticated at "reading" people's emotional capabilities than any intellectual test you or I could devise. When your essential self has located someone who makes it feel safe, you will find it difficult *not* to confide your painful stories. Even people who have experienced horrifying traumas, so bad that they repressed all memory of the events to keep from going crazy, begin to spontaneously remember and recount their experiences once the essential self finds a reliable, compassionate audience.

Second, don't confide everything all at once. Use the "cat on the roof" system. I get this label from a bad joke, which I will now mercilessly repeat for its illustrative qualities:

A man goes on vacation, leaving his pet cat with a friend. When he calls to check on the cat, his friend says, "I hate to tell you this, dude, but Fluffy's dead. Fell off the roof. Sorry."

The vacationer is appalled by his friend's callousness. "For God's sake," he says, "you don't just blurt out something like that! You say something like, 'Dude, your cat's on the roof. We're trying to get her down, but it's not looking good.' Then you could break the news to me gradually, over a few days. I'd have some time to prepare myself."

"Okay," says the friend.

"So, is there any other news?" asks the vacationer.

"Well, just one thing. Your mother's on the roof . . ."

This is how you tell someone about the painful events lodged in your memory. Reveal a bit of your story at a time—not enough to make you feel totally exposed, just enough to require a tiny bit of trust. Then, gauge the reaction. If your listener responds with indifference, scorn, or anxiety, stop. You're in an unsanitary operating room, with an unskilled surgeon. If the reaction is calm, accepting, and empathetic, you'll want to divulge more. Take another small step; then check the reaction again.

One of the reasons I'd prefer that your first confidant be a trained professional is that emotionally wounded people often seek out the worst possible audiences to hear their initial soul-revealing confessions. You'd think it would go without saying that *it is extremely risky to tell your story to anyone who has been involved in inflicting your emotional wounds.* Unfortunately, it's also extremely likely that you'll want to.

Colette was on the verge of quitting a graduate program. She had a tough farm-wife mother who, throughout Colette's childhood, had repeatedly told her she was stupid and would never amount to anything. As it turned out, the chair of Colette's thesis committee reminded her very much of Mommy Dearest. The emotional wounds she'd suffered as a child were crippling her academic performance, especially when she had to interact with this professor.

When Colette made this connection during one of our sessions, she became tremendously excited. She rushed home, called her mother, and poured out everything she'd realized about her childhood wounds and how they were hampering her life. Predictably, Colette's mother became very defensive and allayed her own guilt by launching into a searing diatribe on Colette's innate dullness and incompetence. She might as well have opened fire with a bazooka; Colette was almost mortally wounded. So, what did she do? Without even hanging up the phone, she called her graduate adviser—the Mommy clone—and repeated the whole story to her! The professor's response was cold and brusque. I imagine she was more than a tad freaked out by Colette's passionate, vulnerable, emotional life story.

Mea culpa, mea culpa, mea maxima culpa. I had made a crucial mistake with Colette: I hadn't warned her about the likelihood that she would be tempted to make repeated, ill-calculated bids for her mother's love and support. This is where the essential self's innocent, trusting inclinations must be tempered by the social self's good sense and experience. If someone you deeply love wounded you emotionally, you may spend years in futile efforts to convince that person to change, to see how valuable you are, to treat you as you deserve to be treated. When these attempts fail (because they usually do), you'll feel magnetized toward romantic partners, friends, and sometimes even employers who are similar to the person who hurt you. You'll try to get *them* to treat you right, because that would feel a lot like getting love from the original injuring party. Colette made both these mistakes, took on several more rounds of hostile fire from both her mom and her adviser, and had to spend even more time treating these new injuries before she could get on with her graduate program and her life.

As we'll discuss in a few pages, you may well need to confront your exploitative boss, your abusive ex-boyfriend, or your manipulative stepmother at some point on the road to your North Star. *But don't go to these people when you're trying to heal your wounds.* This is surgery, my friend. You're going to be laying bare your heart, and you don't need the people who broke it poking their grubby mitts into your chest cavity.

EXERCISE

After identifying some experience so painful you generally avoid talking about it, start checking around for a good therapist. If you can't afford that, look for a twelve-step group that addresses your particular issues. Make an appointment with your potential confidant, or go to your twelve-step meeting. You'll need to schedule at least an hour: ten minutes for introductory small talk, at least half an hour for the heart-to-heart, and a few minutes of closure at the end. During the meeting, confide a *little* information about the event that wounded you. Then stop. Gauge the therapist's reaction. Do you feel unheard or frighteningly exposed? If so, wrap it up immediately. Try again in another setting, or with another therapist. On the other hand, if you feel understood and accepted, you'll want to keep talking. Proceed with caution, one small step at a time.

Step 3: Get to the Truth, the Whole Truth, and Nothing but the Truth

It's amazing how hard it can be to tell the whole, true story of an event that injured you. I've seen people with the physical pain tolerance of WWF wrestlers tremble like aspen leaves when they set out to talk about their emotional injuries. We are often caught between the social and essential selves when it comes to recounting our stories: The essential self will want to talk compulsively as soon as it feels safe, while the social self may be paralyzed by shame, grief, anger, embarrassment, or fear of rejection.

As a result, many people end up telling only part of their stories in a therapeutic setting. They shade the details to make things look better than they really were, or paint themselves as victims of evil when they were actually participants, or leave out important details. As I've already said, it makes sense not to reveal more than feels safe. But if you've never found anyone you can trust with your whole, unadulterated truth, you must keep searching. Your emotional wounds won't heal until it's all out there, the very worst of it. Dark secrets fester, spread, and kill. Truth is the only disinfectant that works on them. Eventually, you'll have to tell it all.

This is a peel-the-onion process; it never ends with the first iteration. Every time you divulge some truth, you'll feel light, relieved, and cleansed—but several days, months, or years later, more information can rise to the surface, requiring another phase of healing. One therapist I know has a friend who, years ago, crashed his car and went through the windshield, leaving thousands of glass slivers embedded in his scalp. Surgeons took out all the glass they could find immediately after the accident, but decades later, some of it is still there. Every so often, this guy feels an uncomfortable prickling sensation somewhere on his head, and another bit of glass works its way out of his skin. Emotional shrapnel works the same way. You'll clear out the big, ugly debris in an initial phase of therapy, but mildly painful slivers may come to the surface every now and then for the rest of your life. Gradually, you'll learn to welcome this feeling, since it always mean that your inner life is on the way to being more whole and joyful than ever.

I usually have clients start the process of emotional healing by writing down their secret history on a piece of paper, which they are to burn as soon as they've finished. It's amazing how many of them can't even put down the whole truth about their lives in this most private of venues. They seem to think the paper will magically reconstitute, like children's letters to Mary Poppins, so they end up sanitizing, abridging, and falsifying their accounts. When you can't even write the truth in a letter to yourself, I guarantee you aren't in any condition to reach your own North Star.

Years ago, when I was doing research on addiction, I found that all my interview subjects, regardless of the nature of their addictions, had one thing in common: they lied to themselves. Obviously, they lied about their addictive behavior, but they hadn't become liars because they were addicts; on the contrary, they'd turned to addiction because they'd been telling themselves lies, often since childhood. You may have some of these tricky little truth loopholes in your own belief system. "Of course Mom loved us; she just expressed it by cursing and pelting us with cigarette butts." "No, Uncle Bob was *not* an alcoholic, welfare-cheating sadist. He was just . . . colorful." "I'm fine. Really, absolutely fine. I said *I'm fine, damn it!*" Healing your emotional wounds means shattering the soft-focus lens of denial that pretties up ugly truths of family history and personal experience. It also means taking responsibility for your own misdeeds, whatever they may be.

Once you've got the facts straight, you must also tell the truth about the feelings caused by hurtful events. This kind of truth also comes in layers. Your initial flush of self-righteous rage may blanket a layer of guilt, which holds incredible sadness inside it. Or your deadening depression may be a mask for wild, raw anger you're petrified to feel. Again, writing is a powerful way to begin peeling away the onion skin, exposing the core truths of your emotional life.

EXERCISE

At the top of a piece of notebook paper, write the words "This Is What Happened." Then put down a description of something that hurt you emotionally. Next, write "This Is How I Feel About It," and describe your emotional response to the event. Very nice; that's out of the way.

Now turn to a fresh page and write "This Is What REALLY Happened." Recount the same event, only tell all the shocking, rude, blunt, unkind details you left out the first time. When that's done, write, "This Is How I REALLY Feel About It." Dig deeper into your gut reactions, *taking especial care to describe any feelings you think may be "inappropriate."* Keep writing rougher and ruder and balder and badder versions until your emotional energy is exhausted and no more new truth is emerging from your descriptions.

Now burn the pages, or keep them in a very safe place. Eventually, you'll talk about them, but not until you've digested them yourself. You'll know it's time to tell your support system when you *want* to talk.

Don't do this exercise until you've established at least one supportive relation-ship, if possible, with a qualified therapist. If you know or suspect that you may ever have been physically or sexually abused, a trained counselor is a must.

Step 4: Accept Others' Compassion and Learn to Extend It to Yourself

If you've chosen a halfway decent confidant and told him or her the whole truth about the most painful experiences in your life, his or her natural reaction will be sympathetic and kind. If you have no trouble dealing with that, you're home free. Accepting someone else's compassionate response to your story enables you to feel love for yourself—and *self-love is the single most important tool you will ever use in your search for your own North Star.* I'm not talking about self-obsession, self-importance, or self-pity, all of which signal emotional shrapnel. I'm talking about the healthy self-love that allows you to care for yourself as you would a dear friend. People who maintain this kind of self-love heal quickly from the slings and arrows of outrageous fortune, and since they are healthy themselves, they give far more love to others than folks who are mired in self-hatred.

Learning self-love comes most easily to people who have been well loved by others. However, for people who aren't used to receiving affection or support, this final step in emotional healing can be astonishingly difficult. Such people often find expressions of kindness embarrassing, incomprehensible, or even frightening. People whose hearts have been injured armor themselves against further pain, rejecting anything with the potential to touch them deeply. If you tend to respond to love by running or panicking, don't push yourself. You must eventually get over the problem if you want your emotional wounds to heal, but you can't force this to happen. Just try to accept as much compassion as possible, in whatever form you can stand it. Persist in this effort and, over time, your resistance to love will relax.

This is what happened to Arturo, despite a really rotten childhood. His father was a violent drunk, his mother silent and depressed. By the age of eighteen, Arturo had walled up his badly wounded emotions, dropped out of high school, and set off down the same dreary road of life his parents had taken. Then one day, on his way home from his job at 7-Eleven, he nearly tripped over a mangy, half-dead puppy in an alley near his apartment.

"If he'd whined or been friendly, I probably would have kicked him into a Dumpster," Arturo told me later. "But he growled and tried to bite me. Got his teeth into the leg of my jeans and wouldn't let go. You have to understand, this dog was so small he couldn't have beaten up Tweety Bird, but he sure would've tried. I looked down at this ratty little mutt hanging on to my pant leg, and something happened inside me. It was like I recognized him, the look in his eyes. I thought, Hell, that's *me*."

Arturo took the puppy back to his apartment and named it X. Over the next few weeks, he gradually learned to care for X, and the puppy slowly came to trust him. In fact, as X recovered from the scars of puppy abuse and grew into a really ugly but healthy dog, he started showing his new caretaker the kind of unfiltered adoration for which his species is so justly famous. For the first time in his life, Arturo was deeply and unconditionally loved.

This started a domino effect that transformed Arturo's life. Because he saw the puppy as a reflection of the damaged, confused, scrappy child he had once been, he couldn't love X without caring for himself as well. Arturo entered the emotional "flooding" that often happens when a wounded heart begins to heal. "It was insane!" he told me. "I was falling apart—TV commercials could make me cry like a little girl. Crazy!"

Eventually, things got so bad—or more accurately, so good—that Arturo consulted a psychologist, who became his first human confidant. Short version: Arturo eventually returned to school, earned a B.A., and went on to become a social worker, helping other emotionally damaged children. He grew strong at the broken places, and so did X. The emotional lives of these two creatures, once so badly hurt and neglected, are now extraordinarily rich in love.

Arturo's story is a classic example of how the essential self can guide someone with virtually no social support into a healthy, happy life. If Arturo had gone to a touchy-feely shrink right off the bat, it would have done him no good at all; he wasn't ready to receive that level of compassion. Even a friendly dog would have been emotionally threatening to him. But Arturo was able to accept a hint of empathetic connection with the mangy, aggressive X. By acting on that impulse, he set himself on course for healing and reaching his North Star. No one can make an authentic loving connection, no matter how small, without beginning to heal emotionally.

Step 5: Give Yourself Time

Every time you suffer an injury to your emotions, you'll go through the whole grieving process: denial, anger, grief, acceptance. Actually, it's more like denial, anger, grief, anger, denial, grief, anger, grief, more grief, absolutely blistering anger, denial . . . and so on. Although "acceptance" does come along eventually, the path to it is a wild roller coaster. As you open up and start talking about your wounds, you'll experience the mood swings Arturo went through after he adopted X.

People who don't have safe healing environments stay in the first stage of the grieving process—denial—for a long time. Some never go past this phase, because they sense that the rage and sadness they'll feel as soon as they jettison denial are extremely unpleasant. Many of my clients actually think these emotions—especially anger—are morally wrong. Ironically, accepting and even embracing the grief process makes it brief and cleansing, while denial means that even minor soul shrapnel can stay inside, poisoning your happiness forever.

If you've never grieved a wound, bringing it into consciousness will make you feel an emotional reaction almost as intense as if the event were actually happening. You may feel sadness or rage that takes your breath away. You can express these feelings by writing and talking about them, or by physical actions such as crying or pounding some inanimate object like a pillow (do this alone or with a therapist, who can stay calm and supportive as you express your anger). Remember, though, that long-past events don't absolutely require any changes outside the confines of your own heart and mind. You don't have to force people who hurt you in the past to redress every wrong in the present. For example, you may have a gut-wrenching memory of your mother taking away your favorite teddy bear when you were three. It's necessary to grieve and rage on behalf of that little kid. You might want to buy yourself another teddy bear, a really good one. But you don't need to rush over and demand your mother's apologies, now that you're a line-backer for the Pittsburgh Steelers and Mom's so old and frail she can barely gum down enough Jell-O to keep up her weight.

The intense and scary grieving process has a remarkable alchemical effect on your psyche. It changes the stuff of your personality in such a way that you're less likely to fall into unhealthy situations that mirror past catastrophes. I've had any number of clients with an uncanny knack for winding up in the job situations and relationships that echoed their painful pasts. This "repetition compulsion" has the effect of pulling you back to the source of your pain, so that you have a chance to heal old wounds and learn new, more self-supporting responses to people and events. Once you've fully grieved the original wounds that scarred your psyche, you'll stop unconsciously seeking and repeating them.

THE AFTERMATH
OF EMOTIONAL SURGERY

My friend Lois was another survivor of an emotionally devastating childhood. Her family was so dysfunctional—flat-out abusive in every way—that I'm not even going to tell you about it. Lois emerged from this family like a diamond from the dirt: shining, clear, the strongest substance on earth. I've never met anyone more kind, generous, honest, or brave. Of course, this didn't happen without effort; in fact, it took so much energy that by the time she was forty, Lois had little will to live. Physically and emotionally, she was numb and utterly exhausted. She sought counseling and, over a couple of years, removed an enormous amount of emotional shrapnel.

"It was like dumping a thousand pounds of garbage I'd been carry-ing my whole life," she said. "Before I started feeling good myself, I had no idea that most people weren't walking around sad and angry all the time. Now that I was getting clearer, I could understand what people meant when they said they were happy. Even though I still have prob-lems to deal with, there's an underlying sense of happiness and security.

It's like getting over the flu; I'm so conscious of feeling good that I think it's almost better than if I'd never felt bad."

After several months, Lois began to sense that she was coming to the end of her therapy. There was very little shrapnel left in her, and her worst scars had almost totally healed. At this point, she got a little scared. "I don't know what to do when I don't feel bad," she explained. "All I've done, my whole life, is deal with pain. I go to my job, then I go home and cry—it's always been that way. Therapy made it even more intense for a while, but now the pain is almost gone. Frankly, I'm not sure what I'm going to do with my time and energy."

Never one to shrink from the unknown, Lois forged bravely onward. As the last of her emotional pain resolved, she experienced a sustained explosion of creative energy. Within a couple of months, she applied for (and got) a promotion, redecorated her house, began what turned out to be a highly successful investment portfolio, and started designing her own clothes.

Healing your emotional wounds will have the same effect on you that it did on Lois. Not only have I seen this happen to others, I've been through it myself, big-time. Before experiencing this, I would have said that it sounded too good to be true. It isn't. It really happens. If you're limping along riddled with bullets, you have a major treat ahead of you. From the first time you tell your truths and are truly understood, you'll begin to experience surges of unprecedented happiness. (I've had recovering drug addicts tell me that emotional health feels better than an amphetamine high, but with positive, rather than negative, side effects.) The euphoria of feeling healthy will level out as you get used to it, eventually becoming a calm, sustained sense of well-being. This will sink deeper into your soul the more you learn to love and care for yourself.

As a kind of by-product, you may wake up one morning to discover that you have forgiven the people who hurt you. (By the way, trying to forgive without healing is one way of Band-Aiding a bullet wound: It might make things look nicer, but it doesn't really "take.") As anger and grief disappear, you'll start feeling bursts of enthusiasm and new ideas, along with unprecedented energy to turn your dreams into reality. This will vary somewhat as you go through the inevitable crises of life, but it will return and continue as long as you remain emotionally open, honest, and self-loving.

Though the emotional healing process is sure to make you feel warm all under, it may also blow your outer life to smithereens. Remember Allen, the alcoholic I described in Chapter 2? When he stopped drinking and started living authentically, his boss, wife, and parents threw multiple blue-faced fits. Most emotionally wounded people are living and working in situations that *depend* on their avoiding a healthy inner life. You can't stay well without telling—and living— the truth. That might be completely unacceptable to the people around you. If this is the situation you're in, you are facing a choice: You can start taking on emotional shrapnel all over again, get out of the life situation that requires you to stay wounded, or start changing that system from within. The next chapter will help you streamline the terrifying, exhilarating, forbidden, flat-out wonderful process of transforming your life in accordance with your emotional compasses. Once it's whole, your emotional self won't let you rest until you're moving straight toward your North Star.

8

READING YOUR
EMOTIONAL COMPASS

The navigational equipment that takes you to your own North Star is arranged like a series of concentric circles, or those nested boxes that have a series of smaller boxes inside them. The outermost compass, the easiest to access, is your body. If you're out of touch physically, it's hard to reach the next layer: emotion. When you do connect with your emotional compass, you'll immediately bump into any emotional wounds that may be gumming up the works. Heal them, and you're left with a set of emotional impulses that will not only tell you where your North Star is but also map out a route and describe the terrain you'll have to cover. This chapter will help you interpret and act on the incredibly rich information you get from these emotional compasses.

THE FOUR MAGIC QUESTIONS

Often, my clients have no idea what emotions they're feeling. Their social selves exist in a state of bland pleasantness, or perhaps glum depression, that hides the raw emotional experience of the essential self. To get a general heading from your emotional compass, you might want to use what I call the Four Magic Questions. As you read through the explanations below, try answering each question for yourself.

Magic Question No. 1: What Am I Feeling?

I can't tell you how many times I've stumped intelligent, articulate clients with this one. Ask them what they're feeling, and people with enough graduate degrees to wallpaper a small office building will look at you as though you've suddenly started speaking Klingon. If you have no idea how to identify your own emotional state, go back to the body-sensation exercises in Chapter 6. You can't really inhabit your body without connecting consciousness to emotion, so feeling nothing emotionally is a sign that you need to get physical.

If you're feeling a confusing welter of emotions, try categorizing the sensation into one of four major areas: sad, mad, glad, or scared. Most of my clients, even those with very tenuous attachments to their emotions, can usually put their feelings in one of these categories. Doing so seems to prime the pump, allowing people to get more specific, subtle emotional information. Once you get used to doing this, you may get so good at expressing every nuance of feeling that you start spouting extemporaneous poetry.

Speaking of poetry, another way to refine your emotion-identification skill is to expose yourself to art. You can do this without a dirty raincoat or a lurid leer; just look for works of art—any art—that seem to match what you're feeling. For example, think of a piece of music that matches the mood you're in right now. What comes to mind? Is the melody wistful, triumphant, calming, exciting, buoyant? One of the characters in Anne Tyler's novel *Breathing Lessons* never displays overt emotion but perpetually whistles songs whose lyrics describe his feelings. I had a client who did exactly the same thing. She realized she wanted a divorce after noticing that after every knock-down-drag-out fight with her husband, she found herself humming the tune to "Time to Say Goodbye." Another client, Thomas, became fascinated by Renaissance art as soon as he got in touch with his essential self. One day he figured out that he was filling his life with painted saints and angels because he had a deep-seated yearning for the spiritual practices of his childhood. What about you?

EXERCISE

1. Right now, are you feeling more mad, sad, glad, or scared? Even if your feelings are very mild, try putting them in one of these categories.

2. Now write down at least six different words, besides those listed above, that describe your feelings at this moment.

   a. _____

   b. _____

   c. _____

   d. _____

   e. _____

   f. _____

3. Think of three works of art (songs, movies, images, poems, plays, books, etc.) that resonate with your current emotional state.

   a. _____

   b. _____

   c. _____

4. What do these works of art have in common? _____

   _____

5. Complete the following sentences. Don't think about grammar or spelling; just shoot for emotional accuracy. No one has to see this but you.

   a. I wish _____

   _____

   b. I hope _____

   _____

   c. I'm angry that _____

   _____

   d. I'm afraid that _____

   _____

   e. I'm sad about _____

   _____

f. I'm happy about _____

_____

g. If it weren't so embarrassing, I'd feel _____

_____

h. Even though it's stupid, I feel _____

_____

Magic Question No. 2: Why Am I Feeling This Way?

Once you've begun to get a grip on what you're feeling, it's time to trace your emotion to its source. I like to use a system popularized by the Japanese car manufacturer Toyota, which developed its extraordinarily high production quality by using a system known as the "Five Whys." Every worker on the Toyota assembly line was taught to analyze design or production problems by asking the question "Why?" over and over again, like a two-year-old. ("This bolt fell off." *Why?* "Because the thread is stripped." *Why?* "Because it was misaligned with the screw." *Why?* And so on.) Almost every design problem they encountered could be solved with five "whys" or less. It turns out that this system works beautifully with emotions, too. Once you've identified your current emotional state, ask "Why?" until you've figured out what's making you feel that way. This isn't psychodrama; it's a direct route to a pragmatic action plan for improving your life.

For example, one morning Fred is sitting at his desk, getting very little accomplished. Pushing himself harder just leads to unfocused, fruitless wheel spinning. Time to haul out his emotional compass. When Fred asks himself, "What am I feeling?" the answer is "Nervous, jumpy, and irritable." It's time for the Five Whys.

"Why am I nervous, jumpy, and irritable?" Fred asks himself.

"Because I'm wired on caffeine," he answers.

"Why?"

"Because it took six cups of coffee to get me out of bed this morning."

"Why?"

"Because I didn't sleep all night."

"Why?"

"Because the Becks' fat little beagle started howling at midnight and didn't stop until dawn."

Aha! Now Fred has some information he can really use. He's identified the situation that's diminishing his quality of life. Before reading his emotional compass, Fred felt annoyed at virtually everything: his boss, his secretary, his clients, his dried-up ballpoint pen. He's been criticizing people, barking orders, and swearing at inanimate objects all morning. But now that he's tuning in to his essential self's navigational system, Fred is able to zero in on his real emotion (anger) and its real source (exhaustion and frustration at being kept awake all night).

My clients are often surprised to discover how simple their emotions actually are, once their emotional wounds have healed. (Leftover emotion from bygone trauma can really mess up an emotional compass-reading.) Emotions we'd rather not confront often create the illusion of tremendous complexity. In fact, one way you can always tell when people have lost touch with their emotions, or are unwilling to admit to them, is that when you ask them about their motivations, they'll say, "It's complicated."

The Question	The Answer	The Truth
1. Why didn't you call me last night?	Um . . . it's complicated.	I didn't want to.
2. You seem so distant; what's wrong?	Well, it's complicated.	I don't like you.
3. Don't you want to date me anymore?	It's just so complicated.	No.

Usually, people who use the "complicated" line actually believe it themselves. They think of emotion as a tangled web of contradictory forces. This is because their emotional compasses are pointing in directions that offend their Everybodies or their social selves. The only way out of a "complicated" emotional situation is to figure out which feelings are coming directly from your core and which are being imposed on you by social fears and obligations. The result may unnerve you by presenting you with a choice to either follow your own instincts or obey frustrating social imperatives, but it won't be all that complicated.

So, although Fred initially thought his frustration came from complex sources (his high work standards, his desire to be outside in the open air, his uncertainty about his long-term employment future, a vague disgust for his boss), his emotional compass leads him to a much simpler, more manageable problem: His sleep has been interrupted, and it pisses him off. All those other issues are important, and when it's time to deal with them his emotional compass will tell him so. But right now, attacking problems that aren't really causing today's anger won't help him feel one bit better. In fact, Fred is liable to make a serious mess if he starts changing his work situation without addressing his fatigue.

If Fred can figure out how to use the Five Whys effectively, you can too. Try it in the spaces below.

EXERCISE

1. What was the strongest emotion that emerged as you did the exercises above? _____

   _____

2. Why do you feel this way? _____

   _____

3. Why? _____

   _____

4. Why? _____

   _____

5. Why? _____

   _____

6. Why? _____

   _____

Magic Question No. 3:
What Will It Take to Make Me Happy?

If your primary emotion is happiness, this question is easy to answer: You already have what it takes, and your only problem is keeping things as they are, or changing in positive ways. If you've strayed far off your true path, however, this Magic Question may be very hard to answer. It requires creative problem solving, and many unhappy people don't want to work that hard, even to improve their own lives. They want someone else—their bosses, their spouses, their parents, the government—to figure out what would make them happy, prepare it for them, and serve it to them nicely browned, with an apple in its mouth. I've known people who spend their whole lives in a state of furious self-pity because this never happens for them. Don't make the same mistake. You're the only person who can figure out exactly what would make you happy. It's your job to define and articulate your needs. Even if others were willing to do it, the fact is that *they can't*.

It's crucial to frame your answers to Magic Question No. 3 in terms of *your* own basic needs, *not* external circumstances. In Fred's case, the basic need is very simple: to be happy, he needs to know that he'll have peace and quiet when he's trying to sleep. Notice that *the problem isn't how to get the Becks' dog to shut up; the problem is Fred's need for a quiet environment*. If the beagle went into a soundproof chamber in the Becks' basement, it could howl its little lungs out without bothering Fred one bit. On the other hand, if the dog stopped barking, but Charlton Heston insisted on conducting target practice outside Fred's bedroom window every night, his basic need for undisturbed sleep would remain unsatisfied.

One of the most common obstacles to realizing your dreams is a tendency to answer Magic Question No. 3 in terms of other people's actions. "I'd be happy if Bill loved me and Alice stopped shooting heroin" may be an accurate statement, but it's not very useful; there's no way to force true love from Bill, and ultimately, you can't control Alice's addiction. If your needs are being frustrated by another person's behavior, it's especially important to ask "Why?" enough times to reach the root of your feelings, where they can be expressed in terms of your needs, not other people's behavior. If you feel really stuck, wanting another person to behave differently even though you know it's not going to happen, try imagining how you would feel if you got what you wanted. Then, direct your efforts toward getting that positive feeling *in a variety of ways,* instead of focusing all your energy on changing someone else.

Let's look at a couple of real-life examples. My client Joanna's answer to Question No. 3 was, "I'd be happy if my family would stop stereotyping me as a flaky cheerleader and support me in becoming a doctor." This didn't seem likely, certainly not in the near future. So Joanna and I came up with a more basic and useful description of her desires: "I'd be happy if I were surrounded by loving people who believed in my dreams and encouraged me to become a doctor." This led Joanna to consider distancing herself from her family emotionally and creating a new Everybody by hanging out with friends and mentors who championed her ambitions. It wasn't an easy solution, but it proved to be very liberating.

Scott came to see me a month after his wife, Heather, was diagnosed with cancer. Her illness had made him re-evaluate his entire life; he'd decided he needed to change jobs and had quietly made contact with some corporate headhunters. Scott asked me to help him figure out which of several job offers he should take. The problem was that none of the opportunities really interested him; the more he weighed the options, the more he felt confused and stuck. Not surprisingly, when we read his emotional compass, it turned out that Scott's feelings revolved around his wife, not his work. What was he feeling? Sad, angry, and scared. Why? Because the love of his life was dangerously ill. What would it take to make Scott happy? The answer was "I'd be happy if Heather didn't have cancer." Because that wasn't going to happen immediately, I pushed Scott to go further. What would he feel if his wish were granted, if his wife suddenly recovered?

"I'd feel free," he told me. "I wouldn't be so obsessed with my fear of losing her. I wouldn't have to force myself to take a job so soon. I'd spend more time with my kids." In other words, what Scott really wanted was to fully experience and revel in his love for his family. We couldn't magically restore Heather's health, but clearly, the way to

Scott's North Star did not lie in any of the job offers he was considering. We spent our time together figuring out how he could temporarily reconfigure his present job. When he was ready, Scott went to his employers, explained his situation, and presented a clearly thought-out plan that would allow him to actually improve his performance while working out of a home office. Because he took responsibility for detailing this plan, instead of waiting for some authority figure to offer a solution, Scott's idea was very well received. In fact, his boss was so impressed by Scott's initiative that he became something of a mentor. This helped Scott enormously during the difficult months before chemotherapy blessedly eradicated Heather's cancer.

The concept of framing your desires without trying to control other people's behavior is difficult for many people to "get." Here are some more examples that may help you begin to think in this radical and liberating way. The phrases on the left will leave you feeling victimized, helpless, ruled by implacable circumstances or other people's whims, desperate to control the uncontrollable so that you can be happy. The phrases on the right put you in a position to go ahead and solve whatever problems you may be facing, with or without any given person's cooperation.

Useless Yearning	Useful Yearning
"I want Brad to love me."	"I want to be in a loving, romantic relationship with someone who does not, technically speaking, have fur."
"I want my mommy."	"I want to feel comforted and nurtured."
"I want my cretin boss to reward my ideas for once."	"I want to work for a boss who is at least marginally more intelligent than a potato."
"I want my company to give me a raise *right now.*"	"I want to have more income, soon."

"I want Cassandra to stop making me feel guilty."	"I want to stop feeling guilty."
"I want Percy to admit he was wrong."	"I want to believe that I did the right thing when I ignored Percy's advice."
"I want Everybody's approval."	"I want to know I'm a good person."

EXERCISE

1. Think about a situation that makes you feel angry, sad, or scared. What is it about this situation that you wish were different? _____

   _____

   _____

2. Think about a situation that makes you happy. What elements of this situation do you want to keep? _____

   _____

   _____

3. What do you want most right now? _____

   _____

   _____

4. What do you *really* want most right now? _____

   _____

   _____

Magic Question No. 4: *"What's the Most Effective Way to Get What I Want?"*

So far, almost every action step in this book has focused on silencing your social self long enough to hear the directives of your essential self. However, once you've gone inward to pinpoint exactly what you want, your social self should be invited back to help you complete your journey. Magic Question No. 4 is the point at which this happens.

Figuring out the most effective way of getting what you want often takes the form of a dialogue between your essential and social selves. It's like a conversation between a wacky youngster and his dignified butler (P. G. Wodehouse fans, think Bertie Wooster and Jeeves). The essential self will come up with wild, out-of-the-box, often unworkable ideas. The social self, without mocking or censoring these ideas, gets to modify them with its sophisticated practical knowledge of various physical and social rules for living. As I've already mentioned, the social self is a terrible master—but as a loyal and intelligent servant, its contribution is priceless.

For example, now that Fred has realized he's being deprived of rest by the neighborhood beagle, any number of solutions may pop into his mind. His essential self, being a direct and passionate sort, might suggest that he run home right now, hop the Becks' fence, and wring their beagle's neck. His social self, however, is wise enough to point out that while killing the dog would solve the howling problem, it also presents needless moral—not to mention legal—complications. Fred's social self might approve of some other plan, like putting sedatives in the dog's chow, buying Fred some earplugs, or moving to Canada. Or, of course, Fred could always muster up the courage to have a serious conversation with the dog's owners. The social self's solutions often lack pizzazz, but they tend to work.

A lot of my clients get confused when I suggest that they work within the boundaries set by their social selves. Haven't I been telling them to stop listening to social convention and trust their essential selves? Yes, but *this is the way to figure out what your goals are, not to calculate the best way to achieve them.*

Working within social systems is like playing a game. Some of the rules are arbitrary, even completely illogical, but that doesn't mean they're evil, or that following them will destroy your essential self. For example, if you really wanted to get a basketball from one end of a court to the other, dribbling isn't nearly as efficient as simply carrying the thing. But when you play basketball, you keep the rules without feeling that you've compromised your core identity. You don't become enraged at the meaninglessness of dribbling, even if you're Dennis Rodman. *It's just a game.*

That's the mind-set that allows you to "play" social systems without losing your mind or your integrity. Of course, you should refuse to play social games that are immoral, or toxic to your essential self. There will also be times when, to be true to your essential self, you *must* break the rules of some social system. However, there's nothing wrong with abiding by the rules of a game you enjoy, and the social self, with its cultural savvy, can tell your essential self how to do that. Charting a course set by your emotional compasses doesn't mean acting purely on emotional impulses. It means *acting effectively within your social context, to satisfy your real needs.* You can stretch the rules as far as you want (for example, I know a lot of refugees from China who broke the rules of communism because they didn't believe in them), but if you're going to push the envelope, be very, very careful.

Clarissa was one of the brainiest clients I've ever had. During the time we worked together, she joined a large consulting firm and went off to attend a two-week intensive-training seminar. Clarissa read and memorized all her text materials during the first three days. After acing a practice exam, she asked to be allowed to test out of the training. She was furious when her employers said no. She spent the next several days exuding boredom and anger.

Clarissa was a terrific problem solver, but she was working the wrong problem. She'd been told—and she believed—that she was in training to learn the text material. But that wasn't the real game. The real game was learning to fulfill the social and cultural expectations of her new corporation. As soon as she reframed the problem this way and decided to play the game, Clarissa changed her strategy. Instead of alienating her managers and coworkers by fussing about their failure to acknowledge her genius, she turned her extra brainpower to helping other new recruits master the material. Clarissa quickly became one of the most liked, respected, and highly paid young consultants in the firm.

EXERCISE

1. Think of a very inexpensive item you'd like to own, such as a Popsicle or a shiny new pencil with your name stamped on it in gold-colored letters. *Make*

sure it's something you don't own at the moment. Note what the object is in this space:

_____

_____

2. Now think of six ways you can get the item you just named *without leaving your house.* You can use any communications devices or other technologies at your disposal, and you definitely don't have to go it alone. (Magic question No. 4 is all about working with others to reach your objectives.) Even if the methods you come up with aren't things you're really comfortable doing (like borrowing or calling third parties to ask for help), list them. You may build up some courage, and even if you don't, you'll find that refusing to censor your inventiveness will lead to more solutions.

   a. _____

   b. _____

   c. _____

   d. _____

   e. _____

   f. _____

3. Read over the solutions you've listed, and see if any of them are a) possible, b) legal, and c) morally acceptable to you. If an action plan fulfills *all* these criteria, go ahead and use it.

4. Double-check to make sure your social self isn't ruling out workable solutions. Here are some signs that your social self is acting as your master, rather than your servant:

   a. When you think about putting the solution into action, you find yourself laughing in embarrassment.

   b. You react to the proposed solution with thoughts like "I could *never* do that!" or "I can't just . . ." or "But I have to . . ." These statements tend to reflect social inhibitions, not actual limitations.

   c. You immediately think of some person who'd be upset if you took this course of action, or you stop yourself with the question "What would people think?"

5. If you've had any of the reactions above, consider whether you might want to break the rules of the social game. Be sure you stay within the confines of your own moral system; violating your own integrity will lead you directly away from your own North Star.

9

CHARTING
YOUR COURSE

If you've done your basic emotional compass reading thoroughly, you'll have all the information necessary to move toward your North Star. Using that information, however, can be a little tricky. No, make that a *lot* tricky. Emotional energy always creates change. If that energy is handled well, the change will move you closer to the life you want. However, most of us don't get much instruction about using our emotional power effectively. In the grip of passion, we're about as effective as five-year-olds trying to operate a nuclear submarine. We may end up using that awesome force to turn several tight circles, launch a few H-bombs at densely populated areas, and drive ourselves straight downward to perish in the sludge at the bottom of the sea.

The intensity of emotion, its capacity to destroy when unwisely managed, is the reason why Western philosophy, from the Greeks on down, has encouraged us to act only on our thoughts, not on our feelings. I can respect the rationale, but I think ditching your passions to avoid misusing them makes about as much sense as cutting off your legs because you have a tendency to trip when you run. Emotion is a glorious force that will push you toward your North Star with breathtaking speed and efficiency. When your social self uses its tremendous powers of restraint and guidance to shape behaviors based on your real desires, instead of in opposition to them, you will be astonished by your own power. These behaviors are the vehicle that allows you to move in the direction indicated by your internal compasses. Once you've accessed your navigational equipment by turning your attention inward, you must learn to "drive" by taking wise and positive action in the real world, rather than pouting, weeping, or raging in ways that are likely to get you locked up.

The following chart is a quick-reference emotional-instruction manual. Once you've figured out what you're feeling, you can refer to this chart to see what the uses and misuses of your current emotion might be. This approach to acting on your emotions is much more directive than the advice you'll get from a therapist. It's forward-looking and completely pragmatic. If you find yourself unable to follow the suggestions coming from your emotional compass—for example, you simply cannot calmly express anger to your boss, because you're too scared—go back to the last chapter and work on your emotional wounds. Even better, hire a shrink. As far as this chapter is concerned, we follow the Gospel According to Nike: Just do it.

IF YOUR EMOTIONAL COMPASS READS "FEAR"

If you check your emotional compass and find that you're scared spit-less, congratulate yourself. You're not one of those people who blithely self-destruct by smoking Drāno or trying to ski down Everest. On the other hand, you're probably not a happy camper, at least not at the moment. Fear is an incredibly unpleasant sensation, and your essential self wouldn't produce it without a very good reason. Fear tells you that something in your immediate vicinity is threatening your progress toward happiness. To move forward, you must make some move that will cause your fear to dissipate as soon as possible.

SUMMARY OF EMOTIONAL COURSE CHARTING (WHAT TO DO WITH EACH OF THE FOUR BASIC EMOTIONS)

Once you've determined which of the four basic emotions you're feeling, this chart will give you a basic idea what you can do about it. If you avoid the pitfalls and move forward as your emotional compass directs, your life will automatically become more comfortable and fulfilling for your true self.

COMPASS READING:	FEAR	GRIEF	ANGER	JOY
Function:	Protects from danger	Heals, strengthens	Corrects injustice	Nurtures, expands
Dangerous Fakes:	"False Fear" may show up when the real emotion is something upsetting to the social self—especially anger	"False grief," including depression, is usually a screen for anger. It is most common in women.	"False anger" often appears to hide the real emotion of grief, particularly in men.	"False joy" is euphoria that doesn't last, such as chemical or behavioral addiction or mania.
Recheck Your Compass If:	Your fear shows up as generalized anxiety or worry and doesn't lead to clear action.	You feel utterly helpless or hopeless or lose the ability to experience pleasure.	You find yourself lashing out at people (including strangers) who don't deserve it.	You experience giddiness or a high that is followed by an emotional "crash," leaving you worse off than ever.
Think It Through:	Identify the thing that's scaring you. Investigate to see if your fears are well-grounded.	Identify what it is you have lost. Acknowledge your right to grieve that loss.	Identify what you need that you aren't getting, or what is present that you can't tolerate.	Identify the real source of your happiness. Express gratitude.
Healthy Reactions to the Real Thing:	1. Run from danger 2. Face your fear *See text for instructions*	1. Replace what is lost 2. Mourn what is lost *See text for instructions*	1. Change yourself 2. Change your situation *See text for instructions*	1. Enjoy 2. Share *See text for instructions*

COMPASS READING:	FEAR	GRIEF	ANGER	JOY
You Will Be Tempted to:	Run from your heart's desire	Deny your pain	Resist change	Either cling to joy or push it away
To Go On, You Must Give Up:	The illusion of dependency	The illusion of permanence	The illusion of helplessness	Suffering
If You Go On, You Will Gain:	Courage and confidence	Empathy, wisdom, and resilience	Gentleness and power	Everything your heart desires; your own North Star

PRELIMINARIES: CHECKING FEAR FOR AUTHENTICITY

The first thing to do if you're feeling fear (or any other emotion) is to make absolutely sure this sensation isn't fronting for something else. Fear is a particularly common stand-in for other emotions. This is because small children often learn, from large, threatening adults, that certain feelings are officially Forbidden (these feelings may range from desire to boredom, although anger is often considered particularly naughty, since it leads children to defy adult authority figures). When they grow up, these children experience a jab of fear every time a Forbidden feeling tries to emerge. Their attention is distracted from their authentic emotions by the terror of getting into big, hairy trouble.

This is the dynamic that often keeps people in abusive relationships: The natural response to being abused is anger, but they've learned that acting on anger will get them punished, so all they feel is fear—false fear. Real fear is easy to distinguish from the phony variety, because it has a clear source and motivates clear action. Fake fear is a blanket anxiety or worry that doesn't mobilize; on the contrary, it paralyzes.

Gavin De Becker, a security expert (whose book *The Gift of Fear* should be required reading for every human), points out that worry and anxiety, far from keeping us safe, actually keep us from acting on the clear instructions coming from authentic fear. We'd all be a lot safer, he writes, if we paid more attention to our deep, instinctive fears and ignored anxiety that comes from socialization.

For example, say you're alone in a dark office building late at night, waiting for the elevator. The door slides open: There's a man in the elevator. For some reason, you feel an instinctive jolt of fear—you're scared of this guy. Do you act on this fear? No, you're *worried* about seeming socially odd or impolite. So you voluntarily walk into a sound-proof steel box and push a button that locks you in with the spooky stranger. Would a wild animal ever respond to its fear this way? When was the last time you saw a wild animal in an office elevator? This is De Becker's example, but I used it because I know a guy who was robbed at gunpoint in almost exactly this situation—the only difference being that there were two scary men in his elevator.

EXERCISE

Think of something that scares you. Then answer the following questions:

1. Exactly what are you afraid of? _____

_____

2. Does your fear tell you to do anything specific? If so, what? _____

_____

_____

If you aren't able to answer these questions, your primary fear is of the unknown. Check to see if you're covering up another emotion. If not, proceed to the next step.

RESPECTING REAL FEAR

The point of the elevator story is that once you've determined that your fear is real, you must act on it—even if that means social awkwardness. Take it from my client Oliver. He brought his boyhood friend Clem in to manage the finances for his small firm. Something told him that Clem couldn't be trusted, but Oliver wasn't going to breach the etiquette of buddyhood by confronting Clem. When he hinted around about his worries, Clem acted horribly shocked and insulted, and Oliver backed right off.

The IRS wasn't so squeamish. They audited Oliver's firm and found that Clem had been frolicking unabashedly with corporate finances for some time, embezzling a fair amount and miring the firm in deep debt. Because he didn't act on his fear that Clem might be dishonest, Oliver ended up declaring bankruptcy.

EXERCISE

Is there anything you "don't want to know"? Are you avoiding information (medical testing, a good hard look at your finances, the truth about your romantic relationship) because you're afraid it might reveal something terrifying? Take a deep breath and name your pain by listing the information you're scared to know:

_____

_____

_____

_____

_____

DO YOUR HOMEWORK

As the compass-reading chart will tell you, fear presents you with a couple of options. You can either run away or face the thing you fear. Since fear is the "flight" component of the fight-or-flight mechanism, the first inclination of a scared person is almost always to run away. Before you do that, though, you need to *gather information*. Fleeing in a panic won't cause your fear to dissipate as fast as doing some research will. Let your fear motivate you to pay very close attention to the scary situation.

In Oliver's case, this would have meant bulldogging Clem to find out exactly how their company's money was being used. Would that have disturbed Oliver's friendship with Clem? Without a doubt. But Oliver didn't save the relationship by squelching his uneasiness. The friendship was compromised the moment Clem started stealing Oliver's money.

The urge to find the real facts is destructive only to people or systems (friendships, family dynamics, political dynasties) that are based on lies. The truth can scare you half to death, but it's never as destructive as deception.

Finding information is crucial even when the truth seems to be right before your nose. Tina was raised in an upper-crust New York home, by an upper-crust Wall Street financier who customarily beat the crap out of her upper-crust socialite mother. Not surprisingly, Tina ended up with a guy just like the guy who married dear old Mom. Her first boyfriend, Stan, had the social skills of a scorpion. Like her mother, Tina lived in constant, paralyzing fear—of the world in general, but mostly of Stan. One day, she happened to see a daytime talk show describing the dynamics of abusive relationships. She felt like Saul on the road to Damascus, hit over the head by a blinding blast of comprehension.

"I saw myself," Tina told me years later, after she had long since left Stan and become a top salesperson for a financial-services firm. "I saw how our whole relationship worked. I saw that I had to get out, and I saw that the way to do that was to learn more about what was going on in my life." Moral: If something is scaring you, *learn everything about it that you possibly can.*

EXERCISE

Think about the topic you listed in the last exercise. Today, take one step toward getting more information about this topic. Schedule the mammogram, call your bank, get ready to confront your spouse about the unfamiliar undergarments that have been cropping up in the laundry hamper. Tomorrow, take another step toward full disclosure. Knowing may be scary, but not knowing can be deadly.

DECIDING WHETHER TO RUN OR STAND YOUR GROUND

How do you tell when you should flee something you fear (as Tina fled from Stan) and when you should face it (as Oliver finally did when his firm was audited)? The answer lies in your essential self, which wants what it wants, even if it's scared. The rule is to *follow your desire.* If fear and desire give the same instructions, run away. If fear and desire give opposite instructions, feel your fear and stand your ground.

In other words, you should run from anything that scares you *and* holds absolutely no appeal for your essential self. If the thought of attending medical school makes you queasy with dread and you've never for one second wanted to be a doctor, *stay away from medical school*. I don't care if your parents donated their life savings, their spare kidneys, and your little brother to Johns Hopkins in the hope that you will become an M.D.; your fear and your desire are both telling you that it will never happen. Spare yourself the long scenic road to failure. Run. Now.

On the other hand, there will be many instances when fear and desire point in opposite directions. You want something, but you're scared to go for it. In fact, if you really set out to pursue your heart's desires, you're pretty much guaranteed to feel a lot of fear: fear of failure, fear of commitment, fear of competition, even fear of success. This kind of fear—the fear that accompanies desire—is something you must face, not flee, to reach your own North Star. Put your desires above your fears. Stop running and face it, whatever it is.

FACING FEAR

So you want to be a champion of the World Wrestling Federation, or a professional violinist, or the governor of Vermont. The idea really sets you on fire with hope and excitement, but on the other hand, when you think about actually climbing into the ring, playing your violin for an audience, or making a political speech (not all at once, of course), your blood freezes in your veins. Maybe, you think, you'll just wait until you stop feeling so scared—*then* you'll pursue your dream. Well, champ, you'll be waiting a long, long time. Getting over your fear without doing anything scary is like learning to swim before you go near the water—it'd be nice if such a thing were possible, but it ain't.

One thing your fear may be telling you is that you genuinely aren't prepared to undertake the thing you want. That's why thorough research is such a crucial step. As you find out everything you can about the thing you fear, you'll learn what real threats you'll have to overcome to achieve your dreams. How physically fit do you have to be, and how much choreography do you have to know, to avoid getting your neck broken in the wrestling ring? How well do you have to play to get to Carnegie Hall? Is running for governor of Vermont on the snow-prevention platform just an exercise in futility?

The research phase of facing your fear is like making sure your parachute is properly folded and attached to its harness. But no matter how well you prepare, the second and final fear-facing step is still terrifying. It goes like this: You open the door of the airplane, close your eyes, hold your breath, and jump. You climb into the ring with the Rock, pick up the fiddle and play, put your name on the ballot. You tell that special someone how you really feel. You send your poem to a literary magazine. You . . . well, what do *you* do?

EXERCISE

1. Complete this sentence:

If I only had the guts, I would _____

_____

_____

2. Whatever you just wrote down, do it. Right now. You heard me, soldier—put down the damn book and *do it!*

MAKING FEAR YOUR ALLY

Of course, it's easy for me to tell you to face your fears, as I sit here with my laptop and my latte, far from the dangers that besiege you. Rest assured, I know how you feel. In fact, the reason I have no mercy when it comes to pushing my clients out of their various "airplanes" is that I myself am a thoroughgoing coward. As a child, I was scared of pretty much everything, and by the time I hit puberty, things had gotten so bad that I realized I had a choice: I could either start doing things that terrified me, or I could become one of those women who share their long, apartment-bound lives with twenty or thirty cats. The thing is, I'm allergic to cats. There was only one option left. I made myself a promise: I would do one thing that scared me every day, provided it was something I really wanted to do.

This promise utterly transformed my life, and continues to do so. But it was—is—most emphatically not easy. For example, shortly after I made my vow, I developed a severe crush on the captain of my high school debate team. I wanted to be around him, and one obvious way to do this was to volunteer for the individual competitive speaking events. However, I shared the most common of human phobias: an absolutely devastating fear of public speaking. Close eyes, hold breath, jump.

The debate coach enrolled me in an event called "impromptu," where each speaker is given a topic and allowed one minute to prepare a three- to five-minute speech. I didn't even know how this worked until the very moment that I stood facing my first judge. I was so scared that halfway through an utterly pathetic attempt to make the first speech of my life, I fainted dead away. I opened my eyes a few seconds later to find myself lying on my back, the concerned judge peering down at me and asking if I wanted to stop.

"No," I said, remembering my vow, "I'll finish." And I did.

Naturally, I came in last. But something strange had happened, as I lay there on the floor in my puddle of disgrace. By facing my worst nightmare, and having it come flamingly true, I lost my fear of public speaking. I'd been through the worst that could happen to a speaker, and I'd lived. A few months later, I won the state championship in "impromptu," and I have never been paralyzed by the speaking phobia since.

GROWING UP

If you begin to face your fears, something bittersweet is going to happen to you: You'll grow up. You'll lose your dependency on the grown-ups of the world, because you'll realize that there is no time, no age, at which fear suddenly fades and you become one of these impervious beings. You'll begin to recognize fear when you see it, not only in the shivering of a frightened little kid but in the apparent coldness of a shy person, the viciousness of a bully, the self-importance of your narcissistic boss. You'll realize that the difference between success and failure isn't the absence of fear but the determination to pursue your heart's desires no matter how scared you are. Finally you'll realize that fear is the raw material from which courage is manufactured. Without it, we wouldn't even know what it means to be brave.

Eventually, if you follow your "fear" compass dead ahead, you'll come to see it as a good and faithful friend. It will tell you when you're in danger, sometimes before your conscious mind registers any problem. It will motivate you to do your homework, to prepare yourself for the uncharted territory that lies between you and your North Star. And as you go forward, it will gradually transform itself into confidence and compassion. In the process, it may very well turn you into the kind of unassuming hero who has the courage to make the world a better place.

IF YOUR EMOTIONAL COMPASS READS "GRIEF"

It may seem strange that the function of grief is to heal, because sorrow can make you feel as though you're being torn apart, cell from little tiny cell. Nevertheless, there's a good reason psychologists call sadness "the healing feeling." People who follow grief through its whole course emerge stronger and healthier, more able to cope with the inevitable losses that affect every human life. In the end, they become sources of wisdom and compassion for themselves and everyone around them.

Unlike fear or anger, grief doesn't motivate intense activity. It won't make your glands pump out adrenaline, turn your face bright red, or hypercharge your muscles. On the contrary, grief will tell you that the friskiest thing you should do is lie down, and perhaps dab at your eyes with a moist Kleenex. I once had a client shlump into my office and drop onto the couch like a sack of sand. When I asked her what was going on, she answered in a thick voice, "I'm deeeepresssssed." Because she said it so slowly, I didn't hear "I'm depressed" but "I'm in *deep rest.*" Actually, the two things aren't so different. Sorrow is heavy, hard work. It stalls all your systems in order to force you toward a very, very painful task: coping with loss.

Loss always lies at the root of grief. Every time you lose something you hold dear, you must grieve, and every time you feel grief-stricken, you can be sure you've lost something dear. Considering how ubiquitous and inevitable it is, I don't know why we humans hate loss so much. It seems as though we would have evolved into creatures that just *love* loss, can't get enough of it, crave it, seek it out. Instead, by

some design flaw, we are stunned and devastated by things like separa-
tion, aging, and death, as though these aren't the very constants sure to
affect every single blessed one of us.

Whatever the reason, loss is hard for us, and healing from it takes a
lot of energy. A big loss may require so much energy that our essential
selves shut down every possible function, the way the *Apollo 13* astro-
nauts had to shut down everything on their space capsule to save
enough power to make it home. Grief pushes us into "deep rest,"
weighing down our muscles, wringing tears from our eyes and sobs
from our guts. It isn't pretty, but it's nature's way.

CHECKING FOR AUTHENTICITY

When your emotional compass reads "grief," you should double-check
it, just as you should when it reads "fear." Sadness and depression are
often the disguises we use to dress up our anger or fear so that they'll be
more socially acceptable. In fact, true clinical depression isn't really
grief—it's the numb hopelessness that comes from feeling we can't act
on anger or fear. To be in genuine "deep rest" is good; to be in clinical
depression is most definitely bad.

You can tell whether your grief is real and helpful or false and
destructive by checking for feelings of helplessness and hopelessness.
These two feelings move in when the circumstances warrant anger or
fear—in other words, fight or flight—*but we believe that we must not allow
ourselves either of these responses.* Children who grow up in social systems
that are manifestly scary or unjust often end up depressed, because neither running away nor fighting the system holds out any hope of positive change. Women are more likely to suffer clinical depression than
men, perhaps because social customs make us less autonomous, less
likely to believe in the efficacy of our own fight-or-flight impulses.
Depression is actually a thick, numbing cloud of fear and anger turned
inward toward the sufferer. Its hallmarks include not only sadness but
sleep disturbance, changes in eating habits, lethargy, confusion, and
even thoughts of suicide. *If you feel this way, get therapy now.* Depression
is treatable, and you deserve to be helped out of it.

By contrast, authentic grief has a strange and terrible sweetness. It's like the difference between the poisonous ache in your muscles that comes from a flu virus and the ache you feel after a good, hard workout. Even as real grief breaks your heart, something in you knows that you're being broken *open,* and there is something profoundly hopeful at the core of that sensation.

IDENTIFYING AND HONORING YOUR LOSS

Charting your life course by reading your emotional compass always starts with identifying the source of your feelings. In the case of grief, this means figuring out what you've lost and letting yourself feel bad about it. A lot of my clients, especially men, feel that it's weak or inappropriate to grieve anything but a full-blown catastrophe. They might allow themselves to clench one strong jaw muscle if, say, aliens destroyed Europe or the Rams lost the Super Bowl. They seem to think that grieving more obviously, or for anything less manly, would make their testicles shrink right back into their abdominal cavities. Get to the core of most violent, aggressive men, and you will find a small boy drowning in grief he will not allow himself to express.

Of course, women, too, can feel that it's against the rules to express their authentic grief. I remember being tremendously confused after my son Adam was diagnosed with Down's syndrome. I was full of grief, but I wasn't sure that was okay. After all, I'd chosen to have the baby, rather than getting an abortion. I felt this robbed me of the right to feel bad about Adam's disability. My social self was very clear on this issue. "You've made your bed; now lie in it," said my internal Everybody. "Put up or shut up." The situation also confused the people around me. They felt bad, but there was no funeral to attend, no tried-and-true ritual to acknowledge loss, no ready-made Hallmark card that said, "Congratulations on the birth of your baby! Sorry he's retarded!"

Before I could grieve freely, I had to pick through my feelings, articulating what I'd lost: the dream of the baby I thought I was going to have, the future I'd imagined for him, my own "normal" status as a mother whose children were all made to spec. Every time I was able to clearly identify another loss, especially if I articulated it to the caring people around me, the grief broke over me like a stormy surf—wave after wave of it. Over several months, as grief always does, it washed away the pain and left me to enjoy my beautiful son.

People who don't honor their losses don't grieve. They may lose all joy in living, but they don't actively mourn, and this means that they don't heal. Members of the stiff-upper-lip club tend to get emotionally stuck at the point where their loss occurred. They can't move toward their North Stars, because the path lies directly through grief, and they won't go there.

Remember Ron, the client who made no career progress until he started grieving his girlfriend Gina's death? Besides the general taboo on male grieving, Ron felt he had no right to mourn his lost love because their relationship hadn't progressed very far. If he'd been Gina's husband, Ron would have gotten automatic support from others, and given himself more permission to feel his immense sadness. Because he stopped his own grieving process, his entire life lost direction: His job, recreation, and friendships started feeling empty and meaningless. This is what happens to anyone who has sustained a terrible loss but can't or won't move into the pain of grieving.

EXERCISE

Is there any sadness you carry that has not been honored, either by you or by the people around you? What is it?

_____

_____

Now give yourself permission to grieve this loss, no matter how "inappropriate" or silly it might seem. Processing genuine grief is never inappropriate. It's the only way to your North Star.

CONSIDERING YOUR OPTIONS

As you can see from the handy chart, you have a couple of options when your emotional compass reads "grief." You can either replace what's lost or mourn it. My feeling is that you should *replace everything you can*. I've had clients go into full-scale mourning over things they could easily replace—wrecked cars, fritzed-out computers, even, in one case, a favorite pair of running shoes. If you've lost something like this, turn the energy of grief, that deep longing, toward figuring out how to get what you need. Call the insurance company, ask salespeople about finance plans, research new technologies. You may still be upset by the time and money this takes, but you won't end up lying in bed sobbing for days on end.

Of course, most people know that new objects are easy to find, but you'd be amazed what can be replaced if you put your mind to it. One of my students once showed me a legal contract her attorney father had written up for one of her friends. The document officially reinstated this woman's virginity, which she'd decided to reclaim following a brief and unpleasant marriage. Although this contract might not restore what was lost in a technical sense, the woman who commissioned it seems to have felt much better once she was a legal virgin. Whatever works for you, I say, go for it.

Lost your childhood? So did Belinda, whose horrible upbringing was followed by a horrible marriage, which was followed by an exceedingly horrible divorce. "After my husband left me," Belinda told me, "I stopped feeling sorry for myself and decided that I was just going to go out and get all the things I should have had as a little girl." As she learned to be a responsible single adult, Belinda also had a happy childhood. She spent part of every day riding roller coasters, eating popcorn, reading Harry Potter books, and hanging out with a rapidly growing group of happy-go-lucky friends. She dyed her hair purple ("plum," she corrected everyone) and painted her fingernails blue. She bought the most beautiful doll her fifty-going-on-ten heart desired.

This phase lasted about five years, during which Belinda's essential self blossomed professionally, as well as personally. She went to work for a newspaper with the same childlike zest she took to amusement parks. This eventually landed her a spot as the local movie critic, a career beyond her most optimistic fantasies. "I feel like I spent the first fifty years of my life suspended in a fetal state, waiting for my childhood to begin," she told me. "I guess I regret the years I spent waiting, but I'm having too much fun to brood about it."

Whatever loss you're grieving, examine it very carefully for replaceable parts. Even if you can't recapture exactly what you've lost, you may be able to jury-rig an arrangement that fills all your desires, precluding the need to spend painful hours, days, and weeks in rending grief.

EXERCISE

Cast your mind back to something you have lost, something that left you feeling cheated. Exactly what about this thing do you still miss? Is there any way—*any* way—you could get something to fill this need? Be creative.

WHEN REPLACEMENT IS IMPOSSIBLE

Our deepest grief, of course, is reserved for things that have no acceptable substitutes: loved ones, relationships, health, hopes, dreams. Trying to replace someone special to you, or something you once were, is as useless as trying to replace the sun with a Lava lamp. If you've suffered this kind of a loss, the road to your North Star lies through grieving. There's nothing to do but mourn, and the pain will disappear a lot faster if you lean into it.

Greg came to me for career help, not knowing that his mother was about to die of heart disease. He'd just quit his job, gotten a new one, and set out to prove himself to his new employers when his mother passed away. Naturally, Greg's newly met colleagues sympathized with his loss. They didn't expect him to be really focused and upbeat at work for, oh, a whole week. Maybe two.

"I don't know what's wrong with me," Greg said a month after his mother's passing. "I'm tired all the time, I don't have the drive I should. I've got to pull myself together and start performing at work."

I've seen this kind of thing often, and it always breaks my heart. The human psyche doesn't heal overnight, not from a blow like the loss of a mother. Our reason-over-passion work culture doesn't make room for normal mourning. When Patricia Schroeder of Colorado was running for president, her detractors mocked her because she'd been seen crying in public. "I wouldn't want control of nuclear power to be in the hands of someone who cries," said one of Schroeder's opponents. She retorted, "I wouldn't want control of nuclear power to be in the hands of someone who *doesn't* cry." The way our culture has things set up at the moment, the most powerful and important decision-making positions go to people who are numb to grief and empathy. Psychologists have a name for these folks: They're called sociopaths. In case you don't know already, this is another word for *completely, alarmingly, dangerously crazy people.*

Excuse me. I get a little worked up about this. Let's return to Greg, whom we left in my office obsessing over his failure to perform at work in the wake of his mother's demise. Because the culture at large wasn't going to facilitate Greg's grieving process, he had to do it himself. The first step was to realize that normal grieving follows its own course. You can no more force it to hurry up than you can force a broken bone to knit *right now.* Greg had to consciously grieve his mother when he wasn't at work, in order to have any energy left for his job.

You can do this too, if need be. The process is similar to healing an emotional wound (spelled out in Chapter 7). However, if your loss is fresh, your need for time, peace, and rest will be even greater. Here are the basic survival tools you will need to mourn a serious loss.

EXERCISES
(For those facing a serious, irreplaceable loss)

1. Find or Make a Safe Place to Grieve

It's a real bummer that workplaces aren't safe places to mourn, but it's true. You really will damage your career by floundering around in your sorrow when you're dealing with a colleague, customer, or client. Many people also lack a personal support system that lets them grieve; some cultures or families don't encourage open sadness, even in the face of death.

To get into—or, more accurately, through—your grief, you have to make a safe place for mourning. At a bare minimum, you need privacy and quiet. Ideally, you'll have a warm, comfortable place where you can lie down and wrap yourself in a blanket or two (this creates the sensation of being cuddled, which is very conducive to effective grieving).

You'll also need paper and a pen; expressing your feelings by writing about them can keep them from becoming unendurable. A stereo of some kind and some good sad songs are also very useful. Any song that helps you cry will access your grief, move it through you, and help you release it.

Both listening to sad music and writing down your feelings are ways of connecting with other people. By writing, even if no one ever reads what you write, you communicate your sorrow. Music can make you feel that the singer or composer understands and shares your sadness. Both of these are obviously pale substitutes for a loving person who understands your pain. If you have such a person in your life, talking and crying with him or her can do worlds to ease the grieving process. However, don't expect too much from people who have suffered the same loss you have, or who don't know how to handle their own emotions. Again, this might be the time to rent yourself a kind heart in the form of a therapist.

2. Reserve Time to Grieve

First of all, sadness slows you down. Give yourself more time than you think you need to finish projects, from cleaning your bedroom to writing a computer program. You will not be able to speed up by pushing yourself. However, the more love and support you give yourself—and get from others—the more energy you'll have for the tasks of everyday life.

Second, there may be extra work associated with your loss. For example, if you break up with your lover and you move out, you'll have to rent and move into a new place, hassle over dividing possessions, and maybe take care of the dogs all by yourself for a while. This too requires extra time. Accept that fact, and you'll minimize the drag on your energy.

Finally, you need time to just feel sad. This may occupy as much as four or five hours a day in the period immediately following a huge loss. If grief overwhelms you at a time when you can give in to it, let yourself mourn until the really intense wave passes. If you can't think of any convenient time, you may want to consciously clear out space for grieving in your schedule. Put it in your appointment calendar ("6:00–9:00 P.M.: feel like hell"). Tell yourself, and other people, that you have an appointment. You don't have to give anyone the details, any more than you would if you had a meeting with your lawyer or accountant. One word of caution: Don't mourn all day, every day. At the end of each grieving session, picture yourself placing your sadness in a secure container, closing the lid, putting it on a shelf in a cupboard, and shutting the cupboard door. It will still be there tomorrow when your time to grieve rolls around again.

3. Maximize Comforting Activities

A lot of people try to push their grief aside by "having fun," even if that means drinking enough tequila to float the Disney cruise fleet. These same people may also try to cheer you up by forcing you to go dancing, sleigh riding, clubbing baby seals, or whatever else they do for entertainment. Listen: Doing "fun" things *instead* of grieving is very different from adding comforting activities to your grieving process. You should definitely do things that gladden your heart during a period of mourning, but you'll find that your heart has odd preferences at such a time.

When I asked Greg what his heart really wanted, he said, "I need to find a river." Watching running water soothed and comforted him, as it does many other people. Other clients have chosen such mourning-time activities as napping next to their pets, sitting in trees, or watching educational TV with the sound turned off. Whatever works best for you, add it to your day. It's the best way to get to the time when you really will feel like dancing.

LOSSES AND GAINS

One of the Four Noble Truths taught by the Buddha was that any permanence we perceive, in ourselves or the world around us, is an illusion. Clinging to that illusion, trying to force things to stay as they are, leads inevitably to suffering. I used to think that Buddhists were terrible pessimists. Then I began to experience serious loss myself, and I realized what accepting impermanence really means. It means embracing the world as it is, complete with loss. Refusing to accept change doesn't mean that the pain of losing things you love will never start; it only means that the pain will never stop. As they say in therapy, the only way out is through.

A management-consultant friend of mine, Enrico, saw a truly spooky example of people clinging to the illusion of permanence when he was hired to salvage a company that was coming unglued for lack of good, pragmatic leadership. You'd recognize the firm if I named it, so let's call it "Ugly Duckling Instant Puddn' and Pie." Ugly Duckling was founded by a powerful, charismatic leader I'll call Bertram Flatbottom, who took it all the way from a start-up venture to a corporate behemoth. Everything was going beautifully until the day that the boss, laboring away at various boss chores, suddenly clutched his chest and fell over dead. Exit Flatbottom, stage left.

Five years later, when Enrico the consultant was called in, nothing in Flatbottom's office had been touched since they'd dragged the body away. The papers he'd had been working on that day still sat on the desk. The air conditioner was set to the level he'd chosen. The computer was still on, though the monitor had long since burned out. Apparently, the united workers of Ugly Duckling preferred this strange suspended animation to the emotional and logistical messiness of accepting that Flatbottom was gone.

This is the kind of illusion that you will lose if you move forward into your grief. No moment, however sweet, can last. On the other hand, neither will pain or sorrow—not if you allow them to flow freely. Maybe the reason my client Greg needed to be near a river after his mother died is that rivers exemplify the change that fills our lives. Every molecule of water moves continuously; its relationship to other molecules, to objects in the river, to the land it passes is always changing. You can stare at a spot on the river all day and never see anything stable. That's why rivers are fresh and alive, rather than stagnant and stale. Though everything in the river passes away, the river itself remains constant, and it is constantly beautiful.

Losing the illusion of permanence means that you will accept your losses. It means that you will become well acquainted with sorrow. It also means that you will realize the infinite sources of healing and joy that are available to an open heart. People like the Ugly Duckling gang are made brittle and fragile by their losses. They live in terror of acknowledging openly what their hearts already know. People who don't resist grief, who let it flow through them, come out more resilient on the other side. They are less afraid of loss, more able to soften the pain of those around them, and quicker to appreciate whatever happiness life brings. Ironically, it is those who have accepted the most terrible grief who are capable of the greatest joy.

IF YOUR EMOTIONAL COMPASS READS "ANGER"

Anger, the most reviled and misunderstood of emotions, is the psychological equivalent of the immune system. It is triggered whenever we perceive injustice, giving us strength and energy to change the status quo. Whereas the physical immune system may create inflammation (a "flame" in the body), anger is like fire in the soul. Repressed, it destroys from the inside, by slow burn or explosion. Misdirected, it can blaze a path of destruction through your life and the lives of others. Cared for and properly used, it can warm you, light your path, fuel your progress, and keep hostile interlopers at bay.

Some folks seem to think that an inability to feel and act on anger is a virtue. It isn't. It's the psychological equivalent of AIDS. Most of us know people who destroyed their physical and mental health by staying in unjust and exploitative situations without ever speaking up or taking strong action in their own defense.

Maggie spent her hours with me venting her anger at her acid-tongued mother. This would have been great if she'd been preparing to actually change her behavior with Mom—but she wasn't. By blowing off steam with me, she was taking the edge off her own anger so that she could tolerate Mom's mental cruelty without challenging it or changing their relationship.

Overworked Aaron dealt with his anger by playing victim. Every time he told his wife and kids that he had to slave through yet another unpaid weekend, his Martyr Meter climbed another notch toward sainthood. Angry? Why, no, a saint is never angry. True, he had a long history of severe ulcers, but Aaron just felt weighed down and desperate.

When I tell people like Aaron and Maggie that they need to act on their anger, they look as though they've just noticed the number 666 tattooed on my forehead. They think that expressing anger is the height of destructive immorality. Wrong. In fact, *not* acting on anger is often far more destructive and immoral than using it—in a calm and constructive way, of course. Great pacifists know this. Rosa Parks acted on her anger by sitting quietly on an Alabama bus instead of giving her seat to a white man. Gandhi acted on his anger by going on a hunger strike until the religious factions in South Asia stopped slaughtering each other. Mothers Against Drunk Driving got good and MADD, and have peacefully prevented thousands of alcohol-related traffic deaths. Contrary to what angerphobes believe, well-used anger lies at the heart and soul of making the world a better, more humane place.

THE AUTHENTICITY ISSUE

Anger, with its bright, hot energy, can be a more appealing option to many people than the wrenching pain of grief. Men, who generally aren't given much leeway to express sadness—much less acknowledge fear—often divert these feelings into false anger. (Some women do this too, although this is highly likely to offend Everybody. As we've seen, women are often encouraged not to express their anger, even when it's honest and legitimate.) Instead of weeping over the death of a loved one, for example, a grieving relative might rage and fume and sue every medical professional who ever dealt with the dear departed, no matter how briefly. Of course, this kind of anger never disappears when revenge is finally taken, because the issue wasn't really anger. It was sorrow or fear, and the pain won't resolve until these feelings are given an honest hearing.

EXERCISE
Answer the following questions as honestly as you can:

1. True or False: I have felt anger continuously for weeks, months, or years, with no feelings of sadness or fear.

2. True or False: I've attacked the people who make me angry, but I don't feel any better afterward.

3. True or False: People I trust have told me my anger is misdirected.

4. True or False: I've taken out my anger by yelling or raging at loved ones, my children, my pets, random drivers in traffic, or others who did not cause any injustice.

5. True or False: My anger is absolutely uncontrollable; I can't help lashing out in rage.

If you answered "True" to *any* of these questions, recheck your emotional compass. Another emotion is hiding under your anger.

GETTING TO THE SOURCE: ACHIEVING SERENITY THROUGH HATE AND RAGE

When you're genuinely angry, it means one of two things: either something that your essential self needs is absent, or something your essential self can't tolerate is present. To make the anger go away, you have to change this situation. That isn't possible if you don't know what's making you angry. However, pinpointing the source of anger is often more difficult than identifying the cause of fear or grief. That's because anger is so volatile, so fraught with danger. We may be loath to turn it on a person we love, or a job we desperately need, because we equate anger with absolute destruction of the relationship. The truth, of course, is that we ruin our relationships (to things or people) when we harbor anger without acting on it. No matter how frightening or irrational your anger may seem, acknowledging that you are angry is the first step toward a peaceful and cooperative connection with the world around you.

I preach this to my clients every day, but it's still hard to practice. For example, the other day, as I was working on this book, I suddenly felt a horrendous, stabbing pain in my back, as though I'd been harpooned. I tried to shake, stretch, and rub the pain away, but I've had back problems before, and I knew it wasn't going to be a minor episode. For the next week or so, I spent most of my time lying down, panting, like a sick cow. Then someone gave me a book on back pain by one Dr. John Sarno, a physician who seems almost fanatically convinced that the majority of back pain comes from muscle spasms caused by repressed anger. Acknowledge your anger, Dr. Sarno writes, and the pain will go away.

I was skeptical, but I had nothing to lose by trying the good doctor's advice. Wincing with the effort, I found a spiral notebook in my kids' school-supply drawer. I drew a few flowers, birds, and valentine hearts on the cover and labeled it "Muffy's Hate 'n' Rage Journal." Then I opened the notebook and started writing down anything I could think of that really chafed my foundation garments.

Although I'm used to articulating my feelings, I was appalled by the things I wrote in that notebook. It turned out that I was irrationally angry at some of the nicest people I knew, people who had never done me any harm, people who would have smiled and said they were fine, perhaps even apologized, if I'd deliberately and maliciously set fire to their hair. Just thinking about these ingratiating folks made me absolutely *furious*. I started writing down all kinds of rotten things about them, which culminated in a full-page scrawl in my Hate 'n' Rage Journal: "THEY'RE ALL SO #*&$#* SPINELESS!"

What an interesting word choice. As soon as I wrote it down, I felt a tingle along my own spine, and the pain in my back relaxed significantly. I realized that I had been raging at my own reflection. For weeks, I'd been doing my best invertebrate impression, acting unctuously nice to everyone, not setting boundaries, avoiding the unpleasantness of saying no. I hadn't been using my anger as it was meant to be used, and as a result, my essential self had directed all that discontent into the muscles of my back. It had disabled me to keep me from getting stuck in a sweet, gooey morass of people pleasing. In this case, I didn't have to attack the spineless folks who were annoying me so much. Identifying the source of this particular bad mood was a way of figuring out what I needed to change about myself.

EXERCISE

Make your own Hate 'n' Rage Journal. In this notebook, you can write all your most bitter, virulent, unworthy thoughts and feelings. Once you're clear about your anger and its source, make sure the journal is put away where it can't burn anyone. Then proceed to the next step.

OPTIONS FOR DEALING WITH ANGER

When your emotional compass reads "anger," you once again have two viable options. You can change yourself (as I did after I identified my anger at my own spinelessness) or you can change the situation that's making you angry. A third option—carrying all that anger around with you, not changing anything—is a recipe for disaster. It allows unjust or harmful situations to continue far past the point when your essential self first told you to face and correct them.

The best way I've found to determine what needs to change in an anger-provoking scenario is to use excruciatingly accurate language to describe the circumstances that are upsetting me—the kind of language you might learn in a good assertiveness-training course. Shakespeare wrote up a beautiful example of this in that wacky drama *Julius Caesar.* When Caesar's wife begs him not to attend the Senate meetings in Rome, Julius instructs his messenger, "Bear my greetings to the senators/And tell them that I will not come today. Cannot, is false, and that I dare not, falser; I *will* not come today: tell them so, Decius" (emphasis added). This is exactly the kind of wording you'd expect from someone who'd conquered the known world. Caesar doesn't say, "I can't come; my wife won't let me, I have to stay home." He recognizes that he's not a victim of his wife's demands, even when he's decided to accept her advice. His decision, whether to go or stay, is an act of his own will, not environmental pressures.

To start using your anger effectively, you have to start talking like Caesar. This means refusing to use phrases like "I can't," "I have to," or "I don't have time," unless these statements are literally true. For example, saying "I can't lift that piano by myself" or "I have to breathe oxygen to stay alive" or "I don't have time to walk from Memphis to Seattle today" are statements of fact. However, "I can't come to your party," "I have to call home," or "I don't have time to attend PTA meetings" may not be true at all. It would probably be more accurate to say "I won't be coming to your party," "I want to call home," or "I tend to put other priorities ahead of PTA meetings." Using this kind of language when you are angry will make it glaringly clear whether you need to change yourself or the situation.

"I'm getting robbed blind in my divorce," Eliot told me. "I even have to give my wife the money I inherited from my grandfather."

"Is that legally true?" I asked. "Did the court rule on it?"

"No, but I can't cross Doris when she gets like this," Eliot said. "She'd throw a fit."

"So what you're really saying is that you've chosen to give Doris this money, even though you're angry about it, because you don't want to deal with her reaction?"

"She's making me do it," grumbled Eliot.

"No, she isn't. She's pushing you to do it, but you're the one who's decided to do what she wants, and it's creating a lot of anger."

It would be very nice if Doris decided to be more generous or less vicious, but those aren't things Eliot can control. What he can control is his own behavior: either to stand up for himself or to refuse to do so. While he's ending his relationship with Doris, he will never end his relationship with himself. As long as he allows himself to be treated unfairly, Eliot will continue to harbor a lot of destructive rage.

EXERCISE

For the next twenty-four hours, do not use the phrases on the left unless they are literally true. Substitute the most accurate statement from the list on the right. You'll be amazed how much this will clarify the real source of your anger.

Victim Language	Accurate Language
1. I can't . . .	I won't . . .
	I choose not to . . .
	I don't want to . . .
	I've decided not to . . .

Victim Language	Accurate Language
2. I have to . . .	I will . . .
	I want to . . .
	I've decided to . . .
	I choose to . . .
3. I don't have time to . . .	I'm going to do something else.
	That's not my highest priority.

WHEN YOU HAVE TO FIGHT

As you figure out what your range of choices actually is, you'll feel less anger at others, because you'll acknowledge your part in creating any upsetting situation. That means that you'll be able to change the situation by making different decisions, or at least accepting that whatever is going on, you're the one who chose it. But sometimes, the reason for your anger really will be someone else, someone big, bad, and ugly, someone who refuses to compromise or cooperate. In this case, you may have to "fight" to change the situation. Here are some rules for doing that responsibly and effectively.

Step 1: Burn Off "Hot" Anger Before the Confrontation.

Anger is the "fight" component of the fight-or-flight response. Because this response evolved in the assumption that, any moment now, you might need to stop a saber-toothed tiger from eating your cave babies, it creates immediate, profound changes in your physiology. Blood rushes to your muscles, your body fills with adrenaline, you feel deep-seated urges to yell, kick, punch, and bite. This tends to be counterproductive in, say, a salary negotiation. However, holding in the "fight" response, acting calm and collected when you're itching to tear the head off your enemy's Barbie doll, can be incredibly stressful. It can literally make you sick. You have to release your "hot" anger, but I suggest you do it before you confront the person who's upsetting you.

Physical movement is the best way to do this, especially if you're really, really furious. My client Sanford's parents raised him to become a professional pianist. By the time he was twenty, he'd spent most of his waking life practicing the piano. His essential self was starved for almost everything: freedom, friendship, nonmusical interests and activities. When Sanford's anger finally surfaced, it was gargantuan—way too big to dissipate through mere talk. He needed to take physical action.

The rule for expressing anger is the same here as in any other situation: *Use the energy of rage constructively, not destructively.* Sanford turned his "hot" anger to clearing an empty lot near his home. Every day for weeks he would go out to the field, summon up his anger, and get moving. He chopped up tree stumps and yanked them out of the ground, demolished broken concrete pilings with a sledgehammer, threw rocks and empty bottles into a Dumpster as hard as he could. When he wasn't out standing in his field (har har), he began making other changes in his life. In fact, physical movement—punching, kicking, throwing, heaving, pushing—seemed to clear Sanford's mind, facilitating insights that helped him change the way he behaved in his relationships. During his prolonged physical "fight" with the empty lot, he found the courage to defy his parents, take control of his life, and start building a happy future.

EXERCISE

Think of something that really enrages you. Then, while holding this in your mind, duplicate the actions of fighting in some way that helps the world instead of hurting it. House or yard work does it for some of my clients. You might also try going to a gym or a kickboxing class. Notice how much physical energy you can get from your anger, and how much less upsetting anger is when you're moving.

Step 2: Using "Cool" Anger for Energy, Confront the Person Who's Responsible for Your Anger. Tell Him or Her Exactly What's Bothering You, and Why.

I've said it before, and I'll say it again: You can't expect the people you're angry at to figure out what's wrong. Many of my clients develop towering, sustained grudges against folks who never have the slightest idea there's a problem. *You've got to say it.* Even if you're dealing with someone who won't respond well to your anger, someone with the receptiveness and emotional intelligence of Vlad the Impaler, articulating the exact cause of your anger is extremely important *for you.* If you don't speak up for yourself, you're sending a message to everyone—especially your essential self—that you're too timid to fight on your own behalf. Once that happens, welcome to all the physical and mental stress that comes from misdirected anger. Be sure to stock up on Doan's little pills (for back pain).

By far the best way to stage a confrontation is to have a calm, face-to-face conversation with the person who has upset you. However, this isn't always possible. A lot of infuriating people barricade themselves against such confrontations, either by establishing physical defenses (the supervisor who hides in his office behind his venomous reptilian secretary) or through behavior (the relative who pretends not to hear you, drowns you out by shouting, or walks away). Sometimes you can get through the barriers by making a specific appointment to talk about a problem, even if the other person is reluctant. Phone conversations will do in a pinch, but they tend to be more tentative and less effective than actual "face time." If you can't get someone to meet with you at all, you might want to write down your feelings in a letter. (After you write them, let such letters sit for a few days before you decide whether to mail them. This allows your feelings to settle and clarify, so that you won't fire off a first draft you'll later regret.)

It's quite possible, of course, that the person won't ever read your letter. If this happens—if you've tried every method of communication and gotten no considerate response—you'll end up with a very useful piece of information: This person is not going to cooperate with you *at all*. He or she is completely unwilling to hear why you're upset. To create a situation that resolves your anger, you may need to make changes that increase the emotional and physical distance between the two of you. In extreme cases, this might mean quitting your job to ditch an evil boss or filing for divorce to escape a spouse who has ignored your pain and anger for years. If someone absolutely refuses to hear, discuss, or respect your anger, there's really no way to sustain a workable relationship.

In most cases, though, the person who has upset you will eventually talk to you about the problem. Once you've set up some time for communication, try to follow the rules of engagement below. These will minimize the chance that your anger will destroy the relationship and maximize the probability that the confrontation will improve things.

1. Use examples to support all generalities.

If you go into a confrontation without clarifying exactly what's making you angry, you'll tend to make sweeping generalizations. Generalized attacks are both damaging and useless. Replace them with very clear, specific examples of things that upset you.

Angry Generalities (Useless)	Angry Specifics (Useful)
"You're such a cheap jerk!"	"When you didn't tip the waitress, I felt awful for her and angry at you. You've done things like that before, too . . ." (At this point, you can list other examples. Stay specific.)
"You're always pushing people around!"	"When you told the kids to clean their rooms, you yelled and threatened before you asked them nicely. I'm really pissed off about that, and I'm not going to let anyone treat our kids that way."
"You don't love me enough!"	"You almost never seem to be listening when I speak to you; you look the other way or read the paper and say 'Uh-huh.' That really hurts, and I'm angry about it."

2. Speak only in terms of your own firsthand experience.

You may have noticed that all three of the "angry specifics" above contain facts that the speaker observed directly and expressions of the speaker's own emotions. It's very tempting to go beyond these two areas when you're really angry. You may want to say, "Everybody talks about what a clod you are" or "I know you've been sleeping around behind my back," but unless you have actual evidence, don't go there. There's a reason that hearsay and speculation are not admissible in a court of law. The fact is, they can be wildly wrong. Don't let your anger tempt you into accusations that aren't borne out by firsthand observation.

3. Don't moralize; just express your feelings.

One of the ways we try to control people who are doing something that angers us is to claim that they are breaking some inviolable set of rules, that we are Right and they are Wrong. This approach can give you an almost chemical rush, as you crusade against injustice and evil while casting yourself in the role of moral arbiter. It can also allow you to avoid simply asking for what you want. Instead of naming your needs and asserting that they deserve respect, you can use lofty-sounding moral principles to *force* other people to treat you well. Unfortunately, moralizing is a coercive tactic that almost invariably creates more anger—on both sides of the argument—than it resolves.

The fact is that although we must all define and adhere to our own moral systems, none of us can know what is absolutely right for all people, at all times. (Of course, if You are God, You can ignore that last sentence—but You knew that.) The real issue on the table in a confrontation is not some overarching value judgment but the fact that you are being hurt in some way, and you wish it would stop. Here are two more lists, one of some favorite ineffective, logically insupportable value judgments, the other of rock-solid claims that cut to the heart of the matter. The Top Five Tunes on the left can feel delicious when you're thinking and saying them, but the ones on the right are far more grounded and effective. *Every comment on the left could be more truthfully and effectively expressed by using one of the two sentences on the right.*

Preaching Disguised as Irrefutable Truth	Irrefutable Truth
"Your way is wrong, and my way is right."	"What you're doing is hurting me, and I want you to stop."
"Any sane person would agree that your way is wrong and mine is right."	"What you're doing is depriving me of something I really need, and I want you to stop."

Preaching Disguised as Irrefutable Truth	Irrefutable Truth
"All our friends and your mother think that you're wrong and I'm right."	
"You *have to* admit that you're wrong and I'm right. You *have to!*"	
"It says in Deuteronomy 35:11 that you're wrong and I'm right."	
And so on.	

Framing the confrontation completely within the context of your own felt experience is not only a less aggressive, controlling strategy than moralizing; it also leads you to the next step in solving the issue that angers you. This is a clear, specific explanation of the precise way in which you need the troubling situation to change.

Step 3: Tell The Other Person
Exactly What You'd Like Him or Her to Do.

When you confront the person who's making you angry, you'll need to state *exactly* what changes you want. I remember sitting at a women's faculty retreat as a female professor gave a long speech claiming that her university had created a hostile work environment for women. She didn't really spell out why she believed this, except to say that there was a "general atmosphere of sexism." When her colleagues asked questions like "What would you like the male faculties members to change?" and "How would you like them to act?" the speaker's anger reached blistering levels. *"That's what they're supposed to figure out!"* she yelled. *"They're the problem—let them think up the solution!"* Now, most of us at the retreat, including yours truly, happened to agree with this woman. But if I'd been in the place of the male faculty members, I would have been confused, terrified, and yes, angry. How can anyone meet your demands if they don't know what those demands are? If you can't pinpoint your own needs, how can you expect someone else to do it?

Describing what you want is probably the most important step in any confrontation. If you don't like your spouse yelling at the kids, describe—in detail—the way you'd like parental discipline to work. If you're being underpaid, know exactly how much money it will take to keep you working happily. If you want a loved one to treat you differently, don't use vague phrases like "I want you to let me have my feelings," leaving the other person to guess what would satisfy you. Instead, you might say, "When I cry, you always get very agitated and tell me to stop. I'd feel a lot better if you'd just let me cry, without saying anything."

Present your requests calmly, without any chest beating or whining. You don't need to make empty threats, because you have a real, solid one: You can't go on with a situation that's either starving or poisoning your essential self. The needs you express in a confrontation should be as simple and clear as your need for ample food: Give me less than a thousand calories a day, and I'll starve. It isn't spite, it isn't greed; it's just a fact. This kind of authenticity comes across very clearly to the other party, and is much more convincing than the biggest conniption fit you can throw.

Step 4: Spell Out What You'll Do
If Nothing Changes, and Follow Through.

More often than not, the steps above will yield the results you want, or at least a compromise that feels acceptable to you. Sometimes, though, your enemies will laugh in your face, flick cigar ashes on your shoes, and walk off licking their pointy yellow teeth. If your anger is deep and authentic, it won't let you simply hang your head and go back to business as usual. So it's very important that you decide what will happen if the situation that angers you doesn't change. You need to calmly inform your opponents about what you'll do if you don't get what you want. Think carefully about this, because if things don't go your way, *you must follow through.*

The action you take if your requests aren't honored should be what shrinks call "logical and natural consequences," such as confiscating your teenager's car keys if she's always driving off without asking permission, or refusing to loan money to someone who habitually stiffs you. (Obviously, physical violence is a logical and natural consequence only if you are trying to defend against a physical attack.) The consequence is not something you make up to scare or punish the other person. It's simply the action you must take to stop feeling angry, in view of someone else's nonresponsiveness.

I learned these steps intellectually when I was in my late twenties, but I didn't realize how terrifying it is to act on them until I actually did it. I was teaching sociology at the time, and one of my classes required a large packet of photocopied articles as the text material. I took the original copy of the packet to an off-campus printing store I'll call Ye Olde Printe Shoppe and filled out a little form specifying that I needed copyright permission and fifty copies by the following January, six months in the future. No problem, said the friendly Printe Shoppe manager, a man I'll call Cloyd Liverfluke. No problem at all.

A few months passed, and I phoned the Shoppe to see if my copies were finished. "Almost," said Cloyd cheerfully. "Call back next week." So I did. Still not finished. As fall faded into winter, I began calling the Printe Shoppe every week, then every couple of days. Cloyd always said he just had a couple of things to check before I could pick up my packets. Finally, the week before my January class was to begin, I went to the Printe Shoppe and asked to see my original packet, since I needed it to prepare my first lecture. Well, Cloyd admitted, there was a little problem with my original copy. He couldn't exactly find it.

Blood pressure mounting, I asked if I could look for my papers in the storage area. After searching the room, I found my text material sitting on a windowsill, still in the plastic bag I'd used to carry it in. The bag was covered with thick dust. I went downstairs and had a little talk with Cloyd, explaining that I was very upset and that I needed my copies ready for my students by Tuesday. He apologized profusely, assuring me the work really, really would be done by then. The day of the first class arrived—no packets. "Tomorrow!" Cloyd promised. "They'll be done tomorrow!"

"I really hope so," I said, "because if they aren't, I'm going to bring your shop a lot of really bad publicity. I don't want to do it, Cloyd, but I will." I tried to say this firmly but calmly, as if Cloyd were my own five-year-old instead of a man twice my age.

Right up to the last second, I really thought he would come through. I thought I'd heard the ring of sincerity in his voice. Denial is a powerful hallucinogen. But, of course, when tomorrow came and I phoned, Cloyd had nothing for me but more excuses and assurances. I cut him off in midapology. "Cloyd!" I said. "Tell me the truth! When can you actually have this job done?"

Cloyd was silent for a minute. When he spoke again, it was in a voice between a shout and a whine. "I can't believe you're being so pushy. This isn't an easy job, you know. It's going to take us at least six months."

I hung up. I was pale with anger, but I was even paler with fear, because I knew what I had to do: I had to follow through with the consequences I'd promised. The point was not to punish Cloyd but to act in a way that would channel my anger into something productive. Otherwise, I knew, it would fester and poison me. I had to take action.

Up until that time, I'd never participated in civil disobedience. However, my sociological training had taught me how it's done. First, I phoned the university media center and rented a bullhorn. Then I called the campus newspaper and told an editor he should send a reporter and a photographer to Ye Olde Printe Shoppe at nine o'clock Tuesday morning.

The day dawned bright and cold. My forty students left little plumes of steamy breath in the air as they filed into the Printe Shoppe and sat down, silently, on the floor. I asked the nearest Printe Shoppe employee to get me my packet of text materials, still the only copy in existence. Explaining that I had to disseminate the contents of the packet to my students one way or another, I started reading an essay on the sociology of religion through my bullhorn, while the students sat listening.

So far, this is the closest I've come to being arrested. Cloyd and his Printe Shoppe cronies called the police, who showed up and tapped me on the shoulder just as I was getting to the part about Max Weber's theory of presocial religious experience. I'd already told my students that we would be on private property and that we would leave, quietly and immediately, as soon as we were asked. I mentioned this to the arresting officer. He turned to Cloyd, who was hiding behind a copy machine. "You didn't ask them to leave?" said the cop.

"We were afraid," said Cloyd. "Can't you see she's crazy?"

The cop rolled his eyes and put away the handcuffs, ruining what would have been a great photo op for the campus newspaper ("Lecturer Jailed in Printe Shoppe Pandemonium"). Even so, my rabble-rousing students and I were the front-page headline the next morning.

For a pedigreed people-pleaser, walking around campus with my new notoriety was harrowing—I hated it. Things got even worse when it turned out that (by the account I heard) over a hundred other professors had been experiencing similar problems with the Printe Shoppe. When all these customers read the newspaper article and withdrew their business, the Printe Shoppe folded. Cloyd sent me a letter written in red Magic Marker that accused me, among other things, of being the Antichrist. I was a little startled; I'd always thought the Antichrist would be taller.

LOSING YOUR HELPLESSNESS

If you follow the steps I've just described, your anger will push you toward your own North Star like rocket fuel. It will also rob you of the illusion that you are helpless to change your situation. Many people are loath to relinquish this illusion, because believing you are helpless exonerates you from your responsibility to take constructive action, which is often difficult, strenuous, and risky.

I once saw a woman come completely unhinged when the instructor of an assertiveness-training course encouraged her to avoid "victim" language. "You're wrong!" this woman yelled, her face going red and puffy, like a frightened octopus. "I have no choices! I have to do what other people want! I can't say no! Why are you doing this to me?" She actually got up and stormed out of the crowded room. This woman was using the energy of anger—and let me tell you, she had a *lot* of it—to hammer home her belief that she was not responsible for acting in her own best interests. For years, she had employed this belief as a basis for inaction, self-pity, and the conviction that the world owed her, big-time. It wasn't that she didn't use her anger; it's just that she reserved her rage for anyone who tried to take away her illusion of helplessness.

You can go ahead and try the same approach, if you want your anger to burn holes in your psyche, not to mention your digestive tract (and let's not forget that lower back). Giving up your illusion of helplessness leaves you staring at the raw truth: that no one else is totally responsible for your failures, and no one else can push you into the success you deserve. Fortunately, your anger can give you the strength of purpose to take these truths and run straight toward your own North Star. As you do this, you'll experience a level of power you may never have felt before. You'll lose the need to get destructive and will begin channeling your anger into productive action. Ultimately, you really will achieve serenity through a powerful energy source that once was rage and hate.

IF YOUR EMOTIONAL COMPASS READS "JOY"

There are two rules for using joy to chart a course for your own North Star.

Rule 1: If it brings you joy, do it.

Rule 2: No, really. If it brings you joy, do it.

In fact, if the only thing you ever did was fill your life with the people, things, and activities that bring you genuine joy, you'd find your own North Star almost immediately.

Naturally, this isn't as easy as it sounds.

Suppose I ask you to imitate an animal you've never heard of, like the Australian echidna (if you know all about echidnas, just play along and pretend you don't). To help you with your imitation, I show you a tiger. Then I tell you—this is true—that an echidna is *nothing* like a tiger. Now, based on only this information, do your echidna imitation. Go ahead, I'm waiting.

This is the same type of problem many people face when they try to zero in on joy—real joy. They're attempting to act out something they have never really seen or felt. They know what they *don't* want—quiet desperation, boredom, perpetual low-grade anger, or outright despair—but that doesn't really help them know what they *do* want.

Li Jiang was an MBA student in my career-development class. He was a high-range genius who'd already earned a Ph.D. in physics at a university in his native China before starting business school. He was also a very nice guy. He always wore a nerdy-looking pocket protector and an enormous, engaging grin. One day, Li Jiang stopped by my office and explained that he was trying to choose from among several job options. They all sounded fantastic in terms of money and prestige, so I asked Li Jiang the obvious question: "Which one makes you feel happiest?"

He squinted and cocked his head, like a puzzled puppy. "Happiness?" he said, beaming at me. "I'm sorry. I do not know what happiness feels like."

For a moment, I was too taken aback to answer. Then I said, "You've never been happy?"

Li Jiang shook his head, still grinning. For the first time I noticed that above that enormous smile, his eyes looked a little desperate. "I must find happiness soon," he said in his precise, accented English. "Because I cannot go on living without it." He gave a bizarre little laugh.

Since Li Jiang floored me with this pronouncement, I've met many clients who don't have a clue how to even begin looking for their own North Stars, because they have never experienced genuine joy.

When I told Jessica I thought her life could be joyful, she looked first cautiously optimistic, then a bit concerned. "When I'm happy I get into a kind of frenzy," she said. "I stay up all night doing weird projects—I'm not sure it's good for me." The best thing Jessica had ever felt was a hyperalert manic state, maybe one side of a mild case of bipolar disorder. Manic giddiness can be better than a sharp stick in the eye, but it's not real joy.

"What's the longest period of time you've ever been happy?" I asked Don.

"Well, how long can sex last, really?" Don shot back. "Twenty minutes?"

Even though this was a joke, Don was basically quite serious. The hormone-saturated ecstasy of sex was the only joyful experience he'd ever had. That's certainly a part of a joyful life, but it isn't even close to the whole thing. To chart your course in life by the compass of joy, you must first understand how genuine, core-deep happiness looks, feels, sounds, smells, and tastes.

REAL JOY

If there's any Greek philosophy that really floats my boat, it's hedonism. If you think the hedonists went around snarfing figs, guzzling wine, and fondling themselves, you're wrong. (People who lived for mere pleasure, instant gratification, were called Sybarites, and you'd better remember that, because there will be a quiz in twenty minutes.) Hedonists believed in living for happiness, but they also believed that, due to our basically good inner nature, we can be truly happy only if we live moral lives, complete with integrity, compassion, and sometimes self-sacrifice.

Pleasure and suffering are antithetical; joy and suffering are not. Anyone who's felt the pain of bearing a child, or pushed past physical limits in some athletic event, or struggled to learn difficult but powerful truths understands that suffering can be an integral part of the most profound joy. In fact, once the suffering has ended, having experienced it seems to magnify the capacity to feel pleasure and delight.

When I ask extraordinarily successful and happy people to tell me about their experience of joy, they always talk about it as something that includes the painful aspects of living, as well as the pleasurable ones. Justin, a carpenter and amateur poet, said, "Joy happens when you finally fall in love with the whole span of life, even the parts that hurt. Your love for yourself and others, for the whole process of life and growth and loss and death is so strong it somehow illuminates your suffering and pain. In the end, it's all joyful."

Rachel, a physical therapist, told me, "I became truly happy after I lost everything at once: a baby [who was stillborn], my job, and my marriage. As I lived through that, I broke down completely. But then I began to feel a kind of cushion beneath me, like a net below a circus acrobat. I realized that by accepting my sadness and then going beyond it, I could find a deep source of happiness inside myself, one that will be in my life as long as I am."

Paul, a recovering drug addict, said, "The rush I got from cocaine and meth was so intense, really seductive. But there was always fear chasing it, fear telling me that the high would end and my life would still be a mess. When I stopped and faced that mess, and started bringing it under control, I realized what real happiness feels like. It's solid, it comes right from the absolute center. You don't have to worry that it will disappear if you can't get a fix. Fear is something incidental that I handle when I have to. It's not something that hangs on to the back end of happiness, the way it does with a drug rush."

This kind of joy, the kind that runs deep and broad, requires facing and mastering all the painful experiences we've discussed in the previous sections. It means making yourself stand and face the things you fear long before you've had a chance to develop courage; allowing grief to wash over you when you really think you'll drown in it; channeling rage into compassionate action when you long to commit mayhem. I hate that, but I've never found a way around it. To be a true hedonist, to chart your course by joy, you need a strong moral center and some serious guts.

FAKE JOY

The biggest danger you face when dealing with happiness is mistaking joy substitutes for the real thing. Because our whole life purpose is to experience joy, we are geared to go toward it full throttle, with our whole souls. Putting that kind of commitment into a joy substitute, some chemical or behavioral Joy Lite, leaves us horrendously vulnerable. But for people who have never felt genuine joy, the allure of these substitutes can be overwhelming. Perhaps because he was once a junkie, Paul's description of joy summed up the best way to distinguish a substitute for joy from the genuine article: Phony joy takes you to a place of ecstasy, then drops you off the edge of a cliff. This is true not only of chemical euphoria but of any mood-altering substance or activity.

Susan had a pattern of falling desperately in love with unattainable men. She would become fixated on a man after the briefest contact, say an elevator conversation at work. Before Susan even knew much about her current "target," she would construct elaborate fantasies about the perfection of his character and the bliss they could share together, if only he would leave his wife, girlfriend, boyfriend, cloistered monastery, or whatever. These fantasies would put Susan in ecstasy for a few weeks, then give way to horrendous loneliness and anger when the man did not respond.

The interesting thing was that when one of her targets actually *did* respond, Susan's emotions went into a nosedive anyway. She didn't want the guy—she didn't even know him. She was addicted to the thrill of the romantic chase. Until Susan got over this unhealthy pattern, she couldn't start the long, demanding, infinitely rewarding task of building a genuinely loving relationship. In romance as well as work, real joy is based on real effort. A high flight followed by a crash landing is characteristic of Joy Lite.

Another difference between true happiness and a cheap fake has to do with the way you remember the experience. If you try to cast your mind back to a time when you felt warm and mellow because you'd been drinking, you won't resurrect the pleasure of the experience; you'll need another drink to recapture the feeling, and you'll start scrounging around for alcohol. But if you cast your mind back to a time when you felt real joy, just remembering that experience will light a small, warm flame inside you. The memory of joy, all by itself, is joyful—something that can't be said of imitations.

EXERCISE

List four or five of your happiest memories:

_____

_____

_____

_____

_____

Choose the memory that appeals to you most right now. Close your eyes and recapture this experience in as much detail as you can. Then answer the questions below.

True	False	1. Just remembering this experience creates a surge of happiness.
True	False	2. I feel hollow and exhausted when I think about this experience.
True	False	3. When I remember this experience, my muscles relax.
True	False	4. I can't really remember the good feelings that came with this experience.
True	False	5. I find myself smiling spontaneously when I dwell on this memory.
True	False	6. I get agitated and "hyper" when I remember this experience.
True	False	7. I know that no one can ever take this experience away from me, that it is a permanent part of my mind and heart.

The odd-numbered statements are characteristic of real joy. If you answered them "true," you know how to identify happiness. The even-numbered statements describe the way joy substitutes often affect people. If you answered them "True," then you may not yet be distinguishing between joy and Joy Lite.

FINDING THE SOURCE

Joseph Campbell once commented that "many of us get so caught up in pursuing things of outer value that we forget that inner value—the rapture that is associated with being alive—is what it is all about." When I'm dealing with clients who are basically happy, the best way to chart a course for the future is to help them identify whatever brings them "the rapture that is associated with being alive." Many successful people with hyperactive social selves honestly believe that their happiness comes from money, power, or fame. But when we let their essential selves talk, these people often discover—to their own surprise—that their children, friends, colleagues, pets, hobbies, or environments are their real sources of joy.

Jill came from a family of college professors. She had followed her parents' footsteps into academia and was working toward tenure (a promotion that essentially gives professors lifetime job security) when she began floundering academically. Jill's research and writing slowed to a trickle, then stopped. Her teaching evaluations were lackluster. Jill really thought she wanted to overcome these deficiencies and make it in the university system, but her emotional compass did not point toward a life as a professor.

I asked Jill to search her memory for times when she felt a sustained, peaceful happiness. After a few seconds of silence, her posture relaxed and the lines in her forehead softened. She told me about an afternoon she had spent in a forest. Nothing had really happened there. Jill had just walked around for a while, then gone home. But it was obvious from the new warmth in her voice and her expression that this simple memory brought her more joy than all her academic degrees and distinctions. Every one of Jill's happy experiences shared this striking simplicity. All of them took place in natural settings, when Jill was far away from the rat race she'd been taught to value. Jill's social self was bound and determined that she would spend her life in the hallowed halls of academia, but her emotional compass was telling us that she'd come closer to her North Star as a farmer or forest ranger.

EXERCISE

(For those with a history of happiness.)

1. Take a minute right now to mentally run through everything you've done today. Does thinking about these activities bring on any surges of joy? Which activities are most joyful?

2. Now think about the past month. Have you done anything in the last four weeks that left you with a joyful memory? What was it? List as many joyful moments as you can; then see what they have in common.

REMEDIAL JOY WORK

Jill actually had very few joyful experiences in her memory vaults. Fortunately, those few were real and powerful. When she went back to these experiences in her mind, she felt such a rush of happiness that she finally became willing to make a dramatic change, quitting her college job and thinking about a career devoted to preserving the natural environment. This sort of leap of faith is even harder for someone like Li Jiang, Jessica, or Don, none of whom could access *any* truly joyful memories. If you can't cast your mind back to experiences that make you thrill with joy, you're due for some remedial work.

Sadistic as this may sound, one of the main purposes of remedial joy work is to make you cry. Tears show up as a signal from the essential self that you have fixed your sights on something that *would* bring you joy, if only you could experience it. I remember being bewildered by my tendency to tear up while watching my son interact with his kindergarten teacher. It took me a while to realize that I had spent my entire childhood trying desperately to act grown up. After I'd been in kindergarten for about two weeks, my teachers and parents had decided to move me up a grade. Determined to prove their decision a good one, I'd been so focused on excelling that I had never simply enjoyed school, the way my son does. This realization led me to a habit of watching the Discovery Channel while snacking on graham crackers and milk, a hobby that has brought me hours of humble but genuine joy.

Sometimes my joyless clients tear up at the oddest times: when I'm talking about my car, or they're describing a restaurant meal, or a hummingbird pays a visit to the flowers just outside my office window. These tears are indications that some source of joy is nearby, even if the client has not yet learned to feel it.

REMEDIAL JOY EXERCISES

1. Search your brain for *any* memories that makes you smile spontaneously. These might seem to be "inappropriate" occasions, like the time your brother accidentally ate a wasp or an especially bizarre episode of the Jerry Springer show. No matter what they are, write them down.

2. Try to remember the last time you cried because you were happy, not sad. Births, weddings, sports victories, inspirational stories, movies, books, or television shows may all strum your heartstrings. The ones that can bring tears to your eyes are usually telling you that you need the type of experience you're observing.

3. If neither of the exercises above yields any clear memories, search for incidents where you have felt intense yearning, and perhaps jealousy, about

something you have never experienced: the respect granted to a sports star by his retinue, the intimacy between a loving couple, the relaxed confidence of a performer. Again, write down three or four examples, and look for the common ingredients.

MAXIMIZING YOUR LIFE'S JOY CONTENT

Once you've figured out what brings you genuine joy, it goes without saying that you should immediately begin filling your life with as much of it as possible. Fitness experts are forever preaching that we can tuck exercise into bits and pieces of time: parking at the far end of the lot and walking to the door, hiking the stairs instead of waiting for the elevator, clenching our abs while we sit at traffic lights. This is the way I feel about joy. Putting joyful activities into every nook and cranny of your day is a great way to start toward your North Star. The great thing about this strategy is that it can vastly improve your quality of life almost immediately, without requiring any massive changes.

For example, Geraldine feels soothed and happy when she visits bookstores, so she started going to one during her lunchtime, instead of hanging out at the cafeteria in her office building. Brent loves golf, so he decided to get up early and hit balls at the driving range twice a week. He also added a virtual golf game to his work computer (which he would never, *ever* use during office hours, of course). Marianne's greatest joy comes from being around children. Since her own babies are grown and gone, Marianne volunteers as a classroom assistant in an elementary school, and she reads to children during a weekly "Story Hour" at a public library.

I'm constantly assigning my clients to do the things that bring them joy, and most of them are pleased to comply. However, they tend to see this as a diversion from their professional goals. I beg to differ. When you start doing what you love, you're likely to do it very well, with zest, skill, and infectious delight. Most of my clients' best career connections don't come while they're combing the yellow pages or circulating their résumés. Career miracles happen when you're so in love with your life that pushing yourself is actually easier than stopping, when you "do without doing." Joyful activity adds real value to the world, and adding value is the heart and soul of a successful career.

HANGING ON TO JOY WITHOUT STRANGLING IT

Once you do begin to experience real joy, you will be tempted to cling to whatever brought such happiness into your life. We've already discussed how people who have lost a joy source clutch at situations that have already changed, trying by sheer force of denial to keep natural transitions from occurring. People who haven't felt much joy tend to hang on to every shred of happiness like a drowning victim gripping a rescuer by the neck. They hoard money, friendship, or commitments. They hang on so tightly that they lose their ability to either give or receive. This stops the natural flow of life and quickly kills off the very joy it is meant to protect.

Albert Camus wrote, "In the midst of winter, I finally learned that there was in me an invincible summer." The confidence that your capacity to experience joy is internal and indestructible grows as you let go of joyful experiences and find that they are replaced by others even more wonderful. You can learn to hold your own happiness lightly by remembering that *you* are its source, and that there is an infinite supply.

KICKING THE SUFFERING HABIT

I once gave a speech to a group of devoutly religious women in which I stated my belief that all God really wants from us is an unshakable commitment to our own happiness. I could tell the audience was shocked by this comment. After the speech, several women commented that I'd gone a bit too far, and one said I should be "dragged away in chains." These women seemed to share a religious belief that suffering is the way to paradise, while the road to Hell is paved with happy times.

If you believe the same thing, I encourage you to put down this book and pick up one of those cute little whips with razors embedded in them, because you're not going to find any support for your worldview in these pages. I don't believe in suffering for its own sake. Enduring a thankless, painful life doesn't mean that you deserve happiness as a kind of recompense; it just means you're enduring a thankless, painful life. If I'm going to suffer, it better be for a damn good reason. It better yield me more joy than it costs. If not, I will do anything I can to avoid it, and I advise all my clients to do the same.

This a profound sacrifice for the martyrs among us. I had one client, Tiffany, who had another woeful story to tell me every single time she showed up. Her business was failing, her ex-husband was a stalker, her son was cruel and aggressive toward her, her health was shot. She presented these hard-luck stories with a strange kind of pride, like a cat laying a dead mouse at the feet of its owner. She seemed to think that I would be overwhelmed with pity and devotion if things just got bad enough for her. One week she told me her house had burned to the ground. Later that week, I drove past her home to see the devastation. The house was fine, not a singe in sight.

At our next session, I confronted Tiffany and asked her why she had made up the story about the house fire. As I expected, she eventually articulated the fact that she had always seen suffering as a terrific way— possibly the *only* way—to get loving attention from others. This is a fairly common misperception, especially for people who were ignored during childhood until something tragic happened to them. People like Tiffany believe that giving up suffering literally means giving up love. If you share this worldview, you will most certainly continue to experience disasters. Suffering is horrible, but it's a small price to pay for love, and you'll keep doing it until you figure out that you're operating under a false premise. The truth is that people will love you much more honestly and easily if you give up suffering and fill your life with joy. More important, you'll be expressing love toward your essential self. That will increase your capacity for happiness and spill over into your behavior toward others, so that you start bringing them joy, as well. The happier you are, the more joyful the whole world becomes.

10

ADVANCED COMPASS READING: INTUITION

I'll never forget my first big run-in with my own intuition. I had recently returned to the United States from Asia, where my husband, John, and I had spent the year immediately following our wedding. The evening of my intuitive flash, we were planning to reintegrate into our old college crowd by throwing a dinner party. The main course was to be *katsu-don,* a Japanese version of pork cutlets that is both authentically Asian and easy on Western sensibilities (as opposed to our favorite dish, *natto,* a slimy concoction of fermented soybeans, raw eggs, and seaweed). I was a mile or so from our apartment, walking past a grocery store I rarely patronized, when an idea popped into my head with wondrous clarity.

"I should go into that store *right now,*" I thought—or rather, I *knew.* "They have fresh pork cutlets on sale."

This sudden conviction was so strong I didn't even consider ignoring it. I detoured into the supermarket and straight to the butcher section, where lo and behold, a store employee was putting out fresh pork cutlets, marked down by twenty cents a pound.

As I lugged several pounds of meat back home like a hunter returning from the kill, I pondered the whole experience. I'd never had a psychic flash like that before, and I was puzzled. My primary question was: *Why pork cutlets, for heaven's sake?* If I was going to get just one mystical message in my life, how come it didn't warn me of a potential disaster, or at least a marginally interesting news story? My guardian angel—if that's what it was—hadn't offered a whisper of help a few months earlier, when I'd been hopelessly lost, at night, in a very unsavory part of Bangkok. But it seemed bound and determined to help me find fresh flesh at the best possible price. Who was this friendly ghost—some paranormal version of Julia Child?

I still have no answer to this question. In fact, the whole Cutlet Revelation baffles me at several levels, the grocery-focused aspect being just one. For example, I'm not sure what mechanism conveyed the information so clearly and directly into my mind, or what part of my brain picked up the message, or whether any genuinely "metaphysical" power was involved. Of course, the whole thing could have been a coincidence, but to me, the intensity of the experience argued against that.

I'd almost forgotten this incident a couple of years later. Then my second child was conceived, and something apparently broke loose in my head. Within a very short time, I was besieged by so many odd, apparently paranormal experiences that the Cutlet Revelation paled to insignificance (if it had ever been anything else) by comparison. For example, when John was away on business trips to Asia and I was home in Boston, I'd often see whatever he happened to be seeing at the moment, almost as though the image were being projected on a screen in my mind. I also had "precognitive" flashes—bits of information about what was going to happen in the future—that turned out to be accurate. I spent that entire pregnancy in a kind of altered state, slowly becoming used to a world much weirder and more wonderful than I'd ever imagined.

At the time, I kept this a dark secret. I was a graduate student in social science, after all; this intuitive stuff did not fit into my worldview, or that of the people around me. I had no idea that all the phenomena I was experiencing, known as psychic or "psi" events, are actually fairly common. They have been measured in many laboratory experiments, where researchers have found that human beings can routinely pick up information, communicate with each other, and even influence the movement of objects, using abilities no one really understands, at levels far beyond statistical chance. Things like extrasensory perception (knowing something through some means other than the five senses), remote viewing (knowing what a distant person is seeing), and precognition (predicting the future) seem to be distributed in the population much like musical or athletic talent. Most people have one or two such experiences during their lifetimes, some people get them regularly, and a few are astonishingly, consistently "psychic." Even these people can't do their magical tricks with flawless accuracy, any more than a great baseball hitter can smash a home run every single time he faces a pitcher. But their results are often literally millions of times more accurate than if the subjects were simply guessing.

YOUR FREE PSYCHIC HOTLINE

I don't think you have to have any paranormal experiences to get to your own North Star. Nor would I advise you to consult a professional psychic, except for fun. This isn't because I think they're all charlatans; it's because I believe you have far more intuitive knowledge in your head right now than the most expensive 1 900-number phone prophet you could hire. I know from experience that people who set out to find their own North Stars tend to awaken whatever paranormal skill they may have. In general, the more closely my clients follow their physical and emotional "compasses," the more they begin to sense intuitive guidance. As they draw closer and closer to living in harmony with their essential selves, they often begin to report wildly improbable coincidences, strong impressions of distant events, or a sense of knowing certain things about their own futures.

If and when this happens to you, I want you to be ready to use this most elusive but powerful navigational tool. Your intuition has a more refined understanding of your right life than any other part of your consciousness. This chapter will help you recognize, understand, and deal with its instructions.

As part of my research for this book, I interviewed a number of people who seemed especially happy and successful. Clients tend to come to me for advice when they're at a low point, or when their whole lives have been nothing but low points. One of the differences between these clients and the successful people I interviewed was that the latter talked a lot more about trusting their intuition. Take, for example, the stories of Robert and Ruth.

At twenty-eight, Robert is a tall, dark, handsome, ebullient, and very successful businessman. I met him soon after he purchased the little hair salon I'd been patronizing for a couple of years. The business had obviously been failing for some time, so I wasn't surprised to see that someone had bought out the owner. I *was* surprised when I showed up for my monthly haircut and saw what Robert had done with the place. What had been a dowdy, rather depressing little hole-in-the-wall was now a comfortable and luxurious-looking salon, filled with more customers than the previous owner had ever seen in a month. The feeling in the building had been transformed along with the decor: All the customers were laughing and talking with the hair-stylists and each other. There was a lot of boisterous laughter and a general ambience of goodwill. For the first time, I actually liked being there—and I got the best haircut of my life.

The next month, while Robert snipped around my head, I started asking questions about his life and career. He had grown up in New York, in a family that wasn't exactly poor but definitely was not rich. At seventeen, Robert had seen someone cutting hair in a booth that had been set up right on a Manhattan sidewalk. As he'd watched the procedure, Robert told me, "Something inside said, Hey, I'm gonna do that, and I'll be good at it."

Whatever the "something inside" was, it had its facts straight. Robert proved to be a very quick study at hairstyling. After a little formal training, he literally learned his profession on the streets, cutting hair for a few bucks a head in his own tiny sidewalk booth. "You really learn your stuff that way," he said. "Every type of customer, every type of hair, every type of cut." Since he was paid by the job, not by the hour, Robert also learned to cut hair *fast*. By the time he was twenty, he'd become a maestro with a comb and scissors. He was soon hired by a high-priced salon, where his easygoing personality and impressive skill gained him a loyal customer base. Robert was doing well, saving a bit of money, when one day, with virtually no precalculation, he decided to leave New York and start his own business.

"Why?" I asked him. "And how did you decide to come to Phoenix?"

"I just felt it." Robert shrugged as though anyone would move to an unknown location twenty-five hundred miles away on an intuitive whim. Robert had never even been to Arizona, but that's where his inner compass told him to go. "I got on the first flight out, took a taxi from the airport, and stopped at a real estate agency to find out where properties were up for sale. I spotted this address, and it felt right, so I had the taxi driver come straight here. I took one look and said, 'Okay, this is it.' I didn't even bother to check out any other locations. I just flew home and got ready to move."

This decision-making strategy might come across as cavalier, but Robert is actually a very careful businessman. Listening to him, I remembered my Cutlet Revelation, my absolute matter-of-fact certainty that I'd find what I was looking for in just that place, at just that time. Unlike the rash decisions of impulse buyers, Robert's daring deeds pay off with monotonous consistency. Since his first teenage impulse to learn hairstyling, he has steadily increased his net worth and his quality of life. He now appears frequently on television, doing styling-and-fitness spots for the local news, and his business is growing by leaps and bounds. Robert recently turned down a salon chain's offer to buy his business for several hundred thousand dollars more than he put into it. "But it isn't time to move on, yet," he told me cheerfully. "I'll know when that time comes." He tapped his broad chest. "I'll feel it here."

Unlike Robert, Ruth didn't begin to trust her intuition until she reached early middle age. She was a forty-four-year-old homemaker, raising five teenage children, when her husband died of brain cancer.

"It knocked me for a loop," Ruth remembers. "I'd always believed in the rules: You do the right things in the right ways, and your life works out. My college major was home economics, since I intended to be a full-time, lifelong wife and mother. I supported my husband in his career, had five kids, kept the house. For years, I got up at five o'clock every morning, made twelve sandwiches, stuffed them in six brown paper bags, and sent my family out into the world well washed, well dressed, well cared for. It was inconceivable to me that after following all the rules, I could suddenly become a widow with five scared, grieving kids and no clear future."

On top of her own immense loss, Ruth's concern for her children was almost unbearable. One night, when she was close to utter despair, she was touched by a deep—though irrational—sense of security. "I knew that as I healed, my children would heal," she said. "It wasn't an intellectual knowledge; it was something more fundamental. I just knew that I knew that I knew." In the same ways, Ruth also knew that she would move to another state, go back to school, and become a psychotherapist. She'd never considered this before—never even known a psychologist, much less consulted one—but there was no question in her mind that all of this would happen. Ruth called a meeting of her five children and told them what she was thinking. She had the strange sense that she wasn't so much creating a new plan as following one that had lain buried in her core all her life.

"I told my kids these crazy ideas I was having, and they said, 'Go for it, Mom. We're with you one hundred percent." So we did it. I knew which university I would be going to; I didn't apply anywhere else. After I was accepted—which was far more improbable than I realized—we pulled up stakes and moved. I tried not to let the kids see how terrified I was. The first year of graduate school, I felt as though I were walking through a dark tunnel that never ended."

Ruth kept following her intuition for just one reason: She had nothing else to depend on. Though riddled with doubts, she decided to trust the things she "just knew that she knew that she knew." It worked out as well for Ruth as it had for Robert. She obtained her Ph.D., started a successful practice, and was able to offer enormous support to each of her children as they grew up and left the nest. The more confidence she gained, the more risks she took. Along with helping hundreds of patients as a therapist, Ruth eventually started several successful business ventures and played the stock market with impressive results.

"If my husband hadn't died," she told me, "I would probably have stayed in a life that was very narrow and missed all the incredible experiences I've had over the past twelve years. I lost a great deal, but I got back even more." Chief among the things Ruth gained was confidence in the intuition that has led her to her own North Star.

LEARN TO TRUST YOUR "CAT"

I don't think Robert and Ruth are blessed with far more than the average person's intuitive gifts. The only thing that differentiates them (and the other successful people I interviewed) from my failure-plagued clients is their *willingness to trust* their intuition. Robert seems to have been born and raised to respect intuitive impulses, while Ruth was forced to do so because fate left her with no other option. "Life accidents" like Ruth's widowhood often allow intuition to develop by default: Nothing seems to be working like it's supposed to, so what the hell—might as well trust your gut.

Corbin's "life accident" happened when he showed up at work one day to find that he'd been "terminated," just seven months shy of reaching eligibility for his pension plan. "There I was," Corbin said, "fifty-five years old, with a lot of life left to pay for, kids still in college, and not what you'd call a whole lot of juicy employment prospects." I love Corbin's description of the way he came to trust his intuition in the aftermath of this disaster: "I felt like I was walking along a razor-back ridge on a high, high mountain, in the middle of the night, surrounded by heavy fog. One wrong step in either direction, and I'd fall a thousand miles. And the only way I could tell where I was going was that there was a little black cat walking just ahead of me. If I listened for the sound of the cat's feet, I'd know where to step." Corbin smiled. "Cats have very quiet feet."

The cat, of course, is Corbin's personification of his intuition. As he slowly learned to cope with the fact of being fired and build what he called "phase two" of his career, Corbin became better acquainted with this mysterious creature and its habits. "After a few months, I could 'hear the footsteps' much more easily," he said. "By that time, I'd realized that this 'cat' wasn't just helping me make my way along the cliff—it was actually leading me to safer ground, out of danger. All my life I'd lived with a sense of insecurity, a feeling that everything I trusted could collapse, and there was nothing I could do about it. I was right—that's exactly what happened when the company let me go. But once I began to trust that thing inside, that black cat, I began to take my whole life in a different direction. I decided to go freelance, to be my own boss. The money started slow, but I'm well into the black again, and I have this sense of strength in my gut that I never had when I was answering to corporate HQ. Would you believe I'm grateful to my old firm for canning me? Sure, it was a rotten thing to do. But it taught me to trust my 'cat.' "

KITTY TRAINING

I hope you're never blown out of the water by a life accident of any kind. But if you are, you may find yourself noticing very quiet suggestions that seem to come from somewhere inside your deep self but outside your rational mind. Experiment with these feelings. Try acting on them, and see what happens. The more you do this, the more psychic experiences you're likely to have. In fact, if you want to push this aspect of your North Star navigation instruments, there are reliable ways of increasing your intuitive abilities.

Roma is a client from a wealthy East Indian family. From the moment I met her, she described an overwhelming sense of personal mission and destiny. Though it would be easy for Roma to coast along on the family fortune, she has always been inexplicably certain that her career is supposed to involve helping people improve their physical and mental health. Roma has withstood an incredible amount of personal opposition to follow this dream. She has appalled Everybody and risked losing everything many times, breaking social norms so rigid they make American traditions look about as tough as puff pastry. For example, she ended her arranged teenage marriage to an alcoholic husband, started a small business in a country where women simply do not become CEOs, and later immigrated from India to the United States to earn a business degree.

Roma's reliance on her intuition is truly amazing. She's intelligent, logical, and highly educated in the Western scientific tradition—but she also believes that her schooling should include intuitive training. She matter-of-factly signs up for psychic seminars, no matter how "woo-woo." The majority of them leave her completely unimpressed. "Most of it is just nonsense," she says. But every now and then, Roma learns some new and useful skill: how to clear her mind more effectively, so her intuition can be plainly heard, or how to zero in on important extrasensory information. As a result, she has a very high level of "intuitive fitness." She often astonishes me with her casually accurate accounts of events that have yet to occur, or details about her business associates that she simply "picks up" without being told. Roma is the first client who demonstrated to me how powerfully intuition can lead you to your own North Star, and how pragmatically intuitive abilities can be augmented.

People who allow their essential selves to come out and play often become more intuitive in their field of choice. Writing instructor Natalie Goldberg, who sees her writing as a kind of Zen meditation, accompanied a friend to the racetrack one day and found that she could pick the winning horses—as long as she saw their names in print. The written word is the preferred environment of her essential self, so it's the medium through which she's able to pick up intuitive information. My doctor friend Rebecca has a special intuitive ability to "read" the human body. Accurate diagnoses often pop into her head before she's even had a chance to examine a patient. "The first time it happened, I was walking past a patient who was going into a minor surgery. Without really thinking, I stopped and told the anesthesiologist, 'You can't put this woman under, it'll kill her. Her heart's ready to give out.' Sure enough, she had a heart condition they hadn't even suspected. The biggest problem I have with this kind of diagnosis is explaining to my colleagues how I do it."

Judith Orloff is a California psychiatrist who has written fascinating accounts of her struggle to deal with the fact that she—like most of the other women in her family—is extremely psychic. Orloff recommends that would-be intuitives "train" by setting up trials in which they can repeatedly try to pick up information, then get immediate feedback on their accuracy. The first time I did this, it was completely unintentional. At the time, I was preparing to give a seminar exercise to a group of educators. I planned to have them play the following game: First they would pair off. Then one person in each pair would draw a picture on a piece of paper, not letting the other person see it. Next, person B would try to reproduce person A's drawing, without looking at it, just by hearing person A describe the picture verbally. I'd played this game before, and the drawings had never looked anything alike. The point I had been trying to convey was that visual instruction is as important as verbal instruction.

Before I taught my workshop, I test-drove this game with the help of my friend Karen. I got my piece of paper and went into the next room to make sure that Karen couldn't see what I was drawing. I sketched a fairly complicated scene I'd witnessed just that morning, before climbing on a plane en route to the seminar: the sun rising over a desert arroyo, with a coyote trotting along a dusty path through the sagebrush and cactus. When I'd finished, I yelled that Karen should get ready to draw her own picture, following my instructions. "Okay," I said, when she told me she was ready. "It's a desert scene."

"Stop!" Karen hollered, cutting off further instructions. After thirty seconds of silence she yelled, "Finished!" and burst out laughing. She was goofing off, putting down an absurdly complex drawing after my first clue, just to pull my chain. I thought it was funny, until she showed me her picture—and then my hair stood on end. Karen had reproduced exactly what I'd drawn. Every element of the scene was present—the mountains in the background, the sun, the coyote, every cactus and tumbleweed—and each showed up in the same position on her page that it did on mine.

Naturally, Karen and I were blown away. We figured it was only a matter of time before we could start our own lucrative psychic hotline. We spent the rest of the day trying to replicate our success, but now that we were making a serious effort, we failed miserably. By afternoon, we'd resorted to drawing simple geometric shapes, like circles or triangles. We never got a single match after that first amazing bull's-eye, and we haven't managed to do it since. Anyway, we did get the general idea behind intuition training: try, get feedback, try again. I've listed some classic intuition-training procedures below. Though they're enjoyably useless in and of themselves, just doing them really will improve your intuitive abilities.

INTUITION TRAINING EXERCISES

1. Do You See What I See?

"Projecting" a visual image into someone else's mind, the way I seem to have done with Karen, is a classic ESP setup, replicated in many lab experiments. You might want to try the sketching game Karen and I played, or you can simply sit with a buddy and a deck of playing cards. Take turns trying to "send" and "receive" messages about which card you've pulled from the deck.

2. Personality Profile

Have a friend tell you the names of people whom he or she knows well but whom you have never met. Hold each name in your mind and describe any impressions that pop into your head about the person who owns it. Try not to think; *say whatever comes into your head,* without censoring. "Big red nose, drives a Honda Civic, owns a snake" or "Nasty temper, great legs, hairstyle from Hell." Stay loose, even silly. Your intuition and your sense of humor are deeply sympatico. Get too tense, analytical, or serious, and you'll never hear your little black cat.

3. Psychometry

This word refers to picking up psychic impressions by holding an object. The most common strategy is to hold something that is meaningful to another person and try to pick up information related to the object. For example, you might hold a set of keys and describe the house, office, or car they unlock, or pick up a piece of jewelry and describe the person who wore it last.

4. Going Along for the Ride

You can try "remote viewing" by having a friend call you from some undisclosed location—a phone booth, an office, a cell phone on a boat—at a prearranged time. Try to "see" and describe what's going on around your friend. Obviously, an unscrupulous player could cheat by listening for ambient sounds, so you have to go past generalizations. What pictures are on the wall in the room where your friend is sitting? What color are the flowers in the nearby garden? What other people are visible, and what are they wearing?

STAYING GROUNDED

Finding out that you're intuitively talented, that you can actually do the feats I've just described, can be a heady experience. After my second pregnancy, which was so fraught with magic, I got really carried away exploring the strange new reality I'd come to accept. I was like one of those parents who can't tell their baby's smile from a gas-related grimace; I thought my intuition was speaking to me every time a stray thought wandered into my head. I made a lot of embarrassing mistakes, but these proved very educational. Every time my "intuition" ended up being wrong, I got a little better at telling the difference between a genuine intuitive hunch and, say, sleep deprivation. Mostly, I learned to follow the priorities of North Star compass reading: *body first, emotions next, intuition last.*

This means that if you're sensing some urgent message from within, first make sure your body is healthy, fed, and rested. Then check your emotions for unhealed wounds. Physical impairment or emotional shrapnel, when mistaken for psychic knowledge or the word of God, can lead you off your true path in the weirdest way. Many's the emotionally wounded soul who got swept up in the charisma of some self-declared prophet and ended up slurping poisoned Kool-Aid in the jungle, or vanilla pudding by the light of the Hale-Bopp comet. When in doubt, act on skepticism. Here are some signs that an inner urge is probably *not* a true intuitive message.

1. The thought is accompanied by feelings of fear, anger, or desperation.

Every half-credible psychic I've encountered, in print or in person, describes true intuitive experiences as emotionally calm, peaceful, or a bit detached. Even when they get bad news, people who receive intuitive messages report a sense of warmth and comfort. You may get scared or angry because of the information that comes through such an experience, but the impulse itself is peaceful.

2. You feel the urge to tell other people how they should live their lives.

Because my clients are often uncertain about their futures, I try to stay open to my own intuition during sessions. I almost invariably pick up a sense that the client is enormously loved by some pervasive force that is not me. Often, I get hints about what *I* should do to help clients clarify their own intentions: "Ask about his college roommate," "Mention Alaska," "Be quiet and listen." But never, not once, have I felt impressed to tell people what they should do with their lives—even when these people were begging me for just that kind of advice. I believe that *intuitive information about your destiny, about what you should do, comes only to you.* If you feel you must command another person to obey your intuition, or if other people tell you they have intuitive information about what you should do, you're probably dealing with a brain fart.

3. Your body responds to the intuitive message with revulsion or dejection.

As I've said, your body lies closer to intuitive truth than your brain. If your physical response to a hunch resembles the essential self's *"No!"* reaction, as determined in Chapter 2, don't trust it. When the psychic information is real, you'll get the relaxation response your essential self uses to say *"Yes!"*

TIME TRAVEL

I have found that most of my clients, even the ones who come to me with absolutely no idea what their futures hold, can give me detailed accounts of what's going to happen to them ten, twenty, thirty years from now. Once they're in the right frame of mind, these clients will recite future events they never knew they knew. After waiting long enough to watch a lot of these precognitive stories come true, I've come to believe that we all carry clear, precise maps of our futures inside us. Of course, it may be simply that we build expectations, based on our observations and inclinations, and then make them happen. Or, who knows: Maybe chunks of our subconscious minds exist outside of linear time, in sync with all the information in the universal "holo-movement." (Fans of the paranormal are always invoking physics, because in its current incarnation, the hardest of all hard sciences leaves a lot of room for psi phenomena and intuition.)

For example, my client Daisy's biggest concern about her future is that she will never get married. During her first appointment, we check with Daisy's intuition to see if—and when—her romantic dreams will come true. We do this by having Daisy look carefully at a "future scene" in her mind. You might want to try it yourself.

First, I ask Daisy's age, which is thirty-two. "All right," I say, "I want you to close your eyes and pretend that it's ten years from this very day. It's April seventeenth of the year 2009. You're forty-two years old. Go there in your imagination."

Daisy nods. "All right."

"Now, in your mind's eye, I want you to look around and see what's happening. Where are you?"

She smiles. "I'm in a coffee shop."

"Okay. How does the air smell?"

"Mmm. Coffee, fresh cinnamon rolls. Wonderful."

"Is the air hot or cold?"

"Kind of cool. I'm wearing a sweater."

"What color is it?"

"Blue and purple. It's really pretty."

"Great. Imagine the texture of your sweater on your skin, and listen to the sounds in the coffee shop. What do you hear?"

"Lots of voices. I'm sitting with a few other people, and they're laughing. One of them has a beard. Oh, and there's classical music in the background."

Now I'm convinced that Daisy is really into her future scene, it's time to go for the gusto.

"Okay, in your imagination, I want you to pick up your coffee cup in your left hand. Can you feel how warm it is?"

Daisy smiles. "Yeah."

"Now look at your hand."

"All right."

"Are you wearing a wedding ring?"

The answer comes back instantly, firmly: "Oh, yes."

"Good. Now jump back five years. It's April seventeenth, 2004. You're thirty-seven." We spend a few minutes fleshing out a new scenario. Then I ask, "Is the wedding ring on your hand now?"

She laughs delightedly. "Yes, it is!"

"Now you're thirty-four." We go through the scene-building process again, and then she checks for the ring.

Daisy frowns, her eyes still closed. "Well, I'm not married, but I will be very soon. We're planning the wedding. Oh, my gosh, it's the guy from the coffee shop—the one with the beard!"

"Well, then," I say. "There you go." I'd bet my beer money that Daisy will get married, and that it will happen when she's thirty-four years old.

This exercise has proven amazingly accurate with many of my clients. Though this may well be genuine precognition, I think it's more likely a product of unconscious intention. I think most of us have already decided, at a subconscious level, when the big events in our lives are going to happen. Even though Daisy's conscious mind has been coveting marriage for years, if she unconsciously "knows" she'll marry at thirty-four, her essential self will make a million tiny decisions that will vastly decrease the likelihood of her getting married earlier than that.

The same thing is true of making a million dollars, or changing careers, or getting over a grudge. According to some researchers, just consciously articulating such an "unconscious" goal vastly increases the probability that you'll attain it, even if you make no further conscious effort. "Time travel" can put you in touch with your real plans and help you realize your best dreams, whether they come from paranormal sources or simply deep expectation.

EXERCISE

Think about something you hope will happen in your future. Write it on a piece of paper. Next, pick a date several years away. Write down that date, along with the age you'll be when it rolls around. To get your brain in "future" mode, you might also write down the ages your partner, parents, children, siblings, or friends will be on your target date.

Now close your eyes and create your "future scene." Anchor it in lots of sensory detail: sights, smells, sounds, textures, temperatures (this helps you get into your body, which is close to your intuition, and away from your conscious mind, which often drowns out intuitive messages). Now simply check: Do you have that dream job? The perfect house? A horse? A boob job? (I once had a client whose first comment about her future scene was, "Gosh, I've had so much plastic surgery!")

Once you get an answer, move forward or backward in time to find the approximate date you plan (deep down) to get what you want. This is not a deterministic exercise: If you don't like the answers you get from it, you can change them. What future scenes do tell you, very accurately, is what you now expect. By magic or design, you're likely to make that happen unless you consciously decide to change your future.

SYNCHRONICITY

The term *synchronicity,* which literally means "things happening at the same time," is sometimes used to mean a coincidence so remarkable it seems beyond chance. I assign all my clients to start looking for synchronicities as soon as they begin to get in touch with their essential selves. It's one of the best tools for finding jobs, friends, romantic partners, ideas, and just a general reassurance that life is on your side.

Julia Cameron, a creativity coach and the author of *The Artist's Way,* often sees synchronicity at work in the lives of her clients. When they begin to uncover their artistic sensibilities, she claims, events around them seem to celebrate their efforts and draw them forward. A man decides to become a professional musician, then suddenly inherits a piano; an artist decides to go back to painting just before her eye lights on an ad for cheap studio space; a writer meets an editor at a party the day after finishing his first book. Joseph Campbell, the anthropologist who coined the phrase "follow your bliss," also reported that his protégés encountered helpful coincidences as soon as they began working toward their real life missions.

This happens regularly to my clients as well. Kim, a registered nurse—and the daughter and granddaughter of registered nurses—never even considered another career until shortly before we met. During our sessions, she recalled her passionate interest in her college biology classes, which faded as she began to focus more specifically on medicine and human anatomy. One day she confided with an embarrassed blush that when she was a little girl, she wanted to be a marine biologist. To Kim, this seemed as weird as learning contortionism, growing a beard, and joining the circus. She'd never even seen a marine biologist except on the Discovery Channel—or so she thought. The very next day, one of her clinic's regular patients came into the office with a sea urchin spine stuck in his thumb. This is not exactly an epidemic injury here in Arizona, so Kim asked him how it had happened. Sure enough, he was a marine biologist. He was able to tell Kim everything she needed to know about studying the sea for a living.

This kind of experience is partly a function of selective attention. Have you ever learned a word you've never heard before, and then stumbled across it five or six times within a week? Whenever your mind is focused on a given topic, your attention will sort through the infinite bits of information you encounter every day and zero in on things relating to that subject. This is why it's always a good thing to clarify and specify your desires. Visualizing exactly what you want or need preps your brain to find it in the world around you.

SYNCHRONICITY EXERCISE

Think of a slightly unusual object, like—oh, I don't know—maybe a pink cow or a metal rose. Write down the name of the object you've chosen. You've just made a tracking device out of your own brain. Over the next few days, you are highly likely to see the object you've just named. It may not be in the form you expect: For example, when you say "metal rose" you may be thinking about a flower-shaped pin made of gold, but the first match you see might be a huge, stainless-steel sculpture, or a photograph of a metal rose in an advertisement. But sooner than you think, you'll run across the object you've named.

BEYOND ATTENTION

Sometimes, synchronicities have components that make them more than mere products of selective attention. My clients report a lot of these, and so do the spectacularly successful people I interviewed. Ernie was a computer-graphics specialist who hoped to start a Web-site design firm. One day, out of the blue, he developed a strange, insistent desire to learn more about photography. He had never been interested in this field before, though it was tangentially related to his, but within one day he became so obsessed with it that he phoned me and said he needed an emergency appointment. I thought his sudden passion was a bit odd, but it was clearly coming from his essential self, so I advised him to "do without doing" and follow this new interest wherever it led. On his way home from my office, Ernie saw a leaflet advertising a photography club at a nearby library. He decided to attend.

Ernie felt a sense of excitement, almost urgency, as the night of his first photography-club meeting drew near. He couldn't wait to go— but when he arrived, it turned out to be a complete bust. Aside from Ernie and one twenty-something woman, everyone at the meeting was over the age of eighty. They spent the evening learning to make decorative cut-out borders for pictures of their grandchildren. Crestfallen, Ernie sneaked out of class early—and then, for some reason, felt absolutely driven to go back into the building. "It was the weirdest feeling," he told me. "Like a big invisible hand turning me around and pushing me back." Near the doorway, he ran into the young woman, who was also leaving early. She, too, was a first-time participant in the club, who'd expected it to be more technical and professional. After a few minutes of conversation, Ernie and Sheila ended up sharing a cup of coffee at a nearby restaurant.

The next day, Ernie awoke to find that his passion for photography had abruptly disappeared. However, it seemed to have been replaced by a fervent interest in Sheila. He called her for a date, and four years later, they are an inseparable couple. Ernie's computer work is going well, and now his personal life is, too. Neither one of them ever went back to the photography club.

EXERCISE

Go to a bookstore or library when you have at least fifteen minutes to spare. Wander through the shelves without any particular intention. Try to feel if some books or sections seem to "tug" at you. This "tug" is a wisp of the same kind of curiosity you used to feel when you were a little kid, whenever something really interesting passed your way. It's quite subtle, and you may be tempted to ignore it. Don't. Pick five books that give you the strongest "tug," take them to a table, and page through them, focusing on anything that seems to draw your attention. Sometimes, you'll feel tuned in to a whole book. At other times, you may feel pulled toward specific bits of information. Simply take note of these, and see if they suggest any action. If not, let it go—this activity often acts like a seed, sprouting eventually into something much more interesting than you expected.

SIGNS AND SYMBOLS: NORTH STAR, DEAD AHEAD

Carl Jung, the psychologist who popularized the word *synchronicity*, believed that these kinds of coincidences hinted at his patients' destinies, orienting them in the right direction for self-actualization. He also thought that synchronicities might show up just to confirm that a patient was on the right track. Once, a patient of Jung's had a vivid dream about a scarab, a large, rather rare type of beetle. As the client was trying to figure out what the scarab represented, something began tapping at the window of Jung's office. Jung opened the window, turned to the patient, and said, "Well, here's your scarab." Sure enough, there sat the beetle, waving its antennae at the patient from the palm of the doctor's hand.

Something similar happened to me when I was trying to decide whether to write about my work with clients. I had just finished a memoir, which was in the process of being published. I was doing a lot of life-design counseling and raising my kids, and though I intended (in a vague sort of way) to keep writing, I hadn't actually done anything in months. My editor called me occasionally to tell me how the publication of my memoir was going and to ask what I'd been writing lately. I'd dodge the question by saying something like "Oh, mostly bad checks." Writer's block is bad enough without people asking embarrassing questions about one's output.

One day, my editor called to say she was going to send me something I would like, provided I got writing again. She knew that I collect anything shaped like a turtle (I'd given her a tiny turtle shortly after we met) because turtles have everything I think a writer needs. They have tough shells to deal with criticism; soft, sensitive insides; the need to stick their necks out if they want to move forward; and the slow-and-steady patience to keep slogging away, day after day. So when my editor found a tiny silver turtle in the bottom of her jewelry box—something she swears she'd never seen before—she decided to send it to me as an incentive to write.

No matter how much I do it, writing racks my nerves. Nevertheless, my editor's call intrigued me enough that I reluctantly started sketching out magazine articles, and also a book proposal based on the techniques I was using to help my clients design their lives. I'd been using the metaphor of compasses, charts, and North Stars for years, but I'd never mentioned this to my editor. I was fleshing out the proposal for the book you're reading now when *Mademoiselle* magazine bought my first life-design article. By way of congratulations, my editor finally sent me the tiny silver turtle. I adored it on sight; it was so small—no bigger than a quarter—and so detailed. After turning it over in my palm a few times, I realized that the silver shell had an itty-bitty hinge. I lifted the carapace. Underneath it, set into the turtle's silver body, was a functioning compass, about the size of my little fingernail.

This little silver amulet was like a dream object, combining so many of my own personal symbols and meanings that I could hardly believe it was real. I called and told my editor all about the way I use compass metaphors in my client work. It was news to her. I also made her search her memory to find out where the turtle had really come from, but she insists to this day that it simply showed up in her jewelry box, apparently on its own. I named the turtle Stella Polaris Beck, and took it as a sign that my own internal compasses were steering me right.

Whether or not this is true, believing in synchronicities, time travel, ESP, and the ghost of Julia Child have made my life infinitely more interesting. As you tune in to your physical and emotional compasses, I fully expect you to find your intuition sharpening, and startling coincidences marking your days with wonder and excitement. The more you listen to your intuition, the more it will change your life; and the more bravely you set forth into the territory of change, the more you'll come to rely on it. Eventually, you may learn to trust this ephemeral talent as the most sensitive and sensible of the navigational instruments you carry around inside you. And if you ever need fresh pork cutlets on sale, you will know where to turn.

11

A MAP OF CHANGE

Stay in your present life as long as you possibly can!

This is what I tell all my clients, and I mean it. For hundreds of pages now, I've been telling you to get in touch with your deepest self, learn to read the inner signals telling you where to go and what to do if you want to achieve the life you were meant to live. It is my devout hope that you've discovered that your life needed only a bit of redecorating, at most an extra room or two, in order to be absolutely perfect. You added some fulfilling hobbies, maybe got a little more assertive, and now your essential self is living in its ideal environment. That's what I hope.

Sometimes, my hopes are fulfilled. Surface changes can often make all the difference between misery and contentment. These days, when I'm feeling out of sorts and I consult my inner compasses, I generally find that I need a little more time to relax, a chance to connect with my loved ones, or some interesting escape reading. As soon as I add these components, I'm flooded with feelings of utter contentment. My essential self rolls around beaming like a hog in slop. But there have been several other times in my life when unhappiness wasn't so easy to escape. My essential self was imprisoned in a life that was simply wrong for it. I couldn't just redecorate my life to get out of those situations. I had to raze it to the ground, dig up the foundations, and start the whole thing over from scratch. I'll mention two such times, although these are by no means the only examples.

In my early twenties I was living—or at least aspiring to live—the life of a Harvard academic. I spent every moment plowing through my Ph.D. program, and I fully intended to continue on that same trajectory for the rest of my life. My health was lousy, my mood was bad, and I was dogged by a sense of desperation—but I thought all that would go away if I managed to achieve Ultimate Success as a scholar. The more miserable Ivy League life made me, the more determinedly I pursued it.

I was knocked out of that life by the birth of my son, whose mental retardation and almost tangible spiritual aura turned my whole way of thinking upside down. It was a horrible, horrible experience, one that stripped away most of the hopes and dreams I'd cherished up to that time. And I am eternally grateful it happened. By taking away my identity and shaking me loose from the very structures I thought would lead me to fulfillment, Adam's birth set me free to realize that the world of academia had never made me happy. It would never have been the right environment for my essential self, or allowed me to find the life I was meant to live.

A few years later, everything looked perfect again. John and I had moved away from Harvard, back to our hometown in Utah, where no one cared about the Ivy League and the culture was based on good, old-fashioned, conservative, religious values. Here my decision to keep a baby with Down's syndrome and my newly discovered spiritual side were both more than welcome. I had three beautiful children, a good job, a lovely home, and a close-knit community of people who loved and nurtured me. And once again, I was utterly miserable.

This time, no great catastrophe came from left field to knock me out of a life that wasn't working. This time, the impetus for change arose from within. In the period around Adam's birth, I'd had a taste of what it was like to connect with my essential self. Now I knew I'd

A Map of Change   241

somehow lost it again. Although some aspects of my new life were much more amenable to my true self than Harvard had been, I was still acting a role that wasn't me. My true self didn't fit into the culture I'd rejoined, no matter how much I admired certain aspects of that culture. I hated the fact that my employers in Utah told me a woman didn't need benefits, since her husband was supposed to provide them. I hated having to defend my decision to work at all, in a community where mothers were expected to stay home cleaning and cooking, twenty-four seven. I hated the fact that when I decided to cut off most of my hair at one fell swoop, the hairstylist asked me—quite seriously—to call home and make sure I had my husband's permission.

Discontents like these grew a little every day, like the pressure mounting under a volcano, until the whole thing erupted in a torrent of life change. Within a few months' time, I quit my job, my career path, my religion, my house, my community, most of my friends, and my home state. Even though this change came from inside, not outside, it had all the same characteristics of the transformation I'd undergone when Adam was born. I felt that my identity had been stripped away, leaving me unsure who or what I was going to become. I grieved mightily for everything and everyone I'd lost, even though I knew I'd walked away from them, not vice versa. I was scared, sad, uncertain—and free.

This time, I decided I wasn't going to get stuck in another life I couldn't love. I began to articulate the sense that there was an essential "me" somewhere deep down, and that this core self was always sending me signals about how to find the life I was meant to live. I began paying attention to my body, my emotions, my intuition. They took me places I never expected: to doctors who diagnosed the illness from which I'd suffered for years; to a job teaching business school that I expected to hate but ended up loving; to the task of writing books I barely dared hope would ever be published; to new friends who always seemed to offer the perfect blend of unconditional support and frank debate.

I hope that I never again go through one of those massive upheavals, the transitions from one life to the next that blow every expected and reliable aspect of my existence to tiny smithereens. I hope you never go through even one. Too bad. It's going to happen, to me and to you. As I keep saying, change is the one constant feature of human life, and from time to time, redecorating just isn't enough. We make transitions that uproot the foundations of our lives, and we go directly into the journey of change.

CHANGE HURTS

If you actually do all the exercises I've written into this book so far, you'll end up either pleased as punch or scared to death. If your life is already the right environment for your essential self, every exercise will send you deeper into it. If not, then every little alteration in your behavior, every emotional wound you clean and dress, every hint, nudge, or holler from your internal navigational equipment will be telling you that it's time for a change. A big one.

People who've been living the right life all along simply pick up the pace and intensity when they locate their North Stars. It's usually a lot of fun. But for a person who's stuck in the wrong life, setting out on a North Star quest has all the combined attractions of suicide and child-birth. To complete it, you'll have to kill off the old You and give birth to a different You, someone nobody has ever seen before. Neither side of this process is painless, and they're both scary as hell. I've watched hundreds of folks make dramatic life transformations, and in every case, the person in question experienced alienation, confusion, frustration, and a thousand other forms of acute distress. Granted, the eventual pay-off was tremendous—cheap at twice the price. But change is always difficult.

CHANGE IS PREDICTABLE

Happily, though no one can tell you where your life changes will take you, *the process of life change itself follows a predictable course.* Every major transformation will take you through a similar sequence of events. Knowing how this process works is like having a map of the landscape you're entering as you follow your internal compasses. It allows you to predict some of the difficulties you'll encounter, so that you'll be prepared to deal with them. It lets you know that if you just hold your course, the scary patches will be behind you soon. And it tells you that you are, in fact, headed straight for the destination you want. If you've ever attended a Lamaze childbirth class, you'll remember that the process of having a baby is less painful and frightening for women who know the way labor progresses and have strategies for dealing with it. Allow me to mix up a nice mess of metaphors and promise that having a map of change will yield the same benefits for you, as you give birth to your new self.

So if you've decided you absolutely, positively can't continue to tolerate the life you're in now, the remainder of this book will describe the landscape of change in some detail. We'll look at every phase of the change process and consider how to navigate each one with style and grace (actually, I've never managed the "style and grace" part, but at least I'll help you get through a major transition with as little unpleasantness as possible). This chapter will give you the broad view of change, so that you'll see how all the phases fit together. In subsequent chapters, we'll get serious about the details.

THE CHANGE CYCLE

Life transformation follows a cyclical course, one you've already negotiated several times (though you probably didn't think about it this way at the time). I owe the description of this cycle to my husband, John, who figured it out when we were both in graduate school. After reading through dozens of corporate histories so boring they could be used to sedate patients for surgery, John noticed that all the successful organizations had gone through the same four phases, in the same sequence, whenever they faced a serious transition. In an act of devotion far more onerous than bearing John's children, I offered to proofread the term paper he'd written on the topic. Imagine my surprise when I realized that his "change cycle" helped clarify all my major life transitions.

Since then, John and I have referred to the change cycle often. It's helped us both as we've gone repeatedly into the chaotic disintegration and gradual rebuilding of our own lives. We've also taught it to hundreds of other individuals, as well as groups, organizations, and, in one case, the government of an entire country, Cambodia. The "map" has proved useful in every situation. People who understand the logic of the cycle cope better with change and adapt more effectively, while those who don't understand it seem to suffer more during change and are less satisfied with the results. Here's how it works.

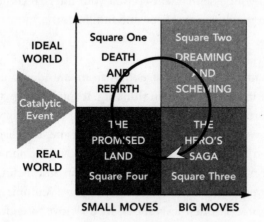

THE CHANGE CYCLE

THE CATALYTIC EVENT

In chemistry, something that starts a reaction is called a "catalyst." In the change cycle, it means any event that pitches you into a major life transition. The change is so big, in fact, that it ends up redefining the way you see yourself.

For example, if you got a couch, you probably wouldn't go from thinking of yourself as a "non–couch owner" to a "couch owner." That's not a catalytic event. But if you got married, your definition of yourself might change from "single person" to "wife" or "husband." In a sense, you'd be calling yourself by a new name. If you were waiting tables and switched to a new restaurant, your work identity would remain the same, but if you then passed the bar and got work at a law firm, your self-definition would change from "waiter" or "waitress" to "attorney." Catalytic changes literally *transform your identity* in your

A Map of Change   245

own eyes, and usually the eyes of others, so that you are identified by a new label.

Catalytic events fall into three types: shock, opportunity, and transition. Each of these offers you a wonderful chance to rethink your life, because each destroys fundamental aspects of your self-definition. They make it necessary for you to chart a new course through life, and they free you to find your essential self, consult your internal compasses, and choose to go in the direction of joy and fulfillment.

Shocks

A shock is a sudden change that comes from outside you, not from changes you've made in your own thinking. It might be anything from a physical disaster like fire, flood, or earthquake to an interpersonal breakdown between you and your beloved. For me, the diagnosis that told me my son had Down's syndrome was a catalytic shock. Not all shocks are bad news, but they are always sudden and major. Within a few seconds, your way of life is rattled to the core. Winning the lottery qualifies as a shock. Though it's a shock we'd all love to endure, people who experience it have many of the same reactions they would if they'd lost a fortune rather than gaining one. They go through denial, fear, and uncertainty. They lose old relationships and form new ones. They grieve as they relinquish the way things were and adjust to the way things are. Like anyone who's experienced shock, they must find their core selves to make the event turn out happily.

Opportunities

An opportunity *always* looks like a lucky break. It happens when you encounter the possibility of making a huge jump toward the life your essential self wants to live. Unlike shock, it's not imposed on you; it simply offers you a chance at something alluring. If your great-uncle offered to let you live in his château rent-free, you could choose instead to go on living in a deceased 1972 Plymouth, but chances are you'd move. Say a corporate headhunter called and offered you your dream job. You might be a little scared, tempted to say no and avoid the headaches of changing careers, but I certainly hope you'd go ahead and accept the offer. If the love of your life turned out—wonder of won-ders!—to love you, too, you could always reject the relationship and head off to live a life of solitary contemplation in a Tibetan cave, but you'd be a damn fool. Some people will avoid an opportunity out of an aversion to change, pure and simple. These people end up bitter and regretful. I urge you not to join them. Take the plunge and grab the opportunity.

As exciting as opportunity catalysts are, you must know that this type of catalytic event will put you into the change process as surely as some unforeseen tragedy. Even prisoners being released from jail go through all the stages of the change cycle, and it is *always* disorienting. Whenever I send clients off to new jobs, environments, or relation-ships, I warn them of this. They invariably nod while their eyes say, "Not this time, sister. Everything's coming up roses for me. This change will be one hundred percent happy." A month into their new lives, they call me in panic and despair. "This is horrible!" they say. "My life has fallen apart! I must have made the wrong decision!" Not at all. They're just going through a normal change process, and this time, they listen while I tell them how to ride it out.

Transitions

Transition events develop much more slowly than shocks or opportuni-ties, and they come from inside you, rather than from the environment. This is what happened to me when I was trying to be a Utah house-wife. Transitions begin, deep down, the minute you set out to live a life that doesn't jibe with your essential self. Over time, the dissonance, the sense of never being who you really are, starts to bother you. A lot. In fact, it finally becomes intolerable. Even though everything may look fine to the people around you, your essential self is torn and dying. Either you end up having a nervous breakdown (which is really just your essential self refusing to continue along the wrong trajectory) or you simply decide that you have to acknowledge your real thoughts, preferences, desires, and identity.

Transition catalysts are much harder to justify than shocks or oppor-tunities. It's easy to explain why you're altering your whole life if you've just lost a limb or inherited a fortune. People (and by people, I mean Everybody) have a much harder time understanding your actions when you go back to school at forty-three because your mind is starving, or you finally accumulate the self-esteem to leave that good, steady job at the Squat 'n' Gobble and head out for Broadway. Sometimes I wonder if the shocks and opportunities experienced by my clients have been arranged by a benevolent fate because they didn't have the social audacity to simply act on the yearnings of their essential selves. Like Ruth, the woman in Chapter 10 whose essential self was set free by the death of her husband, we may find gifts forced upon us by what looks like tragedy.

EXERCISE

See if you can remember three major catalytic events in your life so far. Were they shocks, opportunities, or transitions? Did you use these times to reconnect with your essential self, or did you go along with social pressures?

SQUARE ONE: DEATH AND REBIRTH

Whatever type of change catalyst you experience, it throws you into the first phase of change. I call this phase called Square One, because clients who launch themselves into a new life often tell me they feel that they've gone "back to square one." Though they could've sworn that they were moving forward, they feel as though everything they've ever learned or experienced has suddenly evaporated. They grieve desperately over the loss of familiar roles and situations, all the time bumbling around in their new lives like scared, clumsy infants. Believe it or not, this is a good thing.

Square One is a time of fundamental death and rebirth, the period during which you mourn your old life and begin to explore your new one. The wonderful thing about this is that it gives you a chance to choose a new identity. Freed from your old life patterns, you can seek, find, and embrace your essential self much more easily than you could before everything went haywire. Square One allows you to plot a new life course based on your internal compasses rather than social pressures. *Only if you get in touch with your essential self and go in the direction* your compasses indicate will your life transition lead you toward happiness. Chapter 12 will discuss how you can get through Square One in good, resilient shape.

SQUARE TWO: DREAMING AND SCHEMING

Square One eventually ends, though never as soon as you wish it would. Once you're well and truly sure that your old life is gone forever, and you've dealt with the confusion of starting a new one, you'll enter Square Two, a phase I call "dreaming and scheming." During this part of the change process, you'll start having ideas you couldn't have conceived of before the catalytic event changed everything and you lived through the topsy-turvy roller coaster of Square One. If you've truly tuned in to your essential self and are using your built-in navigational equipment, the dreams you dream during this time will be visions of the life you were meant to live.

At first, these ideas will be wispy and impractical, just idle thoughts about an idealized future. "Wouldn't it be nice to have my own house," you'll think. If this idea comes from your essential self, it will take root in your mind and start sending out little shoots. You'll find yourself visualizing what your house might look like, planting imaginary tulip bulbs in the garden, installing a barbecue grill on the sunporch, creating the ideal environment. As you progress though Square Two, your dream may gradually become more solid. You'll start paying attention to real estate ads, learn about mortgage rates, check with a loan officer to see what kind of house you might be able to afford. Eventually, the dream may become a genuine scheme, a real plan for living.

Of course, the plans you draw up may not have anything to do with literal housing. Square Two is the time to create a blueprint for anything in your new life, whether that means deciding on the kind of person you want to marry, the lean-and-mean physique you'd like to develop, or the business you're going to start in your garage. This always begins with an inner vision and gradually moves into the real world. Chapter 13 will tell you how to make sure your dreams are sound and

A Map of Change

your schemes are coherent, detailed, and feasible. Then it will be time to move into Square Three.

SQUARE THREE: THE HERO'S SAGA

Square Three is where things get brutally pragmatic. It's the nuts-and-bolts phase of change, the time when you put your wonderful Square Two plan into action and find out that it doesn't work. At least, mine never do—not on the first try, and usually not on the second, third, or fourth. This part of the change cycle is a long, often frustrating period of trial and error.

I call Square Three "the hero's saga" because most of the great epics in world literature are the stories of heroes trying to accomplish, in the real world, what they have dreamed of doing. A good hero's saga never goes easily: "So Hercules was given the Twelve Labors, from Flossing the Teeth of the Hydra to Laundering Medusa's Speedo. He found all the labors really easy, finished them in about ten minutes, and went home to whip himself up a mess of baklava." We aren't interested in stories like this, because that's not how we experience life. Making your dreams come true is hard work, and it often lands you right back in Square One, over and over again.

The problem is that no matter how much time you spend detailing a plan in Square Two, you never really know what problems you'll face when you finally put the plan into action. You take all your sophisticated electronic equipment to do research on the mountain gorilla, only to learn that the nearest electrical outlet is four hundred miles away. You go to your fiancée's house, full of love and hope—and your whole new prospective family-in-law loathes you on sight. You build one of the most impressive and expensive architectural structures on earth, then discover that the whole thing is sinking into the sea at a nice brisk clip (this happened to the Japanese engineers who built the Kansai airport, and they're still not sure what to do about it).

Yes, there are a trillion and one ways for things to go awry as you make your way through your own heroic saga, and you'll feel as though you're experiencing all of them. This doesn't mean that your dreams are misguided, or that they won't come true. It just means you'll have to modify the scheme you created in Square Two—possibly several times. That's the nature of any hero's saga, and knowing what to expect makes it slightly more bearable. As Chapter 14 will tell you, Square Three requires the persistence of a pit bull and the resilience of Flubber. But if you continue to manage your own change process, a gritty little miracle is going to happen. Your plan, whether it's plan A, B, C, K, or T, is going to work. You'll move into Square Four.

SQUARE FOUR: THE PROMISED LAND

Like most people of Judeo-Christian heritage, I grew up with the archetype of the Promised Land. I couldn't have been older than three the first time I heard how, after forty arduous years in the wilderness, Moses finally delivered the Children of Israel into a sheltered place full of milk and honey. Once you get to your own promised land, you won't have to expend nearly as much effort as you did during your Square Three hero's saga. Instead of building a new life, you simply have to tend it. Square Four is when your dreams are finally coming true, and you have a chance to stop, rest, and enjoy the fruits of your labor. The whole objective of the change cycle is to get to this point as quickly as possible (though, as we'll see, you can't do this by skipping the other phases of change) and to stay there as long as you can.

Once you've settled into Square Four, the change process becomes very slow and benign. You'll tinker with a problem here, an idea there, making minor adjustments every so often, but you won't have to think about learning anything dramatically new. Now that you're actually living the life you've dreamed about—creating a dream career in a dream environment with dream companions—your job is to refine and perfect operations so that they work more and more smoothly. You eliminate redundancies, cut out unnecessary work, reduce the time it takes to do a given task, and increase your level of enjoyment. In short, you smooth out the kinks.

People who become too complacent about the promised land, assuming that it will last forever, are setting themselves up for a fall. Below the horizon lurks an unforeseen Something, a brand-new catalytic event that will one day bust into the peace and quiet of Square

Four and send you reeling into Square One all over again. Chapter 15 will tell you how to enjoy the promised land without becoming dangerously inattentive.

PUTTING IT ALL TOGETHER

Now that you've had a very brief introduction to each of the phases of change, let's follow some real-life figures through the whole thing. For my examples, I'll use two women we all know unbelievably well, considering that most of us have never met them. (Although men go through exactly the same type of change process, I've chosen these women as examples because so many of us know the details of both their public and their private lives.) The first person we'll consider is the late Diana, onetime nanny, briefly Princess of Wales, now a cultural icon about as well known as the Virgin Mary.

Diana Spencer was nineteen years old when a huge catalytic opportunity came her way: The Prince of Wales asked for her hand in marriage. Well, any girl would be crazy to turn down an offer like that, so Diana said yes. This meant a huge identity transformation for her. Like all women who follow traditional custom, Diana's name changed at marriage, a symbol of the fundamental role switch that transferred her from her father's family to her husband's. Now she was Diana Windsor, though she would be known simply as Princess Diana. She was catapulted into the public eye and had to learn new ways of dressing, standing, talking, and just generally behaving. This Square One, the "death" of Diana Spencer and the "birth" of Princess Di, must have been a doozy.

According to her biographers, Diana got married with stars in her eyes. As she adapted to her new role, she dreamed (Square Two) of a long, idyllic marriage to Prince Charles, happy involvement with her royal children, and perhaps, one day, ascendancy to the position of queen. Diana really tried to put this plan into action. She bore the heir and the spare, became increasingly glamorous and outgoing toward her adoring public, and did her best to make it work with Charles.

Unfortunately, like most first-run dreams and schemes, this one hit white water in the real world (Square Three). It turned out that all along Charles had been in love with another woman. The pressures of Diana's royal role took a devastating toll on her essential self. She hung on for as long as she could, but the plan just wouldn't stick. Diana became depressed. She developed eating disorders, fell in love with the wrong men, and experienced a host of other problems people face when their essential selves are being force-fit into the wrong life. Finally, Diana decided she had to leave her marriage. Back to Square One, big-time.

Once more, Diana's identity was transformed at a deep level. Her name changed again, and she lost the title—Her Royal Highness—that had demarcated her rank while she was princess. This trip through Square One was different from the last "death and rebirth" stage, however, because Diana had finally started paying compassionate attention to her inner life. She'd gotten some good therapy, done a lot of soul-searching, identified her essential self, and learned to pay attention to the signals coming from her body, emotions, and intuition. She wasn't going to play any more social-self games. She told a BBC interviewer that she would like to be "the queen of people's hearts," even if she wasn't part of the royal family. This was a revised version of Diana's original Square Two dream, in which she'd been the queen of England. After her divorce, Diana hadn't given up her vision of the life she wanted—just modified it in a way that felt friendlier to her true self.

With a new clarity and determination, Diana set out to make this revised dream come true (Square Three). She began using her fame to call attention to social issues she felt were important: making the world a better place for the handicapped, finding a cure for AIDS, eliminating the land mines that devastate many Third World populations. This time, because Diana had found her real identity, consulted her internal compasses, and formed a plan based both on her heart's desires and her worldly-wise experience, the whole process worked very well. Diana did indeed become the queen of the public's heart. The life's work she had chosen changed millions of lives for the better, directly or indirectly. According to her friends, she also found true love at last, in the person of Dodi Fayed. She'd made it to Square Four.

Too soon, Diana encountered another really major catalytic event: She was killed in a car accident. It would be nice to think that she took

this in stride and is busily involved in whatever Promised Land may follow this one. Even while we mourned her premature death, we com-
moners were all glad that Diana hadn't been completely destroyed by
the pressures she'd encountered as a young adult. Unlike many people
who get stuck or give up at some point in the change cycle, Diana
negotiated every step, over and over again, until she got it right. Her
legacy, and the world, are richer for it.

ROUND AND ROUND
AND ROUND SHE GOES . . .

Oprah Winfrey is another example of someone who's gone through
the change cycle in style as we all sit around gawking at her. In fact,
she's the perfect person to illustrate the fact that one individual can go
through the whole process over and over again, learning and maturing
more each time. By definition, the change cycle follows a circular
course. But it isn't a flat circle; in three dimensions, it would be shaped
like a corkscrew. Every time you go around the cycle, you move forward a notch, becoming more wise, confident, and capable. We'll look
at Oprah's history from a wider "lens" than we used to see Diana's life,
in order to see broad patterns repeating over time.

Can you imagine what any sane person would have told an illegiti-
mate African American girl, born on a Mississippi pig farm, shunted
between relatives, and sexually abused from an early age, if she'd mentioned that her internal compasses told her she was destined to be a
media goddess? They would have said, "Sure, honey, and after you
become rich and famous, we'll all go back to your grandma's farm and
watch the pigs fly south for the winter." Talk about an impossible
dream! And yet, Oprah set out from this background into the landscape
of change, following her built-in compasses against all odds.

A catalytic opportunity found Oprah when, still a teenager, she was
hired as a radio news announcer. She did the job well and began to
dream and scheme about being a television journalist. Then another
catalytic event occurred: She was hired as a TV anchorwoman. At this
point, the Promised Land was practically within Oprah's reach, right?

Wrong. As she started into the hero's saga, the workaday business of building her dreams, Oprah's producers decided they didn't like her looks or the way she read the news—she was too emotionally responsive to the stories. Eventually, they booted Oprah out of the news-anchor position in what looked a lot like a career-ending demotion.

Like Diana, Oprah refused to let this unwelcome return to Square One keep her from building the life she wanted. She hung on to her dreams and revised her schemes. When Oprah was hired to host a daytime talk show, her essential self responded like a duck let loose in water for the very first time. She was *home,* and like all people who have found the perfect expression of their essential selves, she was magnetically, mesmerizingly good at her new job.

Since finding her niche, Oprah has continued to experience catalytic events, and she has gone through the whole change cycle several times. Against the pundits' better judgment, Oprah's personal maturation led her to change the tone of her show, from sensationalistic ("Preschool Strippers," "Women Who Seduce Their Husband's Lovers," "I Ate My Own Feet," and the like) to socially responsible. She decided to push "loser" topics, like literacy and spiritual development, that appealed to her true self. She's tried any number of hero's saga diet and exercise programs meant to bring her weight under control. Cattle ranchers in Texas dealt her a bizarre catalytic shock when they sued her for mentioning that she didn't plan to eat any more hamburgers. We've watched Oprah try and fail, try and try again, try and win big. I imagine she knows every step on the change cycle as well as I know the path from my bed to my bathroom, and you can bet the pig farm she isn't finished.

SOME GENERAL INSTRUCTIONS ABOUT TRAVELING THE CYCLE

Before we get into detailed directions for each of the four stages of the change cycle, you need to know some general hints about how the whole journey will fit together. First of all, the four "squares" aren't really as separate as they look on the chart. In reality, each phase of the cycle blends gradually into the next. The chaotic aspects of death and rebirth are worst at the beginning of Square One, gradually giving way to moments of optimism as you begin to dream your way into Square Two. This phase begins with rather fuzzy ideas, which become more detailed and informed as you work your way toward the hero's saga in Square Three. Once you've gone through the initial problems of this phase, you'll become more and more efficient and relaxed as you get to Square Four, the promised land.

There are a couple of reasons I've differentiated the four squares graphically in the chart. First of all, defining each phase can help you figure out where you are on the map of change and predict what's coming up. Second, knowing your position enables you to create the best possible strategy for getting through the whole change process. Where would you locate yourself on this "map"?

Wherever you are, your location on the change cycle comes along with a specific set of instructions. As you can see from the chart, the squares form a two-by-two matrix. Squares One and Two, the top two squares, take place in the "ideal world." This means that the work you do in these squares occurs mainly between your lovely little ears. Squares Three and Four, on the other hand, are "real world" areas. You have to roll up your sleeves and *work* in these phases, whether that means going out and digging in the dirt or writing up your essay on theoretical physics, printing it out on actual paper, and sending it to an actual journal.

Besides "ideal world" and "real world," the change-cycle matrix also divides into "small moves" and "big moves." Squares One and Four, on the left side of the cycle, are times for small adjustments, work that won't squander too much effort where it isn't beneficial. You don't want to make huge commitments in Square One, when you've barely started out in this new stage of your life, though people often do so. (Rebound romance is a classic example: You've been bumped by your lover, so you marry the next half-eligible person who will take you to Vegas on a whim.) Square Four isn't the time for big changes either. Remember when Coca-Cola changed its formula, even though sales were just fine? We all hated the new Coke. If it ain't broke, don't fix it.

Squares Two and Three, on the other hand, are the times to make Big Moves. In Square Two, the big moves are still happening in your head—in the "ideal world." That means that you're making major plans, testing them out, then totally rethinking them. You play with all kinds of possibilities, dream big, but remain willing to change your ideas at any moment. In Square Three, the big changes happen in the real world. You actually go to the bank, take out that massive loan, and buy the house. The big dreams you've tested mentally in Square Two become the basis for big efforts in Square Three.

NAME YOUR SQUARE

The biggest problem most people encounter when their lives are changing is that they fail to realize that change has different phases, and that each phase requires completely different skills and strategies. Most people tend to feel more comfortable in one or two of the squares than in the others. They navigate part of a given transformation brilliantly but crash and burn when the landscape of change leads them into a new type of terrain. You may be like any of the following four examples, or you may combine the skills for two or more of the squares.

1. Chaos Commando

Cindy just loves creative ferment. She's constantly having great ideas, and she gets jobs easily because of her strikingly original way of thinking. She performs fabulously for a few months—but after that, she starts getting bored. If she stays in the same routine for any length of time, Cindy's likely to stir up trouble, change horses in the middle of the stream, and fix things that aren't broken, because she's basically a Square One person.

2. Big Dreamer, Little Doer

Falco is a dreamer, a Square Two person all the way. He loves sitting in my office and planning his brilliant career. He does visualization exercises, affirmations, detailed written "mission statements" that his self-help books assure him will lead to fame and fortune. But when I ask

A Map of Change

257

Falco what he's done to actually construct the various castles he sees in the air, I'm met with an offended silence. The truth is, Falco's a lot more comfortable in his imagination than in the real world. He's a Square Two genius, but Square Three makes him very, very nervous. Until he faces up to the need for pragmatic action, his fantasies will never become realities.

3. Realist, Not Idealist

Lauren is a crusader. Give her a dream, and she will make it happen. She's always on a project, like organizing neighborhood associations to keep drugs out of her city, volunteering to serve her favorite candidate's political campaign, or helping her company market and sell a new product. She's a fantastic manager with excellent logistical skills, great at arranging schedules, keeping track of details, and following through to make sure that every assignment gets done. Lauren loves to lead a charge—but don't ask her to come up with the basic ideas. She prefers falling in love with other people's visions and helping make them real. She's a Square Three person, through and through.

4. Rock of Gibraltar

Johann is a Square Four kind of guy. He's had the same job for twenty years, and he's proven invaluable to his company. Steady as the Budweiser Clydesdales, Johann punches the clock every single morning, works until five every single afternoon, and meticulously completes the various physical and bureaucratic aspects of every assignment. But when his firm goes belly-up and Johann is out of a job, he's utterly flummoxed. All he knows how to do is forge straight ahead; he's not used to inventing new responses and coming up with creative solutions. Johann's skills were perfect for Square Four, but he needs a different strategy to get through Square One.

EXERCISE

Read through the examples above and see which ones resonate most for you. If you're like most people, you'll be strong in at least one square, fairly competent in one or two others, and not so great at the fourth. Some people are totally focused on one particular square. Others, even more rare, are great at all four squares. These people are extremely wealthy.

ADAPTING OR ACCOMMODATING YOUR CHANGE-CYCLE SKILLS

If you find that your natural skills and preferences are more adapted to certain parts of the change cycle, or if some of the squares are really abhorrent to you, there are a couple of options you might decide to use. First of all, you must acknowledge that you'll have to cope with all four regions of change, whether you want to or not. Next, you might want to settle down and learn to manage your least-favorite squares more effectively. You absolutely must have at least a rudimentary ability to recognize and traverse each phase of change (and the following chapters of this book are designed to help you do just that).

The other option is to hire, bribe, coerce, or beg someone else into helping you handle the stages of change you like least. For example, I myself thrive most in Square Two. I muddle through Square One reasonably well, and I can force myself through Square Three if I'm really excited about making an idea work. But once I get to Square Four, forget it. I'm a wreck. I am so easily distracted by new ideas and happy fantasies that I completely forget little things like, oh, feeding my children or paying the mortgage. I go to parent-teacher conferences (when I remember them) only to realize that I have no idea what grade Elizabeth is in, or exactly where Adam's school is located. I'm so deeply impaired in this area that people think I just don't care, or that I'm willfully trying to insult them.

Once I went to a psychotherapist to work on this very issue. "I'm surrounded by people who are incredibly good at consistent, effective routine," I told my shrink. "I've got to learn to do it better."

"Why should you learn to do it better," said the therapist, "if you're surrounded by people who are incredibly good at it?"

"You have a point," I said. I went right home and formally requested that my Square Four–savvy friends and relatives help me out in the consistent-routine department. I've been getting logistical assistance from my tolerant, talented loved ones ever since, and my life runs ever so much more smoothly.

STICKING SQUARES, SKIPPING SQUARES

A common pitfall people face as they enter major life changes is getting stuck in one phase of the cycle, where they're reasonably comfortable, and refusing to move on to the next one. This is most common after a catalytic event, when you have to move from the balmy comfort of Square Four, the promised land, to the wild death-and-rebirth ride of Square One. Another popular but misguided approach is trying to skip some phases of the change cycle altogether. By far the most popular mistake is trying to jump directly to Square Four after a catalytic event, without mucking through the scary, disorienting chaos of Square One, the hard mental work of Square Two, or the laborious, two-steps-for-ward-one-step-back drudgery of Square Three. This doesn't work; it leads only to a denial of reality that will end up lengthening the very nastiness you're hoping to avoid.

Lester and Sharon were partners in work and life. They met in the office, stayed on with their company after marriage, and climbed the promotion ladder more or less in tandem. Then, after thirteen years with Lester, Sharon experienced a profound transition. She realized that for some time now she'd felt stifled in her marriage, unable to know her own mind or define her own goals. Moreover, she'd begun an E-mail flirtation, if not an outright romance, with a man she'd met in an Internet chat room.

This transition was Sharon's change catalyst. It led directly to Lester's, which came as a devastating shock: Sharon was leaving him. Since they were still working for the same company, Lester and Sharon had to announce to the whole office that their "perfect" relationship was on the rocks. Naturally, this was big news around the water cooler for weeks. Everyone in the company expected to see Lester and Sharon utterly disintegrate before their eyes.

Strangely, this didn't happen—or, at least, not right away. Sharon moved into an apartment, Lester redecorated, and that was it. They both came to work bright and chipper every morning and went around looking gauntly cheerful. They told anyone who asked that they were absolutely fine, no problems, no worries. Sharon started dating her Internet suitor, and Lester began seeing a lovely woman who'd had a crush on him for years. Within a month, both the divorcés claimed to be happily, permanently committed to their new partners.

Hmm. Do you hear something ticking?

It took about six months for Sharon and Lester to move into Square One, and then, *kablooey!* They'd stored up so much anger, sadness, and bewilderment that it nearly blew them both to bits. Each of them had resisted what they saw as the ignominy of their marital "failure" by pretending—even to themselves—that they had waltzed smoothly and instantly into a new, solid Square Four. Their rebound romances were basically attempts to re-create their original relationship, using other people as stand-ins. Their cheeriness at the office was a desperate charade.

When Lester and Sharon began to internalize what they'd lost, and their new partners turned out to be individuals in their own right, the fantasy Square Four broke down like a stock car hitting the outside curve at maximum speed. The screaming fights their coworkers had expected six months earlier finally began, and they were everything a muckraker's heart could possibly desire. The rebound relationships, lacking any solid foundation, rapidly dissolved. Sharon eventually quit, unable to bear running into Lester or his friends during the workday. Both of them finally faced the enormity of their life changes and began to cover the territory they had to cross.

"METALEARNING"

When I was studying Chinese in Singapore, I met an American linguist who had barely arrived from the States. In a feat that both impressed and frustrated me, this woman picked up more Mandarin in a few days than I did in weeks. She had never heard Chinese spoken, but she had *learned how to learn languages in general,* and that made all the difference.

Knowing how to speak one language is a skill. Knowing how to learn language, any language, is called a "metaskill." Figuring out how to negotiate the change cycle means that no matter what happens to you, no matter what you decide to do, you'll have some idea about what's coming, how it will feel, and how to cope. You'll master the metaskill of personal transformation. People like Oprah Winfrey, who have gone through the whole cycle many times and experienced both failure and success, have amazing metaskills. This is how they manage to remain vital and successful even as they change and the world changes around them.

Once you've begun to develop an ability to manage the whole experience of the change process, the constant fluctuations and disastrous misadventures of life will become far less frightening. Instead of worrying about the fact that society is changing faster than ever before and that tried-and-true institutions are falling apart, you'll see it as a boon. Freed from rigid social expectations, focused firmly on guidance from your essential self, you will stop conforming to any of the pre-designated patterns offered by your cultural environment. Instead, you will turn your own life into a work of art: an absolutely original expression of your unique gifts and preferences. You will be not only the work in progress but also the artist. You will reach your own North Star, and stay with it through any and every change that may ever come your way.

12

SQUARE ONE:
DEATH AND REBIRTH

I am crossing the bridges of sorrow,
Empty with yearning and full of tomorrow.

—OCTOBER PROJECT

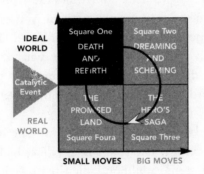

THE CHANGE CYCLE

Somewhere in the Kalahari Desert, twenty teenage boys of the
Xhosa tribe sit together around a smoldering fire. They are nervous,
exhausted, and deeply confused. Everything familiar to these youths has
been taken away from them. They will never return to the homes
where they grew up. Their childhood clothes and toys have been
burned. Their names have been changed. Even their bodies have been
painted with white ash and clay, so that they don't recognize themselves, let alone each other.

This may sound like an alien world to you, but even if you've never been to the Kalahari, you know the territory these boys are crossing. Their most important journey isn't across a geographical landscape; they've got to traverse a psychological one. They are in the first stage of the cycle of change, the place of death and rebirth. Their lives and identities are in the process of transformation. And whether you come from South Africa or South Dakota, you've taken this trip too.

You could probably pinpoint several moments when your life changed utterly, so that you remember everything as occurring "before X happened" or "after X happened." You saw the Space Shuttle take off, and you knew right then that you would grow up to be an aeronautical engineer. You felt your leg snap during a game, and in that one excruciating instant, your career as an athlete was over. Your first child was born, bringing new meaning to everything in your universe. You and Jim-Bob decided to go ahead and rob that liquor store, even if it did have a security camera. Sometimes these pivotal events blindsided you, zooming in from nowhere before you even dreamed they were coming. Sometimes they grew in your heart, little by little, until you finally had to take action. No matter what they were or how they arrived, they disrupted your life so thoroughly that you could no longer be the person you once were. In short, they shoved you into Square One.

The wild and dangerous terrain of Square One is well understood by people like the Xhosa. The young men I described above are undergoing their initiation into adulthood, the rite that will end their lives as boys and begin their lives as men. To help them make this psychic passage, the elders of the tribe have deliberately created conditions that exaggerate the psychological experience of leaving one life behind and moving to a new one. They've obscured the initiates' identities, taken away their names, destroyed their old possessions, and put them in alien territory, not out of cruelty but as a way to familiarize them with the experience of Square One in a controlled, safe environment. It's sort of a Square One simulator, like the machines in driver's ed that re-create various driving situations, so that students can make mistakes, freak out, and learn how to handle a car before they're actually careening around in high-speed metal projectiles.

It's a shame most of us Westerners never get the same kind of training for running our lives that we get for running our cars. Most of our social institutions assume that we'll all march straight onward and upward, building one success upon another, mastering life without any retrenchments into chaos or personal disintegration. This means that when a catalytic event does hit us, we smack into Square One of the change cycle with no warning, no preparation, and no sense of familiarity. It feels a lot like being sucked into a jet engine, without the blessing of quick physical death. Nope, Square One is a death you have to live through. I'm hoping this chapter will make it easier.

EARLY SQUARE ONE: SURVIVING YOUR DEATH

Jennifer bounced into my office full of pride, like a bird dog who'd just retrieved an entire ostrich. After months of soul-searching, compass reading, and good old hard work, she'd snagged a fabulous job offer in an exotic part of the world—exactly what she'd always wanted. After she told me the good news, we spent a few minutes cheering, jumping around the office, and high-fiving each other. Then Jennifer collapsed onto the couch, curled into a fetal position, and spent the next forty-five minutes weeping into a pillow.

After the first flush of excitement, the full impact of Jennifer's "catalytic event" was sinking in. She was thrilled about the job, but it would mean a massive life change. Jennifer was beginning to think about everything and everyone she'd leave behind when she moved overseas, and the loss was already tearing her heart to shreds. There would be no more relaxed evenings with her mom, who'd always lived just a short car ride away. Jennifer would have to give away her dog, whom she loved dearly. Even her old job, which she'd always found frustrating, suddenly seemed comfortingly familiar. The many friends she'd made at work wouldn't be poking their heads into her office anymore. The car Jennifer had driven for three years, the apartment she'd decorated, her favorite restaurants and jogging routes—all these things would soon disappear from her life. Jennifer of the American Southwest was on death row. The execution day was written on her new contract, on her airplane ticket, on the apartment lease she wasn't planning to renew. Jennifer was just beginning to understand that you cannot create a new life without destroying the one you've got.

Letting Go of Your Life

If we can believe people who've "died" and then been resuscitated, we don't have much to fear from our actual, physical demise. True, the part leading up to death—disease, dementia, decapitation—can be horrific. But once you've shuffled off the old mortal coil, you're supposed to go on to a junket of adventures that make a trip to Disney World look like a sentence in Alcatraz. According to those who managed to get a round-trip ticket to the undiscovered country, these activities include floating around without your body, seeing your whole life on "instant replay," and meeting up with predeceased loved ones. (I'm hoping to be met by the luggage I lost en route to O'Hare airport in 1975.) Of course, it may be that the near-death experiencers are wrong, that we just disappear into nothingness when our bodies die. That doesn't sound like nearly as much fun, but of course, we won't be around to care.

Unfortunately, the "death" we experience after a catalytic event isn't nearly so stress-free. Remember, the change cycle doesn't begin when we experience the minor course corrections of life, only when something forces us to *let go of our identities.* This is a very real and profound form of annihilation. The Xhosa youths are losing their identity as boys, a shift so fundamental that the tribe takes away their names and obscures their features to symbolize it. In our culture, loss of identity is a less familiar concept. To help you understand what it feels like, please finish the following sentence with whatever comes to mind:

"I am a/an _____."

Now push it further by listing four or five more things:

"I am a/an _____, a/an _____,

a/an _____, a/an _____, and

a/an _____."

So? What are you? You may have identified yourself by a job description: "I am a tinker, tailor, soldier, spy, corporate strategist, Thighmaster salesman." Or maybe your identity is based on relationships: "I am a devoted lover, caring parent, loyal friend, and a trusted confidante of the pope." You may identify yourself by membership in some group or cause: "I am a homosexual, a Republican, a Jew, a Poultry Rights crusader"; or an avocation: "I am a deep thinker, a ski bum, an alcoholic, a fitness fanatic."

I want you to notice that *you could be everything I just listed, all at once.* You'd be really weird and mighty damn busy, but yes, it's theoretically possible to be all those things, and many more as well, simultaneously. Each of us has infinite roles and identities. But we typically think of just a few, maybe only one, when we say, "This is what I am." This "primary identity" shapes our place in the world, dictates many of our actions, helps us feel that our lives are grounded and meaningful.

Now, looking at the list you just wrote above, imagine that something happened to make it impossible for you to go on being *any* of the identities you listed. I hope to God this never occurs, but it could. You could lose your job, either by being fired or by jumping ship. Your romantic relationship could disappear through death or treachery. You might become disenchanted with your political party, religion, or local Poultry Rights chapter. You might develop hormone problems and pudge up uncontrollably to the shape and size of a manatee. In short, *it could all go away, any time.*

I have spoken to many, many people who have come face-to-face with this awful truth. A few were literally about to die of terminal illnesses, but most were dying in smaller ways. Cliff, who saw himself first and foremost as a committed family man, "died" the day he finally realized his marriage just wasn't salvageable. Hillary's "death" occurred when she knew she had to leave the profession her parents desperately wanted for her, losing her identity as their obedient little girl in the process. Hillary brought her mother, Ellen, to one session, and we helped the older woman grapple with the fact that her nest was now well and truly empty. Ellen had to let go of her primary identity as a mother of dependent children.

I remember each of these people's faces as they told me about their "deaths." Though the features varied, all those faces wore the same expression: gray, tired, empty, inexpressibly sad. I've seen that face on every person I know—including myself—who was facing a major identity loss. Even when the change is what we want, entering Square One means enduring loss after loss after loss. In hindsight, when you're firmly entrenched in a new life of joy and fulfillment, all this pain seems like nothing. When you're going through it, it seems like everything.

The "death" component of Square One, that initial period when you first come to terms with the fact that your old identity is lost, can only be managed by grieving. Psychologists sometimes call it "grief work." I like this phrasing, because it points out that experiencing the pain of loss is a concrete, productive behavior, not a waste of time. Go back to the section on grief in Chapter 9 for reminders about how to "do" grief. A brief recap: Pretending to be happy or unruffled when your primary identity has suffered a deathblow will only lengthen the sadness, while allowing yourself to feel it will help it dissipate as quickly as possible. Grief slows you down, so you'll need more time to do even the most mundane tasks. You'll go through periods of denial, when the sadness eases up a bit, but then it will wash over you again. Identifying your losses, sharing your feelings, and grieving them through is absolutely necessary for preparing you to enjoy your new life. I wish there were another way, but I've never found one.

Different Flavors o' Death

The beginning of Square One, the departure from your old life, will feel slightly different depending on whether the "catalytic event" that shoved you out of your old identity was a shock, an opportunity, or a transition. Chances are you'll encounter all three forms of catalytic event at one time or another. I'll describe each one briefly, so that you'll have a better idea of what to expect, and how to handle it.

Catalytic shocks, as you'll recall, come from some outside source, not from within the person whose life is changing. You may not be even remotely responsible for causing the shocks in your own life, so you don't have many clues about when they'll arrive or what form they might take. Negative shock: Your beloved Auntie Dorcas, who raised you from a baby, is killed by a rogue circus elephant. Positive shock: Though Dorcas lived like a pauper, she had eleven million dollars stuffed in her mattress, and she left it all to you. Your reaction to both these shocks, good and bad, is likely to be "I don't believe this." You will also think, "I don't deserve this," whether the shock is positive or negative—and you'll be right. You really won't deserve it. Shock events have nothing to do with "deserving"; they just happen, whether you earn them or not.

Because of this, people who experience shocks are usually more dazed and confused than those whose lives are changed by opportunity or inward transition. It may take several weeks or even months before they finally really understand that their lives will never be the same. If this is the kind of change catalyst you're facing, be especially kind about giving yourself time to adjust. Don't try to force yourself to do or feel anything just because you think you should. You may be numb and unmoved after a tragedy, or blandly unimpressed by some wondrous windfall. That's okay. Your life has fractured with the suddenness of an earthquake, and your mind will need time to catch up.

One thing you must remember after a shock is that you should *make no big decisions until the dust has settled*. This is true for anyone in Square One, as we'll see in a few pages, but it's especially important if you didn't see your life-changing event coming. There are actually people who seek out folks who've just experienced huge shocks, in order to take advantage of their confusion and muddled thinking. Unscrupulous personal-injury lawyers chase ambulances to the hospital, hoping to latch on to a newly widowed spouse or a client who's just had his head stapled shut. Corrupt financial managers pop in on lottery winners, pushing them to make choices before they know enough to handle their fortunes wisely. If you've been through a shock, *tell these people you need time to think—a lot of it—before you decide on any course of action*. Financial planner Suze Orman suggests that you ask a close friend or loved one to help you pay even regular bills when your life's been turned upside down. Buy as much time as you possibly can simply by telling people you can't commit until you know more about this new life you've barely entered.

This isn't quite as crucial if your change catalyst is an opportunity, rather than a shock. You're more likely to see the opportunity coming, since you probably will have been working to make it happen. This is true even if the opportunity is unexpected. At age thirty-one, my client Tyler had already made a small fortune in finance but was afraid he couldn't succeed at anything else. "I don't know how to create my own career," he admitted, "because everything I've accomplished so far just fell in my lap." It's true that Tyler was recruited right out of college and that he'd received promotion after promotion in his firm. But none of these opportunities "fell in his lap." Tyler was pursued by hiring personnel because he'd worked his proverbial butt off to get good grades throughout his education. He kept climbing the promotion ladder because he'd done his job conscientiously and diligently every single day. If you put in the effort, opportunities are going to come along from time to time. Expect it.

Of course, just because you've worked for an opportunity doesn't mean that it isn't going to rock your boat. Think of Jennifer, curled up on my couch, celebrating her big opportunity with a tsunami of abject woe and fear. Especially fear. In some ways, opportunity catalysts can be even more terrifying than shocks. After all, if fate deals you a totally unforeseen blow, all anyone will expect you to do is survive and cope. A huge opportunity, on the other hand, *always* means a huge challenge.

Congratulations, the adoption papers went through! You're getting a baby! You're flooded with joy—and panic, because you suddenly realize that now you have to raise a child. Wow! You just won an architectural contract to design a massive, innovative, technologically complex building! Oh, my God, now you have to design a massive, innovative, technologically complex building. Hurray! Your book proposal has been purchased by a publishing house! Now sit down to write the actual book. Do you feel just a smidgen of anxiety, the sort that makes you want to puke all over your computer? Yeah, me too. To be a true change catalyst, an opportunity has to stretch you way beyond your limits. And that means *fear.* If you're dealing with a major opportunity that scares you witless, go back to "If Your Emotional Compass Reads 'Fear' " in Chapter 9. Use your passion for this opportunity, your love for your own North Star, and your anger at anything that has held you back so far to help blast through the panic and propel you toward your dreams.

Another emotion that can come on strong after an opportunity catalyst is guilt. As you accept your new challenge and your life begins to change, you'll inevitably leave people behind—people who may be jealous and angry because they want the opportunities you have. Even if you still hang out with your old crowd, you'll find that you don't fit in the same way. You no longer identify with the way your pals think, and the topics that fascinate them now seem irrelevant to you. I've seen this happen to client after client, and it can lead to a period of intense loneliness. Terrence was cruelly frozen out of his social group, a gang of unemployed actors, when he got the lead in a major theatrical production. Byron's friends were all smokers who talked constantly about their need to quit; but when Byron actually managed to kick the habit, his gang began to act uncomfortable and resentful. Sandy's relationship with her girlfriends focused on their mutual inability to find a good man. After Sandy fell in love, her old bosom buddies pointedly avoided her.

If this kind of thing happens to you, keep reminding yourself that the best way to help a drowning person is to learn to swim yourself. By mastering the skills and doing the work to reach your own North Star, you make yourself capable of helping other people reach theirs. Share your life-navigation strategies freely; this is far better than holding yourself back so that you and your loved ones can have matching sets of bitterness, regret, and disappointment. You'll find that some people grab on to the idea of pursuing their own North Stars, jump into Square One with you, and become even better friends. Those who are hobbled by fear, oppressive social selves, or the illusion of helplessness will continue to begrudge your success no matter what you do. Of course, you won't stop caring about these people, but don't wait for them to feel good about your success before you build the life you were meant to live.

Transition events are even more likely to cause social disruption—and intense self-doubt—than opportunities. When you change your whole life because of inner yearning, frustration, or excitement, there's no external force or prize to help other people accept your behavior. I don't think anyone understood when John and I quit our nice, stable university jobs to live on credit-card debt. We heard that the word among other faculty members was that we were trying to negotiate hefty salary increases. A few months later I was offered another, very lucrative academic position. I turned it down. As far as anyone else could see, there was no "good" (that is, external and material) reason for my behavior. Lord knows, my family needed the money. But I had reached the point where I absolutely could not go back into academic life. My body, my brain, and my heart all shut down every time I even considered it. Oh, the anxiety that flooded me as our debts mounted! Oh, the awkward explanations to relatives and friends! I called myself crazy a million times over, but I was finally tuned in to my true self, and it would not let me retrench.

This is what you'll experience if and when a transition pushes you out of one life and into the next. You'll be more fraught with indecision than people who receive shocks or opportunities. The fear of failure will be tremendous. There may also be shame, as you let go of your old status, income, or position in exchange for nothing but inner peace. If you're acting solely on the passions of your essential self, I guarantee most people will not understand—at least not in the short run. "Why can't you just keep your nose to the grindstone?" they'll wonder. "You're earning six figures, for God's sake—how bad can the job be?" Or, "Erma dear, I don't see why you can't make it work with Jack. He's such a polite young man." Or, "All right, if you're gay, you're gay, but why do you have to *tell* people about it? We'll help you decorate your closet so that you'll never, ever want to come out again."

After a time, you'll find these comments merely annoying. After a longer time, they'll just make you chuckle indulgently. But in the first throes of Square One, each accusation, question, or criticism will feel like a killing blow. To keep moving toward your own North Star under these adverse circumstances takes determination, courage, and a lot of hard, proactive work. Instead of hanging out with people who don't understand your behavior, spend a large proportion of your time creating an Everybody who's on your side. Make a daily—even hourly—habit of getting away, going inward, tuning in to your essential self, reading those internal compasses. Imagine going back to your old life, and pay attention to the visceral revulsion in your body and heart. You may even want to return to an old situation, just for a reality check; yes, things really were as bad as you remember them being.

Whatever you do to cope as you struggle to accept your own "death," stay in touch with the real you. Refuse to abandon your essential self, the way a great captain refuses to abandon his ship. Double-check your navigational equipment, plot your course, lash the wheel in place, and ride out the storm. You may take on a little water and lose a rope here or there, but if you're really headed toward your own North Star, you'll make it to smooth sailing with all your important parts intact.

MID-SQUARE ONE: THE THRESHOLD

Once you've gone through the initial task of realizing that your old life is over, you'll find yourself in the center of Square One. Welcome to the middle of nowhere. Since you've lost your old identity but haven't really embraced a new one, you're temporarily a kind of nobody. As old relationships and behaviors change, you'll have no one to cling to, and nothing to do. Nobody nowhere with no one and nothing. Doesn't that sound fun!

The bizarre, formless, zero-identity netherworld of Square One is what anthropologists call a "liminal period." *Limin* is Latin for "threshold," and a liminal period is a time when you're on the threshold between identities, neither inside nor out, neither one thing nor the other. During their initiation into adulthood, the Xhosa youths are not boys anymore, but they aren't yet men. An engaged couple are in a liminal period; they aren't exactly single, but they aren't exactly married, either. A pregnant woman isn't quite a mother, but she's not quite childless. And so on.

Liminal periods sound nice and tidy when you're discussing them in some dull anthropology seminar. Actually living through one is something else entirely. During most of Square One, you'll probably feel panicky, groundless, and desperate. Problems and complications seem to attack from all sides: big ones, little ones, strange and unfamiliar ones. You rush around in frenzied activity but feel as though you're getting absolutely nothing done. Here are some of the things you'll probably think a lot while negotiating this square:

"Oh, no!"

"Oh, *no!*"

"Oh, %★&#!"

"Where am I? What's happening?"

"I *can't* be here! This *can't* be happening!"

"What did I just do?"

"What am I doing?"

"What am I going to do?"

"Ghhaaaaaaaaaaaaaaa!"

This list is by no means comprehensive, but you get the general picture. Again, much of the disorientation, fear, and pain will be similar whether you've just gotten a lucky break (like Jennifer), or been brutally sklonked by some kind of catastrophe. My friend George was in college when his father's company went public, and George came into several million dollars. Because I didn't yet understand Square One, I was baffled when he developed devastating anxiety and depression. Did you see the film *The Shawshank Redemption*? In it, a long-term maximum-security convict tries to kill another prisoner to demonstrate that he, himself, is still a dangerous thug. Why? Because the old man's sentence is almost up, and he's afraid of being released into the outside world. When the system eventually sets this prisoner free anyway, he kills himself. This character is based on research, not just fantasy. That's how awful it can feel to be in Square One, even if your life change seems to be exactly what you should want most. Our whole lives, all the actions we take, are based on our concepts of who we are. Not knowing that one crucial fact undermines everything we feel, say, or do.

Coping on the Threshold

Fortunately, many of the awful feelings many folks experience in Square One come from a mind-set that can be changed. The following "to do" list includes the most important steps that will make your trip across the threshold less upsetting and more fruitful.

1. Instead of clinging to Square Four, read your internal compasses.

People on the threshold will try to crawl back into the past like an adult kangaroo scrambling desperately to fit more than its head into its mother's pouch. They'll try to hold on to the way of life they used to have, or else build an exact replica. Remember Lester and Sharon, the couple I mentioned in the last chapter, who rebounded from their divorce and pretended they were in happy, stable new relationships within about fifteen minutes? Eventually, they both realized it simply wasn't working—and you will, too, if you try this kind of emergency patch job.

When I was about ten, my older brother Tom, an accomplished diver, gave me some advice I've never forgotten. He told me that there are moments in life similar to a backward dive off the high platform, where you jump into thin air without even being able to see the pool, let alone the spot where you plan to enter it. In the middle of such a dive, Tom said, the temptation to twist around and look for the water is almost overwhelming. However, if you do this, you'll belly-flop so violently that your kidneys will shoot out of your nostrils and ricochet off horrified spectators. On the other hand, if you stretch out and hold your position, gravity will pull you around so that you make a perfect, painless entry.

Trying to re-create the recent past after a catalytic event is the equivalent of looking for the water during a dive. The way to create dynamics that will pull you into the right position is to begin paying very close attention to your internal compasses. Throughout this book I've given you lots of different ways to tune in to your essential self and learn how it feels to be on your true path. When you've been trying unsuccessfully to rebuild your old life, consider turning to these exercises instead. They are surprisingly comforting, and they set you up to create the best new life possible. I've never had a client who wasn't scared and disoriented in Square One; but not one has expressed regret about plotting a course based on internal compasses, either. The process works. Try it and see.

2. Make small moves; gather information.

Suppose an alien plasma-transmutor suddenly punctured the ceiling of the room you're sitting in right now, sucked you through an interstellar wormhole, and deposited you on the planet Zorg. Would it make sense to plan your distant future at this point? No. Your natural reaction would be to hunker down, protect yourself, and stare wildly around, trying to figure out what was going on.

This is the same basic strategy you should use whenever you're in an unfamiliar situation, whether that's a job, a living space, a relationship, or a stage of your own life cycle. A man I'll call Ned, the CEO of a multimillion-dollar firm, told me once that his success was based almost entirely on waiting until he had all the data before making any decisions in a new situation. Keep this in mind the next time a catalytic event knocks you out of your identity. I've already mentioned that you should never let someone push you into a major decision while you're going through the uncertainty of Square One. You should also avoid making commitments to *yourself* until you begin to experience symptoms of moving into Square Two (which will be discussed in the next chapter).

One of my first clients, Janet, had a new passion every week for about four months. During her first session, she told me she wanted to be a jazz pianist, and we started researching musical careers. The next week, her focus had shifted to ethnobotany. We went all out getting information on Ph.D. programs in that area. The next week, Janet was all excited about international dispute mediation. Then it was cooking. Then veterinary medicine. I wasted a lot of Janet's time before I understood that she was going through a "threshold" experience: trying on dozens of new identities to see how they fit. I should have backed off on the planning phase of her career until Janet found out which choices took root in her heart and began to grow.

When your whole life is changing, it's normal to have lots of ideas about what you might do. Rapid attention shifts are typical of liminal periods. Now is the time to *play* with these ideas, not to lock yourself into ironclad plans. Wait until an idea has felt right for a number of days or weeks before you commit to making it a part of your new life.

3. Stay present.

If you look at the graph of the change cycle, you'll see that Square One is a time for small moves, not big ones. Part of making small moves is keeping your attention focused on the here and now. Alcoholics Anonymous encourages recovering addicts to take life "one day at a time." If you've just experienced a major catalytic event, I'd suggest that you live about ten or fifteen minutes at a time. Don't even try to think more than a few days in advance, except maybe to plan dental appointments. You simply don't know who or what you're going to be in a few weeks, days, or even hours. You must live in the present.

As a platinum-card-carrying control freak, I know how hard this is. When my son was diagnosed with Down's syndrome, I spent sleepless weeks, before he was even born, trying to anticipate everything he and I might have to go through during his entire life. It's about as close as I've ever come to going completely insane, and believe me, that's saying something. A lot of the things I worried about did in fact happen, but you know what? I always have the resources to deal with whatever challenge Adam and I are facing at the moment. It's only when I try to anticipate the future that I feel like I'm losing my mind.

4. Don't mistake a Square One identity crisis for a signal
that you've made the wrong choice.

I've had many clients who connected with their essential selves, made major positive life changes, and then panicked when the chaos of Square One set in. These folks mistook the confusion of the liminal period for evidence that they'd made a colossal error. The right choice, they believed, would feel simply wonderful, from start to finish. I've seen such people call former bosses—bosses they detested with a fervency usually reserved for parasitic invertebrates—and beg to be allowed back into their old, unbearable jobs. I've watched them reunite with the kind of philandering, insensitive lovers who would give them syphilis, then steal their medication.

A little of this is inevitable, and you shouldn't be too hard on yourself if you "go back" a few times—or even many times. Eventually, you'll get it at a deep level: Your life has changed. *You* have changed. You can't go back to your old routine, your old identity, any more than you can fit into your baby clothes. Since you're not yet sure who you're becoming, you don't really have anything else to wear. You're going to feel mighty naked for a while. Moving forward may be scary, humiliating, and painful, but going back is impossible.

5. Reframe the way you think about identity loss.

Part of the reason Square One is so difficult for most of us is that we see loss of identity, temporary lack of direction, and a sense of unfamiliarity as terrible catastrophes, instead of typical and essential parts of personal growth. Like a woman who can handle the pain of childbirth once she knows it's normal, you can learn to recognize and accept the emotional agony of giving birth to a new you.

I try to describe Square One to all my clients—tell them what it is and how it feels—*before* they start a major life change. Then, when they hit the threshold and freak out, they can calm themselves down simply by saying, "Everything is fine. I'm just in Square One, is all. This is how it's *supposed* to feel." Once they start thinking this way, my clients quickly learn to distinguish the wild, raw, exhilarating feeling of starting a new life from the suffocating, deadening hopelessness of living the wrong life.

6. Remember and repeat the Square One Mantra.

A mantra, as you probably know, is a phrase you repeat over and over again to center yourself. Each of the four squares on the change cycle has its own mantra, but repeating the phrase for Square One is the most important. Here's how it goes:

> "I don't know what the hell is going on, and that's okay."

Say it with me, now: *"I don't know what the hell is going on, and that's okay."* You wouldn't believe how this affirmation can calm you down in the middle of Square One. It really is okay not to know what's happening. The real danger lies in pretending to know when you don't. Which leads me to my next point.

7. Manage the Kindergarten Complex.

My first day of kindergarten was great. There I was, five years old and utterly befuddled, but surrounded by adults who seemed to *expect* me to feel that way. The teachers were kind and patient, explaining everything very clearly as many times as I needed to hear it. All of us kindergartners were novices, but we knew that's exactly what we were supposed to be.

About two weeks later, my teachers and parents decided to bump me up a grade. The first day in my new class was nothing like the first day of kindergarten. All the other kids knew the teacher, knew each other, knew how the school-lunch process worked and where to put the playground equipment after recess. I didn't know any of that. Every time I made some kind of blunder, the other kids pointed and laughed and told me that I belonged back in kindergarten. It was just innocent ribbing—nothing I couldn't handle after several years of therapy—but it filled me with shame and self-doubt. For some time I suffered from the "Kindergarten Complex," the feeling that everybody else knew what they were doing, while I alone lacked the tiniest clue.

Innocent that I was, I thought nobody else felt this way. Now I know better. Almost everyone suffers from the Kindergarten Complex from time to time. In fact, the only people who don't are those who are so terrified of being a novice that they never try anything new. The danger of the Kindergarten Complex is not the sense of confusion or lack of information but the fact that *it tempts you to pretend you know what you're doing when you really don't.* Giving in to this temptation is almost always disastrous. I'm sure, for example, that Cloyd Liverfluke, the Printe Shoppe manager discussed in Chapter 9, lost his business simply because he wouldn't admit that he had no idea how to run it. His glib promises, his show of false confidence, and his belligerence when pressured are all typical reactions of someone who's pretending to understand more than he really does.

The way to deal with the Kindergarten Complex is very simple: Accept that you're a kindergartner. Learning about a new situation or task requires admitting—sometimes only to yourself, but often to others as well—that you are as rank a beginner as any five-year-old. You'll be amazed by how much you can learn if you start from this humble position. You'll also be happily surprised to find that most people react more like kind, sweet kindergarten teachers than bullying, insecure little kids. When you don't know what you're supposed to do—say, during your first day at a new job, or when you're driving around in an unfamiliar city—simply admit your ignorance and ask other people for information.

It's especially easy to mismanage the Kindergarten Complex if you're obsessed with protecting your social status. The higher a person's status, the more likely that person is to fake knowledge and understanding, especially around people they consider "lowly." Most men have a harder time asking for directions than most women do. Managers rarely admit confusion to their secretaries. Older people often struggle to hide their ignorance from youngsters. This is a big mistake. While the "superior" novice goes around looking arrogant and feeling like a scared five-year-old, all the "lower" people (who understand exactly what's going on) watch with hidden contempt. The counterintuitive truth is that if you acknowledge your ignorance to *everyone* who can help you, you'll not only get a grip on the situation much faster but also earn these people's friendship and respect. As Lao-tzu said, "All rivers flow to the sea because it is lower than they are. Humility gives it its strength."

8. Explore the magic of the threshold.

"What am I doing with my life? I don't know what I want to do. I don't know where I want to be. I don't know who I want to be with. And it's been *a whole week!*" I hear this kind of complaint over and over again. We modern Westerners, with our puritanical work ethic and obsession with forward progress, tend to think the limbo of Square One is intolerable and unnatural. We're wrong. Other cultures, whose members think in terms of the cyclical death-and-rebirth pattern that dominates all of nature, have a lot to teach us about this phase of change.

Many "primitive" cultures designate thresholds as magical places, powerful nowhere-lands in which human beings can accomplish things we could never do anywhere else. People on thresholds, both literal and figurative, are acknowledged to suffer terribly from the lonely, uncertain psychological free fall of losing their identity. On the other hand, they're also said to have special powers, like the ability to change shape, become invisible, or travel effortlessly in any direction. Being nobody nowhere, they can become anything and go anywhere. On the threshold, your essential self has more freedom than at any other time or place.

Instead of scurrying around trying to get out of your own liminal period, try exploring its possibilities. Consider just letting yourself relax into the "not-thinking" and "not-doing" Taoist masters worked so hard to achieve. It really is in the still and curious world of the threshold that the true self emerges, that we find ourselves and the purposes of our lives. Some people call this enlightenment. If you're just calling it awful, look deeper. Sit with the nothingness until your fear fades. Watch what—and who—emerges.

LATE SQUARE ONE: REBIRTH

You may remember A. A. Milne's story about Winnie the Pooh, Piglet, and Rabbit getting lost in the Hundred Acre Wood. Under Rabbit's bossy, officious guidance, the three go around and around until they're thoroughly lost and terrified of lurking Heffalumps. Eventually, a disgusted Rabbit leaves Pooh and Piglet and goes to find the way home. He never returns. After a while, Pooh turns to Piglet:

> "Come on, Piglet, let's go home."
> "But we're lost," said Piglet.
> "Yes," said Pooh, "but there are twelve pots of honey in my cupboard at home, and they are calling to my tummy. I couldn't hear them before, because Rabbit would talk."

This is what happens to someone who settles into the threshold of Square One, stops fighting the process, and accepts the strange formlessness of the situation. The chattering, Rabbit-like social self gets so frustrated and disoriented that it finally wanders away. Then something else comes through: a silent sweetness that resonates deep in your essential self, your pots of honey calling to your tummy.

A Love Affair with Your Real Life

I've compared Square One to falling endlessly, because it really does feel that way. Despite the unpleasant aspects of this sensation, there's one kind of "falling" we all want: the experience of falling in love. If this has ever happened to you—and I certainly hope it has—take a second right now to remember what it was like. You probably felt a bit out of control; your feet hardly seemed to touch the ground; you were swept along in a tide of strange, overwhelming new experiences—*and it was wonderful*. In fact, it's probably the best feeling you've ever had, right? Well, if you can hang in there, grieving the losses and bearing the confusion of early and mid–Square One, you're going to start feeling this way about your whole life.

Back when I was doing sociology, I interviewed hundreds of women about major turning points in their lives. I noticed that the women who had been through some sort of identity "meltdown" almost always fell in love during the process. The object of their affection wasn't always another person; some fell in love with a profession, a religious vocation, a style of music, even a sport. Whatever it was, it changed them. It drew them onto a new path, urged them to spend time doing things they'd never done before. I used to think this happened because the people in question were broken and vulnerable. Now I think that their "meltdowns" temporarily dissolved their social selves, setting their essential selves free.

Your essential self *always* tells you what it wants by making you feel absolutely entranced. You get to have that "falling in love" feeling over and over again, without necessarily endangering your current relationship. The magnetism of your own North Star, the life you were meant to live, is close enough to sexual desire to confuse people who haven't learned the difference. Wanda found herself so wildly attracted to a guitarist in a jazz club that she asked him out, "like a damn groupie," she told me. But once she got to know him, Wanda realized that the guy himself wasn't her interest—she felt crazed with longing only when he was actually playing the guitar. From there it was just a short hop to realizing that Wanda herself had a long-buried desire to play jazz. She now performs regularly in the small club where she discovered herself.

I remember when I started writing my first nonacademic book, a memoir called *Expecting Adam*. I was working on my Ph.D. dissertation at the time, and both documents were stored in the same laptop computer. I literally felt as though I were married to my dissertation and having an affair with the other book. I'd turn on my computer, fully intending to work on my dissertation . . . and there it would be, my memoir, blowing kisses and whispering sweet nothings to my essential self. When I clicked on the "book" document instead of the "dissertation" icon, my pulse would speed up. I'd get a little dizzy and short of breath. This may be evidence of something deeply kinky and Freudian, but I have to tell you, it felt *great*.

I truly believe that following this kind of essential-self delirium will not only make you happy but take you straight to the greatest career successes, relationships, and ideas you can possibly have. The people and things that thrill your essential self will be exactly what you need to achieve your highest potential. Can I prove this? Of course not. You're going to have to test my theory yourself, and you'll never have a better chance than when you're in Square One.

As you wander around the nothingness of the threshold, follow your internal compasses *no matter where they take you*. If you feel an irresistible urge to cook lentils, or buy an aquarium, or watch a twenty-four-hour Mary Tyler Moore–athon, I truly believe that's the quickest route to the life you were meant to live. For a while, you might not see how this is going to work. That's okay. Just keep doing what feels most joyful, and eventually, in ways you never imagined, you'll come upon your own North Star.

Going on a Vision Quest: Noticing, Narrowing, Naming

The Xhosa aren't the only people who deliberately create Square One conditions as a way of helping people find their identities. For example, some American Indian tribes send young men out on "vision quests." These men leave their names and their childhoods back at the hearth fire and go into the wilderness alone, surviving as best they can until Something Happens. They aren't told what the Something will be, only that they'll know it when they experience it. It may be a dream, a storm, an encounter with a wild animal, or simply a mental epiphany. Whatever it is, this Something tells the vision quester who he is, and perhaps a bit about his mission in life. Then and only then, he goes back to the tribe. He tells them his new name, the name of his essential self, which he discovered on his own.

Every time a catalytic event forces you to let go of your identity, you have the chance to go on a vision quest. As the world spins crazily around you, pay attention to what I call the "three N's": noticing what you love, narrowing your focus, and, finally, naming the thing you most desire, the identity that fits as though it's custom-tailored.

Deanna did this on her own, almost by accident. She was in her mid-forties when her husband of thirty years left her. As she was groping around the ruins of her old life, she noticed something rather odd. "I started feeling something in my hands," she told me. "A sort of energy. I think it was always there, but I hadn't noticed it before. I knew this energy had to . . . I don't know . . . come out, somehow. I had to do something with it."

One day (and Deanna can tell you the exact date, since it was in a very real sense her "birth day") Deanna's daughter took her to get a massage. Deanna had always been a corporate type, and the concept of someone getting paid to rub other people's backs seemed "different," if not downright strange.

"I don't even remember the massage therapist's name," says Deanna, "but when I left there I felt so good. I remember thinking, 'What would it be like to have a job where people felt great after dealing with you, instead of worried or upset or stressed?' I wanted a job like that."

Deanna had now noticed two key things that obviously (in hindsight, anyway) had a lot to do with each other: the energy in her hands and her desire to make people feel the way she did after a massage. Over the next several months, Deanna found her interests focusing in on anything related to therapeutic massage. This was the "narrowing" phase of her vision quest. When she heard about a type of therapeutic massage called "rolfing," Deanna's new preoccupation finally had the last of the three N's, a name. Though she knew very little about this weird-sounding skill, she sold her home, gave away all her clothes, and drove her blue Honda from Canada to a Colorado school that taught people to rolf.

"It was totally unlike anything I'd ever done before my husband left," Deanna told me. "I wasn't into massage, or healing, or anything like that. I barely knew I had a body at the time—I'd been living from the neck up my entire life."

It turned out that Deanna had a gift for therapeutic touch that went beyond her younger, more experienced classmates. I can tell you this from personal experience. I interviewed Deanna after undergoing my own rolfing session. As a veteran of long-term chronic pain, I've tried just about every kind of physical therapy available. But I've never experienced anything quite like the energy that comes from Deanna's hands. I went to her in the throes of a major back spasm. As soon as Deanna touched me, all the affected muscles in my body began to hum with something that felt like very low frequency sound waves, both subtle and intense.

"Good Lord," I said. "Who are you, Electric Eel Woman?"

Deanna just laughed. "Well, I'm doing what I was meant to do."

When you're doing what you're meant to do, you benefit the world in a unique and irreplaceable way. This brings money, friendship, true love, inner peace, and everything else worth having; it sounds facile, but it's really true. Richard Nelson Bolles, the author of the perennial best-seller *What Color Is Your Parachute?*, puts it this way: "Your mission in life is where your deep joy and the world's deep hunger meet." If you haven't identified your own "deep joy," you can find it in Square One, just by following your internal compasses.

Remember the exercise where you listed the things you "are"? Well, now I'd like to see if you can finish the following sentence:

"I was always meant to be a/an _____."

The moment you can answer this with a sense of powerful, centered rightness is the moment of your rebirth. It will give you your new name, the name you will take back to your people. It signals your readiness to move into the rest of the change cycle. Do this right, and soon there'll be no difference between what you are and what you were always meant to be. You'll be living on your own North Star.

13

SQUARE TWO:
DREAMING AND
SCHEMING

We are such stuff as dreams are made on.

—WILL S.

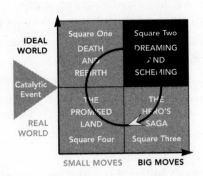

THE CHANGE CYCLE

When you wake up that morning, it doesn't feel like anything special is about to happen. For a while after *it,* you expected something dramatic to come along any minute and make you feel better, but gradually, as the months went by, you stopped waiting for miracles. I don't know what *it* was for you—a breakup, a job loss, a health crisis, that unfortunate incident at the petting zoo—but it killed you, killed your hopes and confidence and deepest beliefs. Since that "death," you've been barely holding yourself together, mustering the energy to put one foot in front of the other when you're not leaning up against a wall to let another wave of grief and longing surge through you. Sure, you've read a lot of stuff like the last chapter, things that talk about rebirth and vision quests and all that. You'd even like to believe them. But frankly, it all sounds a like a smarmy, culturally exploitative fairy tale.

And then, later that morning, maybe while you're on the subway or sipping your favorite Starbucks blend, something different happens. It isn't spectacular, or even obvious, but it's noticeably new. Perhaps a stranger gives you a quick smile, and you find yourself not only smiling back but, just for a second, imagining going out with this person on a date. You pass that restored Victorian house you've always thought was so beautiful, but this time you find yourself thinking, "I wonder how much it costs." You're rewriting yet another report that was ruined by the assistant from Hell when it occurs to you that a pink slip is not just J. Edgar Hoover's favorite undergarment. In other words, tiny suggestions about the future begin showing up in your mind and heart, like the tips of crocuses poking themselves through last winter's mildewed compost.

SQUARE TWO SYMPTOMS

Hope—real, spontaneous hope, with its accompanying excitement and delight—is the key signal that you're moving out of Square One and into Square Two of the change cycle. Hope involves a sense of desire and possibility directed toward the future. During "death and rebirth," you don't feel this. The logistical and psychological dynamics of Square One make the future seem utterly inscrutable, forcing you to act on faith and prior experience, not anticipation. If you try to *make* yourself hope before you've had enough time for grieving, disorientation, and self-discovery, you'll become like those desperately cheerful people who tell everyone how *glad* they are that they were sued by their business partners, or jilted at the altar, or mugged by nuns, because they got rid of so many *illusions* and moved on to so many *opportunities* and where do you keep the vodka?

The visions of the future that signal the beginning of Square Two aren't so self-conscious. They arrive without effort or expectation, from the very core of your essential self. They have an almost ticklish quality; they make you smile or hum even when there's no one around to be impressed. At first, these feelings will make an appearance, then vanish for days or weeks before another sighting. But when you feel authentic hope, even intermittently, you can be confident that the most difficult part of the change cycle is behind you.

Though spontaneous images of the future are the single most important symptom that you've arrived in Square Two, there are many others. No two people experience exactly the same complex of symptoms, and only the spontaneous dreaming is a true indicator. However, you'll probably notice some of these as you arrive at Square Two.

1. You Laugh More Easily and More Often

People in Square One may laugh out of courtesy, or sometimes with a kind of harsh graveyard humor. They don't experience the bubbly laughter you see in happy little kids, who are expressing joy rather than cleverness or sarcasm. In fact, when you're in Square One, laughing tends to feel more obligatory than irrepressible. That changes when you get to Square Two. Your own laughter will begin to surprise you, popping up all by itself when you least expect it.

Diane's controlling parents had never really let her grow up. By the time she reached thirty, she had stored up an enormous amount of anger and resistance, without ever actually defying her parents. After getting in touch with her essential self, Diane began making small independent decisions, a practice her folks did not appreciate *at all*. Diane went through a rough Square One as she abandoned the identity of Docile Daughter and took the accompanying flak.

One day, a few months into this process, Diane was supposed to attend a cousin's wedding. She hated formal functions and barely knew the bride and groom, but there was no doubt her parents would be furious if she didn't show up. In the subway, en route to the reception, Diane bumped into an old high school boyfriend, Tim. They'd barely begun to chat when the train reached Diane's station. She was having a wonderful time, and the thought of saying good-bye to Tim and proceeding to the wedding brought a huge *"No!"* response from Diane's essential self. So she stayed on the train. She and Tim had lunch together at a sushi restaurant, where they sat on the floor in traditional Japanese style.

"Halfway through lunch," Diane told me later, "Tim told some kind of joke—I don't remember it, it really wasn't all that funny—and I started laughing, and I couldn't stop. I laughed so hard that I flopped over backward onto the floor and started rolling around. It went on for at least ten minutes. I could hardly breathe. All I could feel was this incredible rush of joy. I felt so free."

This is Square Two laughter, a spontaneous outburst of effervescent happiness. Some of my clients, like Diane, have little or no prior experience with this feeling. Even in childhood, the forces opposing their true selves were so powerful and pervasive that there was no room for the jollity that produces giggling fits in most babies and toddlers. One of the best things about my job is watching people move into Square Two and discover, or rediscover, this kind of laughter.

2. You Want to Do Things You've Never Done

Don't be surprised if, after surviving a catalytic event and moving through Square One, you suddenly develop an urge to do something utterly new. Very few people can predict what they're going to want to do when Square Two finally arrives. Once your essential self has been freed, it may decide to take up flamenco dancing, or wildlife photography, or French cooking. These aren't necessarily career choices. They're just the things you sample as you begin to realize that you don't have to be controlled by the old pressures and forces, that life is a smorgasbord and you're free to sample whatever looks most delicious.

Stan, a fund-raiser for a nonprofit organization, had a charming exterior wrapped around a core of crippling self-doubt. His insecurity made Stan something of a doormat in his relationship with his wife, an ambitious executive who paid about as much attention to Stan as she did to the planet Neptune. Over thirteen years of marriage, Stan's wife became more and more focused on her job, and Stan grew more and more lonely. It finally got bad enough to push Stan into Square One.

After trying a few months of couples therapy, which turned into singles therapy when his wife invariably failed to show up, he finally filed for divorce.

I met Stan just as he was moving into Square Two, and it was like meeting Ebenezer Scrooge on that famous Christmas morning. After grieving his failed marriage, Stan had entered a period of exuberant self-discovery. He'd rafted the Colorado River, earned a pilot's license, hiked a five-hundred-mile wilderness trail, and made plans for a whole lot of other adventures. This wasn't a desperate attempt to remain youthful or prove something to his ex-wife; Stan was simply having fun. He came to one of my seminars because of the nagging belief that he needed to buckle down and get serious or he'd end up forfeiting his career. Of course, the truth was that Stan's career was in better shape than ever—his new joie de vivre made him an irresistible fund-raiser. The other seminar participants, instead of suggesting ways for Stan to shut down his new life, helped him figure out a way to leave the very next week on a trip to India. He probably went a lot farther than that before he was finished with Square Two.

3. Your Creativity Returns

Along with new activities, Square Two ushers in a host of new ideas. Lila is a sixty-year-old writer who had always resented the fact that her job as a registered nurse gave her little time to develop her endless supply of creative ideas. Her retirement was supposed to be the time when she could settle in and write, but from the day she left the workforce, Lila became utterly blocked. She was afraid that some cruelly ironic muse had destroyed her talent, but Lila's sudden loss of creativity was part of a normal change cycle. She needed to let go of her identity as a working nurse and establish a new one, and her essential self wasn't about to start composing poetry until these crucial tasks were completed. Sure enough, after a year, Lila felt the urge to write again. In fact, her recent trip through Square One made her work all the more inventive and resonant once she reached Square Two.

Creativity is one of the hallmarks of Square Two, the "dreaming and scheming" part of the change cycle. Expect it to show up on its own schedule, and don't panic while you wait. Original thinking comes back to the Square Two mind as reliably as the swallows return to Capistrano, without the guano problems.

4. You Change Your Clothes

I realize that some of my more fastidious readers probably change their clothes on an almost daily basis—but when you get to Square Two, you really *change* your clothes. "I open my closet these days," a client told me just this morning, "and I don't see anything that looks like it belongs to me. It's as though someone else bought those clothes." This is an almost universal Square Two experience. When one of my starched, buttoned-down clients shows up in sweatpants and sandals, or a drab dresser suddenly starts wearing colors that stop traffic, I know I'm watching someone cross the threshold and embrace a new identity.

5. You Change Your Hair

An astonishingly high percentage of my clients not only alter their clothing style as they move into Square Two but also do something drastically different with their hair. I never suggest this, or even mention it. When they come in sporting a Mohawk or a new perm, I ask them why they made the change. They always say something like, "I don't know, I just got sick of it the way it was. I needed something new."

Very few of these folks articulate that they're altering their social identity when they grow a beard or start wearing little satin bows in their hair (or both), but that's exactly what they're doing. Hairstyle isn't a trivial thing from a sociological perspective; it's one of the most important signals by which we tell each other who we are, and where we fit into the culture. Think about it: A hairstyle that would make you a welcome guest on the Christian Broadcast Network would look ridiculous at a gay bar, and vice versa. The way you wear your hair is a major part of establishing your identity.

6. You Remodel, Redecorate, or Renovate Your Living Space

If you've ever had a baby, you might remember a surge of domestic energy hitting you a few days before the first labor pain. If you're male or childless, you'll have to take my word for this. It's weird; you've been lying around for months, exhibiting all the vibrant energy of a salted slug—and then, just as you reach the point where you get exhausted just watching your ankles swell, you suddenly develop an overwhelming urge to, oh, say, dig a new cellar. I know a mother of eight who varnished the entire exterior of her wood-shingled house, single-handedly, two days before her last baby popped out. Her husband tried to stop her, but she was moving too fast. "Nesting" is truly a natural wonder.

I don't know if something hormonally similar accompanies the transition to a new identity, but I've certainly watched a lot of clients go into decorating frenzies in Square Two. Some of them get so excited about it that they bring in snapshots of their apartments for show-and-tell. I always nod and cluck admiringly, knowing that their fixation with home improvement is a sign that their new identity is taking hold, their new life truly beginning.

The psychologist, writer, and former monk Thomas Moore believes that our living spaces are a direct representation of our souls. Every time we choose something to put in our homes, from new wallpaper to a bar of soap, that choice reflects our personalities and psychological condition. Moore sometimes goes to his clients' houses as a way of "reading" their inner lives. I remember telling my client Suzanne about this. "That's ridiculous," she sniffed. "My house couldn't possibly be a reflection of my inner life. I have three kids and a husband to think about. The whole house is arranged around *their* needs, not mine, and—" She fell silent for a long minute, then said, "Oh, my. It's really true, isn't it?"

It really is. When you begin spontaneously choosing a new "look" for your living space, pay attention. You're creating a self-portrait of the new you, and moving solidly into early Square Two.

EARLY SQUARE TWO: THE DREAMTIME

As you begin to notice symptoms of Square Two, you'll also see your attention naturally shifting from small, adaptive moves to longer-term plans. Your grieving periods will become shorter and less intense, then disappear altogether. Some people grow perversely comfortable with the drama and chaos of Square One, enjoying the powerful emotions and the attention they get from sympathetic others. These folks may actually resist when their energy begins to move away from grief-stricken disorientation and into creating a new future. When this starts happening to you, just remember to "do without doing." Let go of Square One and follow the flow of your essential self as it moves into the dreamtime.

Dreamtime is a translation of the word Australian Aborigines use to describe the magical, altered reality of night dreams. (We Westerners prefer the term *REM sleep,* since rapid eye movement, unlike dream content, is something that, by God, we can *measure.*) It's confusing that English uses the same word—*dream*—to denote both involuntary night visions and conscious fantasies. I once saw a magazine ad that proclaimed, IF YOU CAN DREAM IT, YOU CAN DO IT. This is obviously hog waste. For example—this is true—I recently dreamed that I was showering in a luxury hotel when President Clinton climbed into the tub, wearing nothing but a hopeful expression. My first reaction was to think that this man must be really, truly desperate. My next was to say, in a polite but firm tone, "I'm very flattered, Mr. President. But I think you should know that I have a black belt in karate." So Bill climbed out of the tub and went to feed his pet owl, which naturally was living in the fire extinguisher.

Now, I'm sorry, but this is just not going to happen in the real world—I don't think Mr. Clinton even *likes* owls. However, the obverse of the "dream it, do it" statement does work for me, and I'd like you to memorize it right now:

IF YOU CAN'T DREAM IT, YOU CAN'T DO IT.

I've seen this a thousand times with my clients: As long as they can't imagine doing something, it's genuinely impossible for them. I once challenged a very self-sacrificing friend to name a genuine desire. After much thought, she decided that she wanted licorice. We went right over to a store that sold good licorice toffee for two dollars a box, and I urged her to go wild and buy herself some. "Oh, I couldn't," she said—and she really couldn't. She kept approaching the counter, then veering off in a dither of anxiety. Eventually, she put the box back on the shelf and left the store. Only after going home and visualizing herself buying the licorice was she able to overcome her psychological block.

You have to prepare for the major life changes of Square Three by dreaming, and dreaming big. This means valuing and nourishing every dream that pops into your head during Square Two—even if they seem like far-out night dreams rather than plausible daydreams. You'll never miss out on happiness, success, money, or love because you dream the impossible, but you may if you limit your imagination to the possible.

TO DREAM THE POSSIBLE DREAM . . .

Simon was a handsome young man with a life he might have ordered from a catalog. He had a nice nine-to-five job, a nice apartment, several nice suits and ties. The only problem was that Simon felt nice and dead. Against his own will, his essential self was trying to change everything. His performance at work began slipping. He argued with his landlord. He couldn't understand why he was messing up such an ideal situation.

During our first session, I asked Simon to go into his imagination and dream up the wildest, most wonderful life he could imagine. After a few minutes of intense thought, he said, "Well, I guess I'd get up and go to work every day. I'd have a different car. Maybe a Toyota. Toyotas are good cars. I'd work until the afternoon. I'd get a good salary. Then I'd go home and have dinner and go to bed."

I squinted at Simon. "That's the most fabulous life you can imagine?"

He blushed as he realized this was the Wrong Answer. "Well, okay," he said, thinking furiously, "maybe in the evening, after work, I'd watch TV for a while."

That was it: Simon's wildest dream. Feel free to take a whiff of smelling salts if you're overcome by the excitement.

The strange thing was that Simon had a fascinating past. He'd run away from home at sixteen to fish for salmon in Alaska, saved up a lot of cash, then spent a couple of years as a Grateful Dead roadie. He'd had more adventures than three typical people his age—so what had happened to his imagination?

The answer is that Simon had lived through the pain of losing a couple of dreams. A rock band he'd started never really came together, and his first serious love affair didn't work out. This double whammy had hurt so much that since living through it, Simon had poured huge amounts of energy into *limiting* his dreams. He wanted to avoid more disappointments by keeping every hope within the realm of the possible. Judging by the fact that you're reading this book, I'd say there's a fair probability you've done something similar.

A real dream, a wild and strange and true dream like those that occur during early Square Two, very rarely seems possible. When you confide such dreams to the average bear, you probably hear something like this:

CLASSIC DREAM DASHERS

"Why on earth would you want to do *that?*"

"Oh, right. As if you had that kind of talent."

"Nobody's ever done it before."

"Do you realize how much *work* that would take?"

"Do you realize how much *luck* that would take?"

"C+."

"Ha ha ha ha ha ha!"

Most of us run into these dream dashers repeatedly, beginning in early childhood. Virtually every kid runs up against disappointed or frightened grown-ups, powerful authority figures who feel terrible anxiety when they recognize their own, long-lost essential selves in the dreams of a child. Like Simon, these adults have decided that there are certain Rules for Life. Any dream found in violation of these Rules is by definition impossible and must be destroyed. Until you reject this prejudice against your own dreams, I guarantee they won't come true.

GETTING BACK TO IMPOSSIBILITY

In Lewis Carroll's *Through the Looking Glass,* the irascible White Queen has a daily regimen that includes doing "six impossible things before breakfast." You don't have to push that hard, but to reach your own North Star you'll probably have to do at least a few impossible things a month. You'll find out what those things are when you reach Square Two of the change cycle. Here are some exercises I use to help clients blast through internalized limitations and reconnect with their true dreams. (Remember, these exercises won't do you much good if you're still in Square One. They're most effective after you've begun experiencing spontaneous hope.)

1. Repeat the Square Two Mantra

The first step in recovering your dreams is to memorize and repeat the Square Two Mantra:

> There are no rules, and that's okay.

If this doesn't ring quite true to you, you may use the Deluxe Industrial-Strength Square Two Mantra: *Screw the rules.* This doesn't mean that you take all constraints off your behavior; it means that you begin operating out of the curiosity and passion of your essential self, rather than the fear and propriety of your social self.

EXERCISE: WHIZZING ON THE ELECTRIC FENCE

The rules in your mind are like psychological electric fences that keep you from consciously engaging your real dreams. Instead of railing at them, I'd like you to start treating them with profound disrespect, and ultimately trampling right over them. To start, please complete the following sentences.

"If I didn't care what people thought, I would _____

_____."

"If I were sure I'd succeed, I would _____

_____."

"If I had the nerve, I would _____

_____."

"If I could be certain it was the right choice, I would ____

_____

_____."

"If I weren't worried about the future, I would _____

_____."

"If I had the freedom, I would _____

_____."

Now I'd like you to choose one of your answers that is neither illegal nor physically dangerous, and *do it*. Right now, before you're sure that it's fail-safe, or acceptable, or risk-free. When you're finished with that item, pick another one, and do that one too. Yes, I know you'll be breaking the Rules. I don't care. The needs for certainty and permission are the electric fences in your mind. Which would be worse: whizzing all over them or permanently forfeiting *all* of the things you wrote on the list above?

I used to give this assignment to whole classes full of college freshmen, and we had a passel of fun. My students did everything from distributing condoms at Sunday school to singing in the streets. One young woman, raised in an excruciatingly proper household, went home for Thanksgiving vacation and ate the entire holiday dinner with her hands. Her whole family stared in horror, but no one said anything until they were serving the pumpkin pie, at which point the student's father leapt up, screamed, *"I can't take this! I can't take this!"* and rushed from the room. It created quite a follow-up scene, as the family had its first frank and open discussion in memory. Repeat after me: *There are no rules, and that's okay.* Now go.

2. Defrosting

After Simon revealed his dazzling fantasy of being a hardworking, TV-watching Toyota owner, we spent a couple of sessions trying to get him to explore the Dreamtime. During our third meeting, Simon suddenly began to talk about his days as an Alaskan salmon catcher. He told me about a trip where he'd worked around the clock in subzero temperatures and a constant spray of seawater. By the time this ordeal was over, his fingers and toes were black with frostbite. "I didn't feel them after they froze," Simon commented. "But when they thawed out—now, that *hurt*."

As often happens during a life-design session, Simon was unconsciously talking in metaphors. You see, relinquishing your dreams wouldn't be a problem if they simply died, but they don't. The only way to get rid of a real dream is to deprive it of light and warmth until it freezes, then stuff it into the coldest corner of your soul. Unlived dreams don't hurt much as long as they stay frozen. But when they start to thaw—oh, baby. All the pain of that frigid exile comes rushing back. I can tell you from observation, as well as experience, that people don't cry when they lose their hope. They cry when they get it back.

To avoid this pain, you may be tempted to keep your dreams in the deep freeze forever. But it's far better to thaw out your dreams, endure the agony, shed the tears, and regain the full use of your frostbitten heart. Here's an exercise that might help.

EXERCISE: DEFROSTING YOUR DREAMS

This exercise is similar to the popular tool called an "affirmation"—a positive phrase you say to yourself over and over. I don't know about you, but for me affirmations always have a backlash effect. When I walk around saying something like "Every day, in every way, I'm getting better and better," I get steadily more manic for about two hours, at which point something in my brain goes "pop!" and I find myself crouching in a corner mainlining Rocky Road ice cream. I've had far more success with the following version, adapted from an exercise creativity consultant Julia Cameron calls "blurts."

To begin, find a notebook and something to write with. Take these tools to a comfortable place where you won't be disturbed for at least half an hour. Ideally, it should be a place outside your home: a playground, a restaurant, a mountain road. Once you're there, take a few relaxing breaths, climb fully into your body, and focus your attention on your internal compasses. Then search inside yourself for the memory of an abandoned hope. Do you wish your dead mother were here to comfort you? Do you want your amputated leg back? Think of something you truly want that is truly impossible. Write it down at the top of your page.

Now draw a line down the center of the page, below your dream. On the left side of the line, write the following sentence, while holding your dead dream in your mind and heart.

"My dream is coming true."

You will get an immediate response from your analytical mind, which will say something like "COW CRAP." Write that response on the right side of your paper, across from the first sentence. Then, just below the first sentence on the left side of the page, write it again:

"My dream is coming true."

Your brain will give you another negative response: "Get thee behind me, Satan." Write it. Move down a line and repeat the whole sequence. Keep this up for a while, and you'll see that the sentences on the right are different each time. Continue as long as you're getting new answers.

Below is an actual selection from Simon's "defrosting" exercise. The first dream he chose was his lost relationship with his girlfriend, Rose. After breaking up with him, she'd gone on to marry somebody else, making Simon's dream of being her partner solidly impossible. *That didn't matter.* This exercise isn't meant to realize your dreams in exactly the way you expect. Its effect is to free your imagination and revive your hope by embracing the impossible. Here's part of Simon's list:

DREAM:
I WISH I COULD BE WITH ROSE

1. My dream is coming true.	Rose doesn't love me.
2. My dream is coming true.	She's married.
3. My dream is coming true.	You're crazy.
4. My dream is coming true.	Now I'm getting pissed.
5. My dream is coming true.	NO I CAN'T, #*&%!
6. My dream is coming true.	I wish that were so.
7. My dream is coming true.	I wanted it so much.
8. My dream is coming true.	It was her mistake.
9. My dream is coming true.	She really loved me.
10. My dream is coming true.	Hers isn't, but mine is.

You can see how Simon's gut response moved from hopelessness (frozen dream) to argument (some thawing) to anger (serious defrost) to grief (feeling is coming back). Simon's breakthrough phrase is number 8: "It was her mistake." This may not sound like an earthshaking comment to you, but it changed Simon's fundamental outlook. After writing it, he looked up from his notebook as though he'd just solved the riddle of the Sphinx. Immediately, his essential self sent up a couple of truths he'd frozen out of consciousness: 1) Rose had loved him all along; 2) It was her fear, not any failure of Simon's, that had trashed their relationship.

Even though Rose wasn't in his life, this knowledge was deeply comforting to Simon. This wasn't because Simon *wanted* his responses on this exercise to be true, but because they *were* true. I've seen many clients achieve the same deep release when they came up with truths like "I really screwed up" or "My parents don't give a damn about me." Forcing yourself to think happy lies doesn't heal your dreams. Getting to the truth does. For some reason, this exercise speeds up the process more than any other tool I've ever used. It breaks up the permafrost in your soul, so that your dreams can find fulfillment in unexpected ways. In Simon's case, it gave him the confidence and peace to start dating again. Not long afterward, he established a relationship that really did fulfill his romantic dreams.

3. The Interview Game

This is a visualization game similar to the "future vision" I discussed in Chapter 10. First, imagine that you've moved forward in time. It's anywhere from a year to several decades in the future. You've just picked up a fresh, new copy of a glossy magazine, and—oh, look—the picture on the cover is a portrait of you! The headline promises an article, written by a well-known interviewer, that will tell readers all kinds of interesting things about your life and times.

Now I'm going to ask you some questions, and I want you to answer them not by thinking but by opening up this magazine in your mind and reading the answers from it. You might want to write these answers down on a separate piece of paper. Again, *don't think about the questions. Just look at the magazine.* If you can't "see" the answer, just skip to the next question.

1. What magazine is it? *Time? Vogue? Walrus Fancier's Quarterly Review?*
2. Who is the interviewer?
3. What group of people typically reads this magazine?
4. Why do the readers want to know about you?
5. *What* do they want to know about you?
6. The interviewer has written a description of your home, where the interview took place. Read the description. What does your home look like? Where is it?
7. How does the author describe you physically?
8. What does the article say about your clothes? Your manner? The way you move?
9. Is there anyone else in your home? Who?
10. The interviewer asks you about your romantic life. How do you describe it?
11. If you have a spouse or partner, read what the interviewer says about him or her, and any comments about the way the two of you interact.
12. The author writes about the way you spend a typical day. What is it like?
13. The interviewer describes some photographs you have in your home. Who or what is in them?
14. Does the article mention any children, or perhaps ask you about your decision not to have them?
15. The author writes a good deal about your best-known achievement. What is it?

16. There's a motivational paragraph or two about the hard times in your life and how you worked through them. What does it say?
17. The interviewer asks you what advice you would have given to your younger self. What's your answer?
18. What gem of wisdom do you have for your readers?
19. What's the most interesting part of the article?
20. The interviewer asks you about your plans for the future. What are they?

If you really like this exercise, try writing the article out in full. Don't edit, ponder, or worry about writing style; just take dictation from your intuition. When my clients do this, the results often turn out to be spookily predictive. Just remember not to censor or edit the article dictated by your essential self. Nothing you can say is too grandiose or improbable for the Dreamtime.

MID-SQUARE TWO: TRANSITION TO REALITY

Once you've let go of some internalized rules and breathed life back into your frozen dreams, it's time to begin the transition from the ideal world to the real world. This means taking your impossible dreams and putting them into pragmatic, attainable terms. At this point, I join forces with all those motivational speakers who flash their enormous teeth on TV infomercials and tell you that just specifying your goals is a huge step toward achieving them.

I've believed this ever since I was fourteen years old. That's when I first wrote down a set of Wildly Improbable Goals. One day while writing in my journal, I listed three things I really wanted but didn't think I could have: I wanted to learn to ski, own a ten-speed bicycle, and go to Europe. The first two items seemed prohibitively expensive; the third was utterly out of the question. Still, I had a gut feeling that somehow all of these things were possible—barely. I labeled them "Wildly Improbable Goals" and pretty much let them go.

The thing was that, even though I didn't really think I could attain these goals, from the day I wrote them down I had something in my little brain that scientists might call a "search image." A search image is a subconscious alertness toward something you hope to find. All predatory animals have internalized search images of their prey species, so that they can pick out the shape of a deer or mouse in a microsecond, even from a long distance. Your brain uses search images in many situations—for example, when you scan a shelf full of different shampoo bottles looking for your favorite brand. You don't have to carefully scrutinize every label; your brain ignores everything that isn't the right color, shape, or size, freeing your attention to zoom in on the thing you're "hunting."

Forming a goal, especially if you write it down and visualize it, creates a search image that programs your brain to focus on anything resembling or leading to that objective. From the moment I wrote my Wildly Improbable Goals, I began noticing advertisements for ski equipment and bicycles. I also picked up on ways of making money, and I had an internalized incentive to defer gratification and save what I earned, rather than spending it. Within a few months, I was able to afford a pretty nice ten-speed. Only weeks later, I overheard a friend say she'd gotten some new ski equipment and was looking to sell her old stuff. I signed up for a community class that bused me up to a nearby ski resort on Saturdays.

To top it all off, one day I came home from school to find that a friend, an Olympic basketball player from Yugoslavia, had sent my family two surplus round-trip tickets to Europe. The tickets were part of his yearly travel allowance, but they were about to expire without being used. My little sister and I were on a plane the next morning, and my Wildly Improbable Goals were all done deals.

I could have passed this off as a coincidence, but I've been setting Wildly Improbable Goals ever since, and damn if they haven't all come true. It seems to work like this: I find a goal that makes my essential self say, *"Yes!"* Then I go into a "hunting" frenzy, turning over every rock and twig to learn about my goal and spot clues that might help me reach it. Then I work like hell. Then I work some more. Finally, I reach the limit of my ability—and next, with amazing reliability, something or someone shows up to help me bridge the gap between impossibility and reality. I once saw a cartoon where two scientists are looking at an enormous equation written on a blackboard. In the midst of all the numbers and symbols, right in the center of the equation, is the phrase "A miracle occurs." That's how Wildly Improbable Goals work for me. I'm delighted to report that they work the same way for my clients. There's not a doubt in my mind that they'll work for you as well.

EXERCISE: MAKING YOUR OWN WIGS

Setting Wildly Improbable Goals (hereinafter referred to as "WIGs") is a learned skill, something like centering a lump of clay on a pottery wheel or driving a car with a standard transmission. You have to get a *feel* for it. The feeling you need is a desire, a genuine heartfelt longing, for something that lies right on the border between possibility and impossibility. Your internal compasses will tell you when you articulate such a goal. You'll think, "Gosh, maybe I really *could* join the PGA tour / go to chef school / live in the South of France," and immediately your pulse will quicken. Your energy will surge. You'll feel a kind of nervous elation that simply can't be faked. Your essential self won't respond this way to something that isn't really part of your own North Star. Nor will it get all fluttery and excited about a goal that's either easy or truly impossible—but remember, a lot of things you believe to be impossible are actually well within your reach. Your body and emotions will tell you they're possible by yelling, *"Yes!"* when you think about them.

With this in mind, I'd like you to focus your attention on some activity you enjoy very much. It can be any aspect of your work, relationships, hobbies, or leisure pastimes. Now imagine pushing this favorite activity to the boundary of what you think possible. For example, if you wrote down "surfing" as your activity, your WIG might be "Winning the World Surfing Title" or "Living in Sydney and surfing at Bondai Beach every day" or "Traveling to every great beach on earth and surfing all of them." Don't choose what you think is logical or impressive to others. Setting a WIG is all about finding a dream that thrills your essential self. Here are some examples of WIGs from my clients, to help you prime the pump (by the way, every single one of these WIGs came true for the person who set it).

SAMPLE WIGs

Beloved Activity	Wildly Improbable Goal
Exploring the Internet	Starting my own dot-com company
Making people laugh	Doing professional stand-up comedy
Being with my European lover	Marrying my lover and moving to Europe
Volunteering for political campaigns	Running for office
Jogging	Finishing a marathon
Watching TV	Becoming a TV producer
Visiting sub-Saharan Africa	Helping African countries with their socioeconomic development

Looking over this list of WIGs, I note that very few of the dreams listed above get even the teensiest rise out of *my* essential self. In fact, some of my clients' most cherished dreams would be my worst nightmares, and vice versa. It's enough to make you believe that there really is room for everyone's wishes to be granted. What are yours?

Your beloved activity: _____

Your WIG: _____

Go ahead and repeat this exercise a few times—I've found that WIGs work best when you have between two and four going at once. Remember to stick with things you truly enjoy, not things you think someone else would admire. Write your WIGs below:

MY WILDLY IMPROBABLE GOALS

Date these goals were set: _____

1. _____

    Date achieved: _____

2. _____

    Date achieved: _____

3. _____

    Date achieved: _____

4. _____

    Date achieved: _____

You can see that I've left a space for you to note the date on which your WIGs become realities. I ask my clients to let me know when this happens for them. Every few weeks I get a postcard or a phone call from some former client, saying, "It happened! It happened!" The thrill I get from hearing this never fades. "Well, hot puppies!" I think, every single time. "It *works!*"

Unfortunately, this doesn't mean that you'll achieve all your WIGs without effort. I don't get those celebratory postcards from the clients who set goals, then sit back and do absolutely nothing but wait for the Goal Fairy to zap their dreams into reality. Miracles really can and will occur when you connect with your dreams, but they're both more likely and less necessary if you do everything in your power to reach your goals. As the saying goes, "Trust Allah, but tie your camel to the post." That means moving on from the Dreamtime to late Square Two: the Scheme-time.

LATE SQUARE TWO: SCHEMING

The dreaming you do in early Square Two helps you identify clear targets at which to aim your efforts. Once you've done this, you'll find yourself naturally moving from dreaming to scheming. This is basically the shift from *wanting* to do something to *intending* to do it. If you think this is a trivial difference, think again. Any first-year law student can tell you that if you occasionally want to kill other drivers in traffic, you're normal—but if you really *intend* to kill them, you can be legally incarcerated. Human intention is such a powerful force that in legal terms, it's often more important than actual behavior. That's because whatever we intend has a very high probability of actually occurring.

Compared to the exercises I've described so far in this book, the instructions for late Square Two and the rest of the change cycle will sound less like psychotherapy and more like an instruction manual. That's because (as you can see on the graphic of the change cycle), we're moving out of the purely ideal world and edging closer to the real world. Identifying your own North Star is a deep psychological and spiritual art. Actually getting there is more like following a recipe: Find the following ingredients, put them together in this order, heat them to this temperature, wait for this length of time, and so on.

While pragmatic, hands-on people become much more comfortable at this point on the change cycle, others start to balk. These folks like the introspection and emotion of Square One, and they love the Impossible Dream phase of Square Two. They absolutely hate it when I start pushing them to do anything practical, even the practical thinking required to create a good Square Two scheme. Sorry, Charlie. Reaching your own North Star requires both flights of fancy and good old-fashioned work. If you don't feel quite ready to do some hard-headed, realistic planning, go back to the exercises I've already mentioned. When you're sure that you've got your own North Star in your crosshairs, you'll eventually have to move on to the steps below.

1. Post-it Passion: Setting Up Your Scheme

I love Post-its, those little rectangles of paper that can be stuck and restuck to pretty much any surface. I mean I *love* them. Post-its are the perfect medium for creating a Square Two scheme. Like a good life plan, they're solid and tangible but also easy to rearrange, throw away, or replace. To create a scheme that will get you to your own North Star, you'll need a bunch of Post-its and a place to stick them, preferably a flat surface at least three or four feet across, such as a white board, a strip of butcher paper, or a blank wall.

2. Setting Up the Equation

On the far right side of your planning space, stick a Post-it on which you've written a brief description of your Wildly Improbable Goal. Many of my clients like to surround this particular Post-it with pictures that represent their ideal lives. They'll cut images out of magazines, collect postcards, or use snapshots they've taken themselves, gluing all these things into a collage representing their own North Stars. This is so touchy-feely that just writing about it makes me feel like a New Age aura therapist, but it actually seems to work. I learned it from a client, who did it at a training seminar for a major corporation and has since become very, very rich.

Once you've got your WIG on the far right of your planning space, go to the far *left* side—and this may be a good ten feet away—and put up another Post-it recording today's date and time. I mean right now, as you're reading this. Check the time, write it down, and stick it up there. You have now set up two sides of an equation, like this:

My life as it is at

_____ (time)   +   X   =   My Wildly Improbable Goal

on _____ (date)

All you've go to do now is solve for X. In order to realize your goal, what must you get that you don't already have? Generally, your first answer will be fuzzy at best. You know it'll take a lot of work to win that Nobel Prize, or that date with the entire Swedish gymnastics team, but you're not really sure what steps you'll have to take. Finding the solution is simply a matter of logic and research, and that's your next task.

3. Visualizing the Process

Remember, if you can't dream it, you can't do it. This doesn't just mean that you have to have noble goals. It means that if you can't mentally detail every step of an activity, you probably don't know how to make it happen. My whole childhood, I had this vague idea of how adults drove cars—but if you'd asked me *exactly* how it was done, the details would have been mighty fuzzy. I had to learn them one step at a time, until every action became second nature.

Try to visualize every step you must take to realize the WIG you've got stuck on your planning board. If you don't know exactly—and I mean *exactly*—what you must do to achieve your WIG, your scheme still needs elaboration. You may not even be sure what you need to learn, but that's just another question you must research. It's time to play detective.

4. Doing Your Homework

If you've ever watched a semirealistic detective show, like *Law and Order*, you know that real detectives rarely have a nice Miss Marple scenario, involving one tidy dead body, half a dozen possible suspects, and a host of ready clues. Mostly, investigators start with a big mess of extraneous detail and virtually no useful information. Most cases are solved not by brilliant deductions but by thorough, plodding, unromantic persistence. Investigators go over crime scenes in infinitesimal detail, analyze the hell out of every little hint of evidence, ask a lot of experts for assistance, and interview dozens of ordinary people, the vast majority of whom can't or won't help them.

This is exactly the kind of research you're going to have to do to create a solid, workable scheme leading from your life at this moment to your own North Star. Remember that old joke where the man stops to ask directions from one small town to another and the locals tell him, "You can't get there from here"? That's absurd; you can get anywhere from anywhere. You just have to find out how. I can't tell you how many of my clients think that not knowing how to accomplish their dream-scheme is an excuse to give up on it. I blame this attitude on the

Kindergarten Complex. If you're suffering from it, I'd like to say to you, in the most loving way possible, "Suck it up and do your homework."

EXERCISES

Homework Exercise No. 1: Book Larnin'

Go to the nearest public library or bookstore. Choose any one of your WIGs and start looking around the establishment for any information that might help you achieve that goal. I guarantee, the clues are right there waiting. You might begin your "hunt" by asking the store clerk for guidance, or simply browse likely looking shelves of books or magazines with your search image in full operation.

You're hunting for at least two types of information: 1) explanations of how to achieve your WIG directly (such as how-to books on method acting or making a fortune in the stock market); and 2) leads that might put you in touch with experts who can advise you.

For example, my client Alissa wanted to work on a cruise liner. She found an ad for Holland America Cruise Lines in *Travel and Leisure* magazine, called the 800 number included in the ad, and explained to a confused sales agent that she was doing research on the travel industry and needed to speak to someone who could tell her all the ins and outs of running a major cruise line. She eventually got through to several different managers, all of whom agreed to short "information interviews" and gave Alissa the information she needed to move toward her WIG.

Homework Exercise No. 2: Reach Out and Touch Someone

Sit down with a telephone, your Rolodex or address book, and a copy of the phone book (including the yellow pages). You're about to start a manhunt that may set thousands of minds in motion, all to solve your problem. First of all, get your WIG firmly in mind. For illustrative purposes, let's use the example of my client Clark, who wanted to be a forest ranger. We went through a list of Clark's friends and family, looking for the names of people who might know something about how to do this. We didn't find any, so just started calling the people he felt most comfortable asking. It turned out that his sister's former boyfriend had gotten a degree in forestry. She gave Clark the boyfriend's name and telephone number. Clark called and left a message on the answering machine.

Clark's next lead came in when a friend said he sort of thought there was some kind of government involvement in forest management. Clark checked the blue governmental listings in his phone book, and sure enough, there was a Forestry Department listed right there. By calling it, Clark got the name and phone number of an actual forest ranger. He also left a message saying he'd appreciate a call back from the deputy head of the department. The next day, Clark got calls from both the deputy and his sister's ex. He also managed to get in touch with the real, live ranger. It was time for his informational interview skills to swing into action.

During person-to-person research, you want to avoid sounding like a needy job seeker, even if that's exactly what you are. Neediness is a huge turnoff, so if you're feeling it, pretend otherwise. Don't ask anyone to give you employment or solve your problems for you. Just tell them that you are researching a certain field (whatever your WIG may be) and you'd really appreciate it if they could take ten or fifteen minutes to answer a few questions. This taps directly into a universal human longing: the desire for attention. Most people absolutely love being asked honest questions about something they know well. My clients sometimes have a terrible time getting these people to shut up.

Paradoxically, informational interviewing is one of the best ways to make folks want to hire you, befriend you, or move in with you. It's way more effective than asking for these things directly. My favorite story comes from Leroy, an unemployed recent college grad who had the *cojones* to call a bank president and ask him if he'd mind being interviewed over lunch—Leroy's treat, of course. Leroy had eighty dollars in the bank. He blew seventy-six on the lunch. The next day, the bank president was talking to another CEO, who happened to be looking for a likely young assistant. Leroy had the job by the next day, and he's now making a fat six figures.

Homework Exercise No. 3: Untangling the Web

I have here an article from the *Arizona Republic,* our fine local newspaper, recounting the story of a Phoenix woman whose husband was diagnosed with leukemia. This woman had no medical or scientific training, and she was completely computer illiterate. But that didn't stop her. When her husband got sick, she figured out how to use the Internet and began researching leukemia with all the energy that comes from threatened love. This very ordinary woman became so well-versed in the latest research and treatments for leukemia that her husband's doctors ended up apologizing for knowing so much less than she did. They deferred to her superior knowledge on a number of treatment options, and everyone concerned believes that this woman saved her husband's life.

If your WIG really matters to you and you have any sort of access to a computer, the Web can literally turn you into an expert in your field. Try every key word related to your dream, on every search engine you can find. Get references for pertinent books and articles and order them from an on-line service, or call the publisher and ask for copies to be mailed to you. Get the E-mail addresses and phone numbers of people who can teach you how to achieve your goal, and write or call them (about one in three will respond; don't worry if some of them don't).

Homework Exercise No. 4: Wild Invention

You may try all the avenues of research I've just mentioned and discover that no one really knows how to achieve your Wildly Improbable Goals. Maybe no one's ever done it before. Well, now, you're just going to have to get creative. Be sure your dream is crystal clear, remember that *there are no rules,* and start brainstorming ways to get to your WIG.

The summer I graduated from high school, my friends Carrie and Phil and I decided that we wanted to get jobs in the same organization, so that we could hang out together. We pounded the pavement looking for jobs waiting tables or cleaning hotel rooms, but no one was very excited about hiring kids who'd be off to college in a few months, and no one would hire the three of us together. Our job skills were a bit esoteric, anyway: Carrie played the viola like an angel, Phil was an incredible poet, and I loved to draw.

We considered our raw material and our WIG and came up with a scheme: We'd start a summer creativity workshop for kids, a place where children could expose themselves to art. Unfortunately, one of them did exactly that—we had to call his parents to report the incident—but otherwise, our scheme worked out unbelievably well. We had to elaborate many interim steps, from finding a space to starting a corporate bank account, but we researched and conquered every one. Our workshop operated for two summers, drew more business than we could handle, and closed over the protests of loyal customers. It still blows me away that I actually got paid for doing exactly what I most enjoyed, in a job I just sort of made up, with people I adored. Hmm. Come to think of it, that's exactly what I'm doing now.

I used to play a game with my business-school students in which every student had to come up with a different way to get a job. The students who lucked out and got called on early took the easy way out: "Check the want ads," "Send out résumés," and so on. By the time we got to number fifty, people would get really creative. They'd be developing theoretical technologies, threatening to blackmail high-placed executives, sending Candy-Grams to former bosses. When everyone had taken a turn, we'd go around the room *again*. The interesting thing was that the first students in line would have many more ideas than they'd been able to imagine at first. Once your brain is in "dreaming-scheming" mode, the possibilities are infinite.

5. Fleshing Out

I find it incredibly easy to flesh out in the latter stages of Square Two, but let's not talk about my thighs. Let's talk about filling your planning place with Post-its, one little sticky note for every single step required to achieve your dream. You business types will recognize this as a "flow chart." You want it to be as detailed as possible. For example, the scheme below is really just a sketch. A fleshed-out chart would show every aspect of every step. Instead of "follow recipe," you could actually add each step of the recipe to your scheme. The single step "Borrow

Oven" could be broken down into many smaller steps, such as "Think of people who might be willing to loan me their ovens," "Get phone numbers of potential oven lenders," and "Call these people and ask about oven loan."

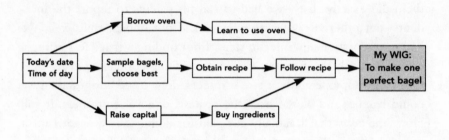

If it's starting to sound as though I want you to list ridiculously small steps on your Post-it plan, you're getting the feeling of what it means to create a really solid Square Two scheme. As your plan becomes more thorough, your research more complete, and the steps to your goal easier to envision, you'll find yourself developing a kind of impatience to actually go out and *do it*. Congratulations. You've finished your time in Square Two, the time of big plans in the "ideal world" of your imagination. It's time to start the actual, flesh-and-blood journey to your own North Star.

14

SQUARE THREE:
THE HERO'S SAGA

The journey of a thousand miles begins from beneath your feet.

—LAO-TZU

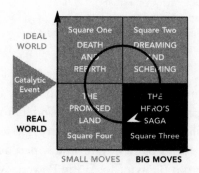

THE CHANGE CYCLE

Hey, do you remember that really great book—or maybe it was a movie or a TV show or something—where the good guys have to do that thing by a certain time or something really bad is going to happen? And then their gizmo breaks, so they don't know how they'll keep going, but they think of a new plan, and then that person who's supposed to be on their side turns out to be working for the bad guys? And then they lose that other thing, and their leader gets injured, and the villains take over that strategic area, and you *really* don't think they're going to make it, but then that brilliant idea occurs to them and at the very last minute they save the day? Remember that one?

Of course you do. The paragraph above describes about ten thousand stories you've heard, read, or watched during your life. The movie section of your daily paper lists several more of these stories, now playing at a theater near you. Your local library has thousands more. Flip through your cable-TV channels at any given minute, and you'll zip over still more versions, from the latest episode of *Pokémon,* to an *Oprah* guest's account of her victory over cancer, to VH1's *Behind the Music* ("When we return: The Snot Machine band members slide into drug abuse, then enter rehab, as their second album goes platinum."). All of these stories and dramas, fact or fiction, are "hero's sagas." They share the same basic formula:

1. Protagonist sets out to achieve a goal.
2. Protagonist runs into a mess of trouble.
3. Protagonist struggles through adverse conditions.
4. Protagonist achieves the goal.

Oh, how we humans love this story! It abounds, in infinite variations, throughout every culture, language, and historical period. In prosperous times, when there's no need to struggle for mere survival, we retell or invent stories of desperate straits, perilous journeys, and fearless champions, from Beowulf to Austin Powers. We think up contests and sports to create simulated sagas—and we want the contestants to have as hard a time as they possibly can. If we don't see all-out effort, total exhaustion, and the occasional gory accident, we become bored and set off in search of a more exciting saga.

Why do all people seem to share this obsessive desire to see the same plot line repeated, over and over and over? Simple: because the hero's saga is the story of every human life. Each drama of danger, discouragement, and derring-do mirrors what each audience member experiences each day. Mystery writer Lawrence Block once wrote that all fiction is the story of someone dealing with "one damn thing after another." Doesn't that come pretty close to describing your day so far? Well, it sure describes mine.

Listen: My daughter missed her bus this morning, so I had to get dressed and drive her to school before I even had any coffee, which made me grumpy. Then I had to return several phone calls, some to people who really intimidate me. After that, even though I was cold and tired, it was time to walk my beagle, Cookie. Naturally, he found a disgusting mildewed pizza under a bush and inhaled half of it before I could drag him away. (Later, after he metabolized enough of the pizza to punch out the few remaining dents in his skin, Cookie barfed the remainder onto a prominent part of our living-room carpet. It's not bulimia; it's interior decorating.) Now it's time to write, even though I have a painful hangnail. And then . . .

Oh, all right, so this is not *The Iliad*. It's a whiny little story of a whiny little person having a whiny little day. But it still contains the elements of a hero's saga. So does your day—or any part of it that requires you to exert any energy or overcome any obstacle, from the most trivial to the most overwhelming. I used to have a cartoon taped to my wall, showing a man in the process of writing his "to do" list. The list said, "1. Get Up. 2. Survive. 3. Go to Bed." There are days—I know you've had them—when just accomplishing that much is a genuinely heroic act. Setting out to achieve a big dream, to claim the life you were meant to live, is inestimably more challenging.

This is what makes Square Three the most daunting region of the change cycle—and the most exciting. Nothing you can anticipate in the "ideal world" of your intellect and imagination can fully prepare you for everything that will happen once you set about realizing your dreams in the material world. If your goal is true and heartfelt, the journey through Square Three is guaranteed to be terrifying, exhausting, and incredibly exhilarating. You'll be telling the stories for generations to come, and they'll be the kind of stories people genuinely want to hear.

NUTS AND BOLTS

Square Three is the nuts-and-bolts phase of finding your own North Star, and not just because it drives you nuts and makes you want to bolt. Compared to anything we've discussed so far, it's practical and hands-on and not nearly as pretty as you'd like it to be. I've read dozens of books with breezy titles like *Do What You Love, the Money Will Follow*, and I'm always struck by the fact that although these books are crystal clear about the ideal-world task of deciding what you love, they're mighty vague about the exact real-world process by which the money will follow. It's not that the authors are wrong—I absolutely agree with them—it's just that they have no way of knowing how your particular dream will come to fruition. If they did, then maybe they could be a little more specific. You'd get titles like this one: *Figure Out What You Love, Keep Your Day Job to Pay the Rent, Come Up with a Really Good Entrepreneurial Idea, Take Out a Second Mortgage for Investment Capital, Get the Training to Create a Marketable Product, Produce the Product, Convince People to Buy the Product, Work Incredibly Hard for Much Longer Than You Ever Thought You Could, Work Some More, Keep on Working, and the Money Will Follow. Probably.*

Unfortunately, a lot of readers think that just loving or wanting something means you don't have to take any prosaic, real-world action to "manifest" it. I've had many clients of New Age–ish sensibilities who fully expected to get the perfect job without ever seeking or applying for one. It's like that old joke where the drowning preacher turns away rescuers in a rowboat, a motorboat, and a helicopter, telling them that he doesn't need them, because he has absolute faith that God will save him. Then he drowns. When he gets to Heaven, he asks God, "Why didn't you answer my prayers for help?" "I tried!" says God. "I sent you a rowboat, a motorboat, *and* a helicopter!"

Let's get this straight: All dreams are realized through pragmatic action. Magic really does follow longing and intention, but it usually ends up looking quite ordinary. Some of my clients really "get" this. These Square Three types just love pragmatic action. In fact, they prefer it to dreaming and scheming. My biggest problem with these folks is keeping them from acting on barely formed ideas and incomplete plans. But most of my clientele are more like Cecelia.

Cecelia was a thirty-five-year-old social worker when she began to feel a restless desire to change the whole system. To that end, she quit her job and went back to school in pursuit of a doctoral degree. Cecelia had a wonderful imagination, and she loved to visualize various aspects of her own North Star. Some of her goals were purely personal: She wanted to live in Texas and ride her horse every day. Others were professional: She imagined teaching and training a generation of social workers who would change the discipline and touch thousands of lives. Over several sessions, Cecelia clarified and elaborated these goals until they were as sharp and clear as cut diamonds. She made a wonderful collage representing the life she was meant to live, and she created a detailed scheme festooned with dozens of colorful Post-it notes. Her next step toward completing this scheme was obvious to both of us: Cecelia had to finish her doctoral dissertation.

"Okay!" I said to Cecelia, on the day her scheme was complete. "You're moving out of Square Two and into Square Three. No more planning—you've gotta slog through some real-world work. The next time we meet, I want to see five pages of a rough draft for your dissertation."

"Right!" Cecelia gave a purposeful nod, like a boxer headed into the ring. Two weeks later, she came into my office glowing with excitement. "Look!" she said. "I added more pictures to my collage!"

"That's nice," I said. "Where are the five pages of your rough draft?"

"I called three colleagues and had *great* conversations about how the field has to change!" exulted Cecelia.

"Where are your pages?"

"I'm thinking of taking a watercolor class to increase my creativity," she said. "Everyone says that's a good idea."

"I'll tell you what's a good idea," I growled. "Five pages of your dissertation."

Of course, she hadn't written them. When we met again two weeks later, she was still bracing herself for the attempt. Two more weeks, and Cecelia said she'd been terribly busy categorizing her herbal tea bags and crocheting a sweater for her cat. She hadn't managed to squeeze in one minute of writing.

"Look," I told her. "You're paying me to help you reach your goals, not make excuses. You're spending money you can't spare on medicine you won't take. Now go away, and don't come back until you can show me five pages of your rough draft." I stood up and opened the door.

Cecelia's eyes filled with tears of shock and anger. Where was the nice person who had helped her envision all those wonderful horseback rides? Who was this brass-plated bitch that had taken over my body? She seemed so upset that I finally sat down again and told Cecelia a little hero's saga. It was about how I'd managed to finish *my* Ph.D. dissertation—and how, in the process, I'd learned a number of tricks for getting through early Square Three.

EARLY SQUARE THREE: ACCELERATING FROM ZERO

The very beginning of Square Three is like standing at sea level and staring up at Everest. The task ahead of you, if it's worth doing, is probably long and hard. Even worse, it's unknown. If you've truly locked on to your own North Star, you will want desperately to achieve your goal, and that means the fear of failure is likely to be overwhelming. None of these factors makes it any easier to dredge up the enormous energy it takes to accelerate from zero. It's much harder to get something moving from a dead stop than to keep it moving once it's on its way. Think of a locomotive starting up—all the groaning, puffing, screeching, and straining—and you'll have a nice image of what you'll go through at the beginning of any hero's saga. For that reason, the following strategies—which can actually be used at any point in Squares Three and Four—are particularly useful at the start.

1. Break Every Task into Turtle Steps.

The story I told Cecelia began the day I took my two-year-old son, Adam, to the "occupational therapy" recommended for kids with Down's syndrome. At the time, I was supposed to be busily churning out my own Ph.D. dissertation; but the truth was, it had been weeks since I could even stand to think about it. The project was like an invisible, bloated monster that sat on my head day and night, leering at me, growing new tentacles, and gaining weight.

That day, Adam's therapist decided that it was time to start potty training. "The way we're going to do this," she said, "is to break the task down into manageable bits, so that Adam can master them one at a time."

"Oh, I see," I said. "Like, one day we work on Number One, and the next day we work on Number Two?"

She smiled indulgently. "Not quite. We'll start with gripping." And she spent several minutes teaching Adam how to pinch the front waistband of his training pants, just below his belly button, with the fingers of his right hand. "Excellent!" she crowed, once he caught on. "Now, that's enough for today—if he has too much to deal with, he'll get overwhelmed. Just go home and work on that right hand for a few days. Next week, we'll start teaching him to grab the back of the waistband with his left hand. That will take longer—it's a harder skill to master. A couple of weeks after that, he can start learning how to actually take off the training pants."

Remember when I said your Square Two scheme should be very detailed? You had no idea how detailed I want you to get. Most of my clients will fill their dream-schemes with steps like "Get work as an actor" or "Apply to medical school," as though these things could be accomplished in one fell swoop. In my case, the social-self imperative was "Write that damn dissertation." The immensity of this task had sparked an impressively successful rebellion from my essential self and stopped my education dead in its tracks. That day in occupational therapy, I realized that Adam wasn't the only one who needed to take things in small doses.

When we got home, I set about breaking down the task "Write my dissertation" into manageable steps. This was one of the first times I noticed the feeling of my essential self saying "Yes" or "No." I began by deciding that I'd try to put in only about six hours of solid writing each day. This was much less than I thought I should be doing, but I could tell right away that my body and brain were resisting even this level of effort. So I knocked my expectations in half: I'd write for just three hours a day. Still, I felt as though I were trying to give a piggyback ride to a woolly mammoth. Ninety minutes a day, then? No go. An hour? Forget it. Half an hour? Nope. But when I got to fifteen minutes, I noticed a dramatic shift in my body and mood.

My muscles relaxed, and instead of numb resentment, I felt downright willing.

I spent my first fifteen-minute workday just hauling out all my notes and glancing at them. Then, true to my plan, I punched the clock and took a nap. It certainly wasn't much, but it was more work that I'd been able to make myself do for weeks. The next day, I wrote a single sentence. The following day, I managed a whole page. And that is how I eventually finished my deadly dull, bulky dissertation: fifteen minutes a day, over the course of a year. Some days I'd write several paragraphs. Some days I would get inspired and finish two or three whole pages. Other days, the most I could do was look up the phone number of an adviser and place it near the telephone. But as long as I didn't bite off more than my essential self could chew, I kept inching forward toward my goal.

I've already mentioned that I collect turtles as my writing totem. A "turtle step" is my label for the largest possible task that your essential self can do easily. That last word—*easily*—is very, very important. We're not talking about how much you can do when you're pushing a deadline, ignoring all other responsibilities, fueling yourself with gallons of caffeine, and receiving a fortuitous visit from the muse. Even on a bad day, when you contemplate your turtle steps, your immediate, genuine gut reaction should be, "Oh, yeah, sure. I can do *that*."

Most people are unwilling to take turtle steps, for the odd reason that they're too small. When I recommend turtle steps to clients like Cecelia, the typical response is "That's not enough! I'll never get anything done at that rate!" And so they go on, month after month, doing absolutely nothing. Trust me, slow and steady wins races a lot more often than paralyzed and inert. String together enough steps—even turtle steps—and you'll eventually make it to the top of Everest.

EXERCISE

Think of a goal you really want to achieve, and write down one step you know you must take to attain it (if you made a dream-scheme after reading the last chapter, pick out a step on your plan). Now break that step down into smaller components. Then pick one of those components, and break it down into even smaller subcomponents. Keep going until you find a ministep that you're sure you can accomplish *easily*. Pay close attention to your internal compasses: You will feel changes in your body and emotions when the tasks become small enough to earn the coveted "turtle step" designation.

Today, take one turtle step toward your goal. Just one. Then STOP! *You are not allowed to take another turtle step until twenty-four hours have passed or you feel a strong desire to move on, whichever comes first.* At that point, take one more turtle step. Then stop again, and so on. Step, stop, step, stop, step. It may not look impressive, but it will get you anywhere.

2. Bribe Your Essential Self.

When I told Cecelia I wouldn't see her until she finished five pages of a rough draft, I was basically trying to extort work from her essential self. I knew that our sessions were among the very few instances where that true self could come out and frolic, and I figured that by threatening its playtime, I might scare it enough to get the dissertation moving. This works fairly well in a pinch—it ended up working for Cecelia—but positive reinforcement is a much more powerful motivating force than punishment. So whenever possible, I prefer to use extortion's cuddly cousin, bribery.

Every Square Three hero's saga will include tasks you really, *really* don't want to do. Obviously, I don't want you to head away from your North Star and fill your whole life with hated tasks, but to reach your dreams, you'll probably have to jump several unpleasant social hoops. There are also some items on your plan that can't be broken down into turtle steps. If you have to give a three-hour presentation, you may chop up the preparation for it into small bits, but at some point you'll be up there in front of people for the whole three hours. Other jobs are so horrendous that even the smallest unit of effort is unpleasant. All of this requires essential-self participation, or at least willingness. When turtle steps won't work, bribery can really help.

Suppose that I asked you to do some really gross task, like cleaning a gas-station rest room. For this, I offered you five shiny pennies and the satisfaction of a job well done. Here's your brush and plunger! How is your essential self reacting to this proposition? Imagine that I'm serious, that I'm really sending you into the field of combat right this minute.

Can you feel yourself shutting down, getting resentful, developing a little lower-back pain? Well, then, let's up the ante. How would you feel if I offered five whole dollars to clean that rest room? Five hundred dollars? Five thousand? Fifty thousand? Five million?

Depending on how much you need money and hate janitorial work, you'll begin to feel more friendly toward the task as the reward increases. Most people sense a transition, from "Hell, no!" to "Hmm. Maybe," right around the five-hundred-dollar mark. I've never had a client who wouldn't cheerfully clean a gas station rest room for five million dollars, and if I did, I'd send the person directly to therapy. At that level of remuneration, I personally would skip to the loo with a smile on my lips and a song in my heart.

The point is that the essential self can be bought, and there are times when you'll need to buy it. You may not have millions of dollars to dangle in front of your own nose as you set out to accomplish an unpleasant task from your dream-scheme. But if there's one thing I hope you've gotten from this book, it's the ability to recognize and articulate what your essential self wants. Assuming that you've at least begun this process, I want you to use something your essential self loves to bribe it into doing something it hates. Offer your essential self various rewards for doing an aversive task, and pay close attention to what your inner compasses are telling you. It goes like this:

"I have to go ask my scary boss for a raise. If I go through with this, I get to buy myself the latest John Grisham legal thriller."

If your essential self thinks this bribe is worthy of the effort you're demanding from it, you'll feel the "Yes!" response. If not, you'll feel a "No!" response and you'll have to up the bribe: "Okay, if I ask for that raise, I not only get to buy the John Grisham book, I get to spend two hours reading it this evening." If that doesn't work, throw in a meal at your favorite restaurant, a massage, or a whole "sick" day. Keep upping the reward until you feel your essential self say "Yes!" to this deal.

Sometimes, if a task is truly wrong for you, no amount of bribery will induce your essential self to participate. This is usually a sign that the step you're trying to take is leading you directly away from your own North Star. If that's the case, don't do it. But if the task is merely an unpleasant step toward your destiny, you'll eventually come up with a bribe that makes both your selves happy.

EXERCISE
Consult your list of dream-scheme tasks for a step that is difficult to break down into turtle steps, or that you *really* don't want to do. Figure out how much of a favorite reward would be needed to bribe your essential self into completing this step. One crucial caveat: *Once your essential self agrees to a deal and completes the assigned task, you absolutely must pay the bribe in full.* Otherwise, you'll lose the trust of your own true self.

3. Do a Terrible Job.

I believe with all my heart that if a thing is worth doing, it's worth doing badly. Almost all my clients are willing to work very hard to do things well. That's a laudable approach to life. However, it often means that once we've amassed enough life skills to get by without daily egregious mistakes, we stop growing, experimenting, and learning new behaviors. We limit our whole range of activities to things we already do well. Refusing to do a bad job is a leading cause of North Star Deficiency Syndrome.

If you're going through a major transition, your hero's saga is absolutely certain to include unfamiliar situations and new skills. The first few times you try any of these things, from tying flies to negotiating a contract, you're probably going to do it badly. Terrific! That shows you're still expanding the horizons of your own capability. With time and practice, you'll do your North Star tasks brilliantly. But being willing to make a mess is a prerequisite to gaining that skill.

EXERCISE
Find a turtle step you've never done before, or something that's difficult for you. Do this thing really badly. Misspell words. Draw stick figures. Get hopelessly lost. Ask for instructions, then forget them. Then, instead of scolding yourself, give yourself a reward for trying something new and being brave enough to mess up a few times. Now you're living like a hero.

MID-SQUARE THREE: FAILURE

A willingness to make mistakes and recover from them is absolutely essential gear for getting you through the rocky, treacherous territory you'll hit once you get past the initial acceleration phase of Square Three, pick up a little speed, and move into the middle of your hero's saga. As you implement your brilliant, well-researched dream-scheme, you're almost bound to discover that—*ta-da!*—it isn't working! And it isn't going to work! There are about four thousand unforeseen problems that make it totally impractical!

At this point, it's crucial to remind yourself that Square Three is the region of trial and error, not perfection. Failure at this stage of the change cycle is pretty much inevitable. High adventure entails high risk, and more often than not that means things are going to go wrong. Learning to see failure as a step toward success is crucial to surviving the rigors of Square Three. Here are some suggestions for getting through this often grueling phase of change.

1. Hang Loose.

We can learn much about the muddled, trial-and-error process of mid–Square Three from the experience of the early Chinese Communists, who kept coming up with Five-Year Plans that were absolutely certain to propel China to wealth and prosperity, except that these plans contained tiny little flaws that ended up causing tens of millions of people to die of starvation. But we won't, because I had way too much of that kind of talk in graduate school.

What we will do is examine an experience John and I had when we started toward a Wildly Improbable Goal by going to China on a research grant in 1984. The People's Republic was still an exotic destination for Americans back then, and we discovered that it was impossible to arrange travel within China until we were actually in the country. Our plan—our dream-scheme—was to fly into Beijing, then schedule subsequent visits to rural areas.

The first step went beautifully, and although it was a little unnerving to travel on a commercial airliner with live ducks in the overhead compartments, John and I got to Beijing without incident. We proceeded to the foreigners' travel bureau to buy our airplane tickets to the southern city of Guilin. All the way to the travel bureau, I practiced various phrases I'd need to explain our plans to the agent, while John extolled the virtues of demand-driven commerce.

When we reached the bureau, we found it completely filled by a long, circuitous line like the ones you see at Disney World. At the head of this interminable queue was a lone Chinese woman sitting at a tiny wooden desk and filing her fingernails very slowly, as though she were doing Tai Chi. About fifteen minutes after John and I parked ourselves at the back of the line, the woman gently set the nail file on her desk, took a few slow, deep breaths, and said, "Next?"

The man at the front of the line, who had grown several inches of facial hair during his wait, spoke to her in Oxford-accented English.

"Yes, I've come to pick up my ticket to Shanghai. I was told it would be here."

The woman took his name, leafed through a card file for several minutes, and then said, "Your ticket is in that drawer." She pointed to another tiny wooden desk across the room.

The Englishman waited several seconds, then said, "May I have it?"

The woman breathed in through her lower teeth and said, "Well, it's in the drawer, and the drawer is locked."

"Would you mind opening it?" The Englishman sounded a bit tense.

"I'm sorry, sir," said the woman severely. "That is Mr. Liu's desk. He is the only one who is allowed to open it."

"All right." The Englishman's voice was getting shrill. "Where is Mr. Liu?"

"He went to lunch."

"When will he be back?"

The woman shrugged.

"Well, when did he leave?"

The travel agent pursed her lips and looked at the ceiling, deep in thought. "I think it was Tuesday," she said at last. "We haven't seen him since. Sometimes he's gone for weeks."

At this point, the Englishman just snapped. *"Oh, my God!"* he screamed, gripping his greasy hair with both hands. *"What am I doing in this country? What kind of barbarians are you? Oh, my God! Oh, my God!"*

The travel agent picked up her nail file and said, in Chinese, "There is no God."

At this point John and I, who had been watching the whole scene with the fascinated horror you feel passing a fatal traffic accident, burst out laughing. The travel agent's head snapped up—the first rapid movement I'd seen her make—and she caught our eyes. Then she began to laugh, too. A few minutes later, a young bureaucrat came up to us and asked, very politely, what he could do to expedite our travel plans. Everyone there was so pleased with us for knowing a little Chinese that they bent over backward to help us.

I try to keep this experience in mind every time I find myself in Square Three. It helps me remember that when you're in alien territory, whether that's a literal place or just a phase of change, you can't predict what will work and what won't. If you become too fixated on forcing your plan to work *exactly* as you anticipated, you're certain to make dangerous mistakes and miss a lot of useful information that could help you operate on this new turf. When you hit mid–Square Three, try to relax, observe, and relinquish your expectation. Stay open to failure, as well as success; see what's working and what's not. Then flow into the rhythm dictated by the situation, not your preconceptions.

EXERCISE

This week, go into an environment that feels alien to you. If you're a clean-living religious type, spend an hour in a bar. If you tend toward chains and leather, go to church—and make sure you pick a religion you've never belonged to. You will enter this situation as a "participant observer" (a term used by social scientists to get professional credit for writing journal articles about strip clubs). Your objective is simply to notice what happens in these alien environments, so that you can describe everything later to a friend. How did the people sit, walk, smile at each other? What would you have to do to fit in? You don't have to do it, just describe it.

As you do this exercise, you'll find that your initial unease will become mixed with detached interest and amusement. Analyzing the social environment will decrease your discomfort and increase your confidence. The next time you hit Square Three, remember this feeling and return to it, no matter how stressful the situation. It will help you hang loose.

2. Learn from Your Mistakes.

My favorite college art professor used to say, "The sooner you make your first five thousand mistakes, the sooner you can move on to the next five thousand." This was his drolly depressing way of noting that we learn to succeed by failing. What he didn't mention is that as you solve harder and harder problems, you eventually reach a level where your mistakes are the problems of a master, rather than a beginner. This is true, however, only if you learn from every failure.

When I was a little kid, I used to wonder why an airplane crash was always followed by a desperate search for the plane's "black box" flight recorder. After all, finding a box wouldn't undo the accident or save any of the people who'd died. It took me a while to realize that every plane in the air is safer because analysts have spent thousands of hours figuring out exactly what went wrong in those crashes. Of course, no one wants mistakes to happen and tragedies to occur. But when we do fail, we might as well learn from it.

Most people don't take a "black box" approach to their own mistakes. We like to put failure behind us, avoid thinking about it, and hide it from others. To reach your own North Star, you must examine your mistakes from all angles—including other people's vantage points. This means seeking honest feedback, both positive and negative, from the people around you. Many of my clients self-destruct every time they get to Square Three, because of problems or preconceptions that are as obvious as daylight to everyone around them. They make it clear that they don't want to be "criticized," so this wealth of helpful information stays in other people's heads and never makes it to theirs. Instead of looking for the black box, they bury it with hardly a glance and end up turning small, isolated errors into big, repetitive failures.

I remember attending a karate class with a dozen other people of all ages and ability levels. Though I wasn't yet a black belt, that day I happened to be the *senpai,* or the highest-ranking member of the group after the instructor. We were all doing a punching drill when an eight-year-old kid wearing a lowly yellow belt yelled at me across the room. "You're not twisting your wrist enough," he said. "That's why you're so slow."

My first reaction was to blush violently and hope that the child would get kicked really hard, in the head, before the hour was over. The instructor, horrified that one of the lowest-ranking students had publicly corrected the highest ranking, gave the kid a scalding lecture on the spot. As he did this, something occurred to me: The kid was right. Only my pride had made his advice an insult rather than a gift. During the next water break I went over to the eight-year-old, thanked him, and asked him to show me exactly how I could improve my technique. Later, when someone kicked him in the head, I tried not to be happy.

EXERCISE

You may recall that a few pages ago I asked you to do something badly. Now I'd like you to figure out exactly why your performance was so bad. Ask for feedback from two or three people you trust. If the task was to make something, show them the product and ask them what's wrong with it. If you were doing something interpersonal, ask for feedback about how you come across to others. If you were solving a problem, let someone show you where your logic failed. Then thank them for their feedback and get your essential self a treat. As Plato said, "Man gains his first measure of intelligence on the day that he first admits to his own ignorance." Congratulations. You're looking smart.

3. Go Back to Square One.

Ray stormed into my office, livid with anger, after a failed job interview. "I can't believe AmEx didn't offer me the position," Ray grumped. "I was way more qualified than the other applicants I met."

"But I thought you said you'd rather die than work for a big corporation," I said.

"Oh, that's true," Ray nodded. "But they should have at least offered me the chance."

The reasons for Ray's failure in Square Three was that he hadn't based his plan on solid Square One efforts. His life plan wasn't based on an understanding of who he really was and what he really wanted. People can sense ambivalence, especially when they're looking for it, as most job interviewers are. Ray could have saved himself a lot of time and effort by not applying for work he didn't want.

The way to analyze a failed Square Three effort is to let it knock you back—or, rather, *on*—to Square One. A major failure should be a "catalytic event" that jolts you into letting go of your agenda and returning to the strategies you used at the very beginning of the change cycle. Was your failure a result of inadequately defining your dreams? If so, Square One techniques are necessary to correct the problem.

If you return to Square One and find that you really *were* on course for your North Star, the reason for your failure may lie in the "dreaming and scheming" stages. Carol, one of my first clients, told me she really wanted to live in a small, rural community in the southwestern desert. She got a job in just such a town and moved there to enjoy her dream-come-true. Six months later, she was back in my office full of complaints about her new living situation.

"The people I've met are so provincial," she said. "They all vote Republican and eat Jell-O salads."

"What did you expect them to do?" I said.

"Well, I thought they'd be liberal and experimental. I thought they'd spend their time creating art and sipping coffee at little sidewalk cafés."

"And you expected to find that in a tiny desert town?" I asked incredulously.

Carol's dream was a city dweller's romantic fantasy about small-town life. Her real dream was to live in a community of creative artists, which she was more likely to find in the world's very largest cities than in a one-horse town. Her Square Three breakdown stemmed from her failure to check this fantasy for flaws. Carol is now living in New York City and loving it.

If your dream is solid and your research sound and complete, you may have a problem with your scheme. The steps included in your plan may be ineffective or counterproductive. Some are probably missing altogether, because you never even knew they existed. The only way to perfect a scheme is to bumble through those first five thousand mistakes and refine the steps in your plan to reflect your ever-increasing experience. Leave yourself more time than you think you'll need for every Square Three activity, and revise your scheme to reflect reality as you learn from the school of hard knocks. This is the adventurous heart of the hero's saga, and you're going to live to tell the tale.

EXERCISE

Make something you have never made before, anything from a potato patch to a model airplane. As you make it, count the number of unexpected problems that arise and the number of new skills you have to learn in order to succeed. Write them down. Reward your essential self for having conquered so many obstacles. If you can learn all that, you can learn everything it takes to go, turtle step by turtle step, all the way to your own North Star.

4. Repeat the Square Three Mantra.

The Square Three Mantra, like the mantras for the first two squares, is something you should say to yourself at moments of discouragement or frustration. It goes:

"This is much worse than I expected, and that's okay."

One of the successful people I interviewed, a computer programmer named Felix, suggested this to me after I marveled at how calmly he accepted the frustration of debugging an incredibly complex program. "Of course, you push yourself to make the code as perfect as possible," he said, "but there are always errors and delays. *Always.* The reason I'm making a ton of money doing what I do is that I welcome every bug in my programs. I kind of like the little critters—you have to chase them around, track them down, and then figure out what to do about them. It's fun, as long as you're not hung up on everything being perfect right away." As in the virtual world, so in the real world. The Square Three Mantra may help keep you in the hunt.

5. If You Can't Figure Out What's Wrong, Just Do Something Different.

The Alcoholics Anonymous *Big Book* defines insanity as "doing the same thing over and over again and expecting a different result." This is typical of people who don't analyze their mistakes or accept feedback. Mid–Square Three is the point where such people really flame out— over and over again. They lose job after job by failing to organize paperwork, or they date the same destructive personality in six different bodies, or they run themselves ragged, a dozen times a week, by promising more productivity than they can sustain.

In his book *Do One Thing Different,* psychotherapist Bill O'Hanlon recommends that if you can't figure out what you're doing to create a pattern of failure, you should just change something—anything. Go through your whole dream-scheme again, but this time do one thing you didn't do before, such as (this is a real example from O'Hanlon's book) wearing a hat. Any change at all will change your perspective and help you break the pattern.

This works both in strictly task-oriented processes and in the more subtle, complicated realm of interpersonal interaction. For example, O'Hanlon describes a married couple who kept having the same vicious argument over and over. He told them to go ahead and fight, but under the following conditions: Every time the argument began, the man was required to sit, fully clothed, in the dry bathtub. His wife could fight only if she was sitting (also fully clothed) on the toilet. According to O'Hanlon, this disrupted the couple's pattern of useless conflict; they felt so absurd crouched on various porcelain conveniences that they abandoned their animosity and joined together in plotting to assassinate their marriage counselor. No, no, I'm kidding. What really happened was that they both became critical observers of their own communication styles. From this perspective, they were able to analyze their own assumptions and revise their schemes for interacting with each other.

Doing one thing you've never done before is a way to enlarge your perceptions every time you implement a dream-scheme. If getting feedback, analyzing your "ideal-world" steps, and studying in the school of hard knocks don't help you pinpoint your mistakes, repeat what you've been doing—but add at least one new behavior. If you continue to adapt your scheme, you'll eventually make it through the "failure" phase of the hero's saga and on to the truly gratifying part of Square Three.

Think of a pattern you'd like to break: a bad habit, a tendency to procrastinate, saying yes when you want to say no. The next time you feel this coming on, don't fight it. Just go right ahead and repeat the pattern—*but this time, you must wear a hat.* If you are a habitual hat wearer, do something else while you commit your little sin. For example, you could try squatting, holding a raw egg, or speaking pig Latin. From now on, you must add something new every time you indulge in your unwanted pattern. Enjoy.

LATE SQUARE THREE: SUCCESS

Max wandered in that morning with a stunned expression on his face. I took one look at him, drew a deep cleansing breath, and prepared to help him deal with yet another disappointment.

Max wanted desperately to be a writer. He'd been sending letters and manuscripts to publishers for months, and he'd received dozens of variations on the theme "We have reviewed your submission and found that it does not meet our needs at this time." Every writer can read between the lines of such notes; we know that what the publishers really mean is, "You can't write, you can't think, and everyone hates you. Also, you're ugly." I guessed from Max's blank, bewildered eyes that he'd gotten another rejection.

"How's it going, Max?" I said gently as he sat down.

"My article. The *New Yorker*," Max stammered.

"I'm listening."

"They took it. They bought it." he said. "I'm a writer."

334 FINDING YOUR OWN NORTH STAR

We looked at each other for a long, silent minute. I was almost as dazed as Max. We'd both gotten so used to slogging through his hero's saga that we'd stopped even wondering what success would feel like. Max was used to rejection. Success had taken him completely by surprise.

When you reach this moment, the moment when your dreams first connect to your real life, I want you to stop and record it for posterity. Write journal notations, take videotape, gather your friends and family to tell them how it feels when a dream comes true. Pay attention. This is one of the best experiences life has to offer. This is what it's all about.

Of course, the first instant of real-life success is by no means the end of your hero's saga. Quite the contrary. When your plan begins to operate the way God intended, you'll go through a period of working harder than ever. After selling one story to the *New Yorker*, Max followed up by creating several more article concepts and suggesting them to his new editor. He quickly revised his résumé and several query articles to other publications, mentioning the fact that his work was being published in a prestigious magazine. On the strength of his initial success, he got the interest of a literary agent who could help him sell a book proposal.

Are you getting the picture here? A hero's saga doesn't end with a single triumph; the sooner the hero slays his first enemy, the sooner he gets to meet the dragon, and the Orcs, and the evil sorcerer. It's just one damn thing after another. So after taking time to savor the sweet taste of victory, get set to do the following:

1. Work Like a Dog.

Whoever coined the phrase "work like a dog" obviously hadn't met Cookie, who hasn't done one lick of work in his entire life, unless you count the interior decorating. We use "work like a dog" to refer to thankless, wearing toil—but have you ever actually watched a dog at work? I mean a professional dog, a retriever or a drug sniffer or a herder. Those critters absolutely *love* their jobs. They'll beg to be allowed to work, go at it hour after hour with big doggy smiles on their faces. A pet-store manager once told me that if border collies aren't allowed to herd livestock, they become clinically depressed. Her own collie dealt with his anxieties by herding groups of neighborhood children from yard to yard, hoping desperately that some adult would show up and shear them.

Late Square Three is a time when you should work like a dog in a very literal sense. Dogs are bred to do certain tasks; they're literally created with a passion for their life's work encoded in every cell of their bodies. You, too, were born to love some types of work and detest others. When you're headed for your own North Star, you'll find yourself doing the work you were meant for, the work that was meant for you. You, too, will bounce out of bed clamoring to get on with it. You'll work long hours without even noticing they've gone by.

I could give you hundreds of examples, but I'll stick to just a few. When Lorraine was a paralegal assistant in a bad marriage, she suffered from constant fatigue and repeated viral infections. Now that she's a single clothing designer, she often forgets to leave work until the janitor turns out the lights in her building. Jude almost always slept through his engineering classes, but since he decided to study zoology, he wakes up, full of energy, before his alarm clock has a chance to go off. And Max, who never could follow up on a good performance review in his old job, has developed and applied good, hard-core business habits, now that they support his writing. All these people are working like dogs really work. It's a challenge trying to get them to slow down.

EXERCISE

Find a dog. Watch it work. Now forget Ebenezer Scrooge, John Henry, and the titans of industry: Fido is your new role model.

2. Play Like a Dog.

I suspect that the reason dogs work so hard is that they really know how to play. The common belief in our culture, with its Protestant work ethic, is that play and successful work are antithetical. This is a perversion of the natural order. The truth is that nature bestows superior work and problem-solving skills on creatures that love to play.

I once saw a series of *National Geographic* photos that showed a raven trying to crack open a walnut. The stakes were high, because it was winter and food was scarce. The raven stood at the top of a small, snowy hill, holding the walnut with one claw and prying at it with his beak. He worked so hard that he finally fell right over on his back and skidded, headfirst, all the way down the hill. At this point, the raven forgot all about the nut. He spent the rest of that afternoon walking up the hill, rolling over on his back, and sliding down again. This, my dears, is nature's way.

My clients usually believe that in late Square Three, as work pressure mounts, they should reduce the time they spend playing. Actually, the opposite is true. The more intensely you have to work, the more you need to take play breaks. Playing improves your creativity and problem-solving skills, minimizes burnout, and maintains high-level performance. Iron-willed self-discipline may be just the right thing if you're planning to be a ruthless psychotic despot. Otherwise, let the games begin.

When I was teaching business school, I'd often assign hardworking students two hours of play every day during final-exam week. They invariably reported that their performance improved as a result. The reduction in study time was more than compensated for by a dramatic increase in the speed and effectiveness of their work. I'd like you to do the same thing this week: two hours a day not just vegetating or fulfilling social obligations but having genuine, all-out fun. Ask your essential self what it wants to do during playtime. See how much your productivity increases and your desire to commit mass murder recedes.

EXERCISE
Establish an official play time, and honor it.

3. Hang Out with Your Favorite People.

A really successful Square Three hero is always someone who plays well with others. I don't mean you have to get along with everybody or be a "people person" to navigate a successful saga. What I mean is that you should seek out people you enjoy and spend as much time as possible simply being friends.

I have a few acquaintances, most of them people from John's business-school days, who clearly put a lot of effort into networking. They go to hundreds of cocktail parties and really work every room, handing out business cards and memorizing names. They call all their contacts every six months. "Hello, Martha!" they'll say when my name pops up on their Rolodex. "I haven't seen you since the Blatherspoons' Christmas party! How the heck are you, John, and your children, Katherine, Adam, and Elizabeth?"

I hate these people. I hate their cocktail parties. I hate their Rolodex relationships. The bottom line is, I hate networking—at least the way a lot of businesspeople seem to define it. Furthermore, I've never seen this kind of networking succeed in any major way. Real networking— the kind that improves every aspect of your life, not just your Rolodex list—isn't about slick company manners or mutual advantage. It's about love. Does that sound weird? I could say "friendship," but I want to cut right to the heart of the matter. The fact is that you'll find your own North Star peopled not with folks you merely like but those you genuinely adore. These people will share your passions and ideals. Their essential selves are likely to fit beautifully with yours. They are your tribe.

I've been in my business long enough to know that true friendship is the kind of "network connection" that leads to real success. For starters, it's the best way to decide whom you want to include in your career. It can yield job offers, entrepreneurial opportunities, alliances, promotions, incredibly powerful team performances, and myriad other prizes. But connecting with the people who are meant to be part of your own North Star is much more important than any aspect of business. It's the essence of happiness, the full realization of your potential for joy. Remember back in Square One, when you were nobody nowhere with no one and nothing? By the end of your incredibly arduous, disappointing, stressful journey through Square Three, you'll be your true self, in a place you belong, with friends who truly understand you and bring all sorts of opportunities your way. Every aspect of your life, whether it's a task or a relationship, personal or professional, will be based on love and joy. And when you get right down to it, nothing else really matters.

EXERCISE

Call your best friend. Schedule time to play together. Keep the appointment, and when you're enjoying yourself thoroughly, stop and pay attention. This feeling—the feeling of ease, contentment, trust, and above all, fun—is what you should experience on a regular basis as you lock in on your own North Star. The closer you get to the life you were meant to live, the more work and play, "connection" and friendship will blur together and eventually become one. This is the taste and texture of your hero's saga. Enjoy.

15

SQUARE FOUR:
THE PROMISED LAND

*On the path to excellence, the gods have placed many obstacles, and
the way is steep and hard to climb. But when you get to the top, then
it is easy, even though it is hard.*

—HESIOD

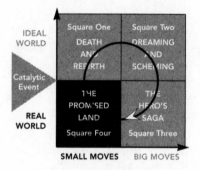

THE CHANGE CYCLE

Moses never got there. For forty years, he wandered around with
the Children of Israel, looking for the green pastures, the still waters,
the milk and honey of the Promised Land. Then, when he'd finally
come within shouting distance, God decided to haul Moses up to
Heaven. Maybe this is another example of the capriciousness of the
Old Testament deity, who sometimes sounds like the Big Pubescent
Boy in the Sky, alternately blessing his followers and using them as sub-

jects in highly unpleasant experiments. But there may be more benefi-
cent reasons. Maybe Moses was a voyager, born to thrive in the wilderness, not interested in a stable, uneventful life. Maybe he went on to
new adventures in another dimension. Or maybe the storytellers who
wrote the Bible just knew that once the hero's saga ends, he's no longer
nearly as interesting to readers.

We really aren't interested in hearing how Moses moved into a nice
split-level temple, came up with a fabulous recipe for milk-and-honey
shakes, and made a bundle in fast foods. We want our heroes struggling,
beleaguered, put-upon. But I can assure you that while Square Four is
less pleasurable to hear about than Square Three, it is far more pleasurable to live.

You'll know you've arrived in Square Four when your dreams have
not only come true but demonstrated some long-term staying power.
Your small business is turning enough profit to survive; the person you
love has agreed to marry you; the contract is signed; the statute of limitations has run out on your more serious crimes. The ingredients necessary for a joyful life are yours to keep. You're done wandering through
the wilderness, not really knowing where your next manna meal is
going to come from or whether it will show up in time. It's finally time
to slow down.

EARLY SQUARE FOUR: SLOWING DOWN

As we've seen, Square Three requires an enormous amount of forward
momentum. To get to Square Four, you've powered your way through
enough obstacles to level an NFL linebacker. It can take so long that
you eventually come to consider this a permanent lifestyle. When you
hit Square Four and there are no more barriers in your way, you may
not know how to handle the situation. Don't worry. This is the good
part. Here are some instructions that can help you enjoy it.

1. Put On the Brakes.

Have you ever encountered a salesperson who convinced you to buy
something, then continued to push you so hard that you got annoyed
and started rethinking your decision? Once you've reached Square Four

and things are going your way, for heaven's sake, ease up. I encounter a lot of folks who have trouble doing this. Even after they've become very successful, they take on too much work, certain that bypassing a single opportunity will end up trashing their futures. They go out of their way to do things that didn't have to be done, for people they don't really like, in order to make sure they never run out of friends. In Square Three, such efforts can add up to success. In Square Four, they actually create failure.

Most of us overshoot a bit when we come out of Square Three into Square Four, and that's okay. You'll put on the brakes in plenty of time if you pay attention to outside feedback and, even more important, keep a weather eye on your internal compasses. When you reach early Square Four, your essential self will begin to pull back a little, trying to keep you squarely aligned with the life you were meant to live. It may take you by surprise that your inner drive toward work and achievement has suddenly switched over to rest and relaxation, but you must listen to it. In Square Four, less effort equals more security and accomplishment.

EXERCISE

Think of a joke you really like. Find a friend who hasn't heard it. Now tell the friend your joke. Isn't that fun? Okay. Now, right away, repeat the same joke to the same person. And while you're at it, *explain* why your friend should laugh. Comment on the joke's amusement value: "That was funny, wasn't it? Oh, boy, was that ever funny!" Before you know it, your friend will stop laughing and start edging away with a slightly curled upper lip. The moral of this exercise is that *there is a time to deliver the goods, and there is a time to let things be.* The next time a dream-scheme seems to be succeeding, give it some space. Check your compasses. Dare to stop pushing.

2. Focus on What's Working; Drop Everything Else.

Seymour was a client who ended up in financial Square Four very early in life almost accidentally. At the age of twenty-nine, he inherited over a million dollars. Without really thinking about it, he formed an assumption that he had a charmed life, that his monetary luck would never change. Seymour went through that million bucks like a pig through pasta, buying boats and houses and sequined love slaves and whatever else he wanted. By forty, Seymour was bankrupt—and he had not a single clue as to what he should, or could, do about it. As far as he knew, the only way to find his own North Star was to lie down and wait for another million bucks to fall out of the sky.

I have many other clients whose thinking is exactly the opposite of Seymour's. These people are like my dog, the lauded Cookie, who thinks that he creates food donations in much the way a rain dancer creates precipitation. Actually, he gets fed twice a day no matter what he does, but don't try to tell him that. After every meal, Cookie devotes his entire brain—both cells—to retracing each and every behavior that immediately preceded the Great Event. He repeats all those actions, in order, the next time a human crosses his path, thinking, "Let's see, what did I do last time—purse lips, go *Woowoowoo,* sidestep twice to the left, twice to the right, turn around, *flap* the ears—flap 'em flap 'em flap 'em—oh Lord now I'm dizzy—roll over, stand up, repeat: *Woowoo-woo . . .*" This goes on for about five minutes. If it doesn't happen to be mealtime, and he therefore doesn't get any food, Cookie eventually slinks off, thinking, "Damn. I must've left something out."

Do you see the common issue here? Neither Seymour nor Cookie understands exactly the mechanisms necessary to get what he wants. Seymour's problem is that he assumes he doesn't have to do anything to be rewarded, while Cookie thinks he has to do an enormous amount of work that is, in fact, completely unproductive. Once you get to early Square Four, it's important to watch for both of these errors of judgment.

If your journey to the promised land was easy, count your blessings. I mean that literally. Stop and thoroughly examine the circumstances of your unusual good fortune. Calculate the odds of its happening again. Make sure you understand just how lucky you are, so that you don't take your success for granted and assume that it will continue indefinitely, with no effort on your part. If Seymour had done this at thirty, instead of forty, he might have invested his money instead of squandering it and stayed in financial Square Four for the rest of his life.

On the other hand, if you've been pouring absolutely every ounce of energy into doing absolutely everything you could to make it to the promised land, you're probably expending more effort than you need to maintain your success. Around the time I started publicizing my first book, a best-selling author told me that I shouldn't bother to get up at two o'clock in the morning to do live call-in radio shows in other time zones. "I used to kill myself doing that, and it really didn't change things all that much," she said. "If a book is going to sell, it won't be because of one predawn radio show. If the book's going to bomb, that one radio show won't save it. Caring for your health and your family is more important." In other words, don't throw your precious time and energy into low-yield strategies. (I'm pretty sure the marketing people at my publishing house will disagree with this, but they will be wrong.) If something drains you dry while contributing very little to your success, don't do it.

One of the primary tasks of early Square Four is figuring out which strategies and activities have the best ratio of effort to effect in your particular version of the promised land. It's different for every person. For example, my friend Mary Ann is an incredible money manager. She has a coupon file, cross-referenced by subject, date, and dollar value, that makes the Library of Congress look like it was organized by illiterate drug addicts. Mary Ann's coupon file saves her thousand and thousands of dollars a year. At one time, awed by its splendor, I tried to duplicate Mary Ann's methods. I spent several hours learning her system, then clipping and filing coupons. I think I once actually remembered to take them to the store, where I promptly dropped them onto a patch of wet linoleum. After a few more feeble efforts, I realized that my coupon cutting was saving a lot less money per hour than I could earn by seeing clients for an equal amount of time. For me, the effort-to-effect ratio of cutting coupons isn't worth it. For Mary Ann, it is. *Vive la différence.* Do whatever works for you.

3. Slide Down the Learning Curve.

In Square Three, you confronted dozens of tasks and situations you'd never even imagined before. You stumbled through these unfamiliar experiences, making lots of mistakes, returning frequently to Square One, and learning an enormous amount. In Square Four, once you've figured out which of these efforts are most effective and discontinued any unproductive behaviors, it's time to focus on becoming really, really good at the things that will sustain your success.

At first, this process is excruciatingly slow. That's because you're not only learning new skills you're also *learning how to learn* this new field. Whether it's career management, architecture, gracious company manners, emotional I.Q., the arts, the sciences, the Funky Chicken, or any other skill, the early learning is the hardest. Once you've got that licked, you'll catch on to the more advanced levels faster and faster. Force yourself to bumble, repeat, and above all, *practice* your way through the beginning of Square Four. Before long you'll become an expert at stuff you thought you could never master. You'll be doing-without-doing it in your sleep.

4. Chunk Your Turtle Steps.

The reason we broke your dream-scheme down into "turtle steps" during Square Three is that you were making huge changes, undertaking unfamiliar tasks, and probably expecting too much from yourself before you'd had any experience in these new areas. Once you're in Square Four, your definition of a turtle step (the largest amount of work your essential self can do easily) will begin to cover more and more territory. Activities you once had to break into several steps will blend together. You won't have to think, "Okay, I shall take this egg and hold it lengthwise, then rap it sharply—but not too sharply—on the side of this bowl, then separate the shell into two parts while letting the contents drop *into* the bowl, then throw the shell away, then grasp this spoon thus, by the narrow end, and thrust the large, shallow-bowl end into the mixing bowl, then circulate the spoon 'round about the interior of the bowl, like *this* . . ." Instead, you'll think, "Beat one egg." Much better, no?

This capacity to combine many small steps into one larger step is called "chunking." Our brains do it automatically every time we learn new information. Suppose I asked you to memorize seventy numbers in a row—say, the value of *pi* to the seventieth digit. Unless you're an autistic savant, you'd have a hard time doing it. But you probably know at least ten phone numbers off the top of your head. That's a minimum of seventy digits, all in perfect order. The reason you can remember so many numbers is that they're chunked: each group of seven to ten digits is attached to a certain person or place in your mind. Every individual phone number is also divided into chunks. One reason we write these numbers with parentheses and dashes is that our brains find it much easier to store and recall chunked information.

The first time you arrange a business trip to Bangkok, or paint an oil portrait, or solve a quadratic equation, every aspect of the task will go very slowly and leave you feeling righteously exhausted. By the fiftieth time, you'll be doing the whole thing with your toes while you give yourself a manicure. Keep pushing yourself, gently but firmly, to incorporate more work into each turtle step. You will eventually reach the point where everything necessary to maintaining your Square Four prosperity is not only manageable but easy. You will have reached the solid center of Square Four.

MID–SQUARE FOUR: WALKING BESIDE THE STILL WATERS

The other day I spoke to a taxi driver who hailed from a country that's been invaded more than Elizabeth Taylor's privacy. The country is independent at the moment, but my cabby friend was dubious about its future. "My people are very good at fighting oppression," he told me. "The problem is that it's all we know how to do. We've had so much war that we don't know how to govern in a time of peace." A lot of my clients are like this. Those who grew up in chaotic, unpredictable environments (children of alcoholic parents seem especially vulnerable) aren't comfortable with the peaceful, bountiful steadiness of Square Four. They don't know how to stroll by the still waters, and they often end up destroying their very own promised land. If you're one of these people, here are some pointers for mid–Square Four.

1. Don't Hoard Your Toast.

I once read a memoir by a man who'd escaped from a Soviet prison in Siberia, then walked across the Gobi desert to China with nothing to eat but the occasional venomous snake. When he finally made it to freedom, he was more dead than alive and had to spend several weeks in the hospital. Throughout this hospitalization, the man kept stuffing toast into his pillowcase. He knew intellectually that this was unnecessary, but deep down, he just couldn't believe that this incredible abundance—toast everywhere!—could possibly last.

A lot of people end up hoarding all manner of "toast" in Square Four. Exhausted and fearful after their long trip through the change cycle, they cling desperately to the good things that are finally coming into their lives: money, relationships, attention, power. They don't delegate authority, pay their employees generously, or donate time and money to philanthropic causes—no, no, then there won't be enough good stuff left for them! Ironically enough, this type of thinking and behavior acts as a promised-land repellent. A hoarding mentality actually keeps you from experiencing joy, reduces your ability to make money, and scuttles both personal and professional relationships.

One November first, I woke up to find that I had enough leftover Halloween candy to rot the teeth out of every man, woman, and child in America. I dumped all the candy into a big salad bowl and put it by my office door. When I told one of my newly successful clients to help himself, he set to work like some kind of starving rodent, stuffing all his pockets with as much as they'd hold until he'd emptied the entire bowl. Even at the time, I knew this man's psychological motive was fear and insecurity. But that didn't soften my reflexive reaction, which was: *"You are an icky person, and I will never offer you anything ever again."* Insecure people—toast hoarders—tend to get kicked out of the promised land because they fail to trust their own well-being.

Buddhists say that when we cling to good things, we not only choke them to death but render ourselves incapable of embracing all the effusive grandeur the world offers us in every present moment. Become obsessed with keeping one person's love and you'll drive that person away while remaining inaccessible to other rewarding relationships. Hanging on to every penny, rather than taking the slight risk involved in cautious investment, could rob you of enormous financial benefit. Stinginess isn't just unattractive; it's counterproductive. If you find yourself giving in to it as you enter Square Four, you must retrain yourself.

First of all, you may have a lot of grasping lies in your head, put there early on by a miserly Everybody. You may be unintentionally, unconsciously repeating little sermons like "Money doesn't go on trees, you know" or "The other shoe is bound to drop soon" or "Fool! Do you think all this toast is going to last forever?" If so, you must recondition yourself with the same techniques you use to replace any other negative Everybody-talk.

EXERCISE ONE: CLING-GUARD AFFIRMATIONS

Despite my doubts about affirmations in general, this is one situation where they work beautifully. Below are some statements you should post all over your walls, including the walls of your mind, whenever you start feeling greedy and anxious. If you've followed your internal navigational equipment through every step of the change cycle, all of these statements are absolutely true. Repeat them until you believe them.

1. There is more than enough wealth, love, and happiness to go around.
2. I am succeeding because of my choices, not blind luck.
3. If something goes wrong, I'll figure out how to make it right.
4. I created this situation once, and I can create it again—and again, and again . . .
5. If I lost everything, lots of people would be willing to help me.
6. I can deal with my life at this moment—and that's all I'll ever have to do.
7. Nothing can take my destiny away from me.
8. There's much, much more good stuff where this came from.
9. I will always have plenty.
10. I have free access to infinite richness.

Even if you have a very generous internalized Everybody, you may develop psychological tentacles after going through a period of deprivation. This is a natural tendency, possibly even a physiological one. The Soviet toast miser's need to save food was an instinctive body-and-brain reaction to near starvation. My favorite remedy for this kind of thing is what I call "divine decadence."

EXERCISE TWO: DIVINE DECADENCE

To practice divine decadence, simply get yourself an oversupply of something your essential self really likes. Don't just get as much as you want; get twice as much, five times as much, more than you could use in a month of Sundays. Obviously, unless you're very wealthy, you won't be stocking up on luxury yachts or highly trained servants; but the essential self is a simple soul, and it can feel divinely decadent with relatively inexpensive rewards.

For her first divine decadence exercise, Lillian bought herself twenty bars of pretty, perfumed glycerin soap in various colors. She was so thrilled that she brought them to a session as show-and-tell. I don't think her essential self could have been more pleased if they'd been solid platinum. Matthew loves mechanical pencils, so for his exercise he bought himself ten different kinds, with extra leads. Emily was almost broke but very resourceful; she went to a "damaged and discarded" sale down at the freight yards and got several gorgeous scarves and dresses for a dollar or two apiece. I personally maintain a permanent supply of boxed chocolates, the kind with caramel and nuts. I like to have at least five pounds on hand at all times.

When I assign this exercise, my clients always look at me as though I've asked them to help me rob a nursing home. That would be a dreadful thing to do, they say; it's self-indulgent and swinish and scandalous! Yeah. Ain't it grand? That's exactly how divine decadence should feel—at least when you start out. But after a while, you'll find that flooding yourself with good things has a peculiar effect on your psychology, as inevitable and involuntary as the toast-hoarding reaction. Once you've been living in the midst of plenty for a while, your psychological grip will loosen. You'll stop worrying about running out. You'll begin to let go.

People are always telling me that if *they* had a five-pound box of chocolates, they'd just keep eating until their abdominal walls ruptured. I believe this is because they've never given themselves permission to have an infinite supply of chocolates. As long as a treat is scarce and forbidden, you're going to feel compulsive and greedy about it. When you give yourself free access to it, you may indeed go a little crazy for a while. The first time I got myself chocolates, I ate nothing else for three days. At that point, I became bored and started hankering for salad. Really. If you've had all the chocolate you can eat for as long as you like and you know you can have more whenever you want it, the obsessive need to gobble goes away. Even if you run out of your favorite thing, there's no sense of panic or deprivation. Peace and plenty go together; give yourself one, and you get the other.

When you think you're over feeling graspish about your divinely decadent item, try a little test: Give some of it away. Pack some of those scarves in a bag for the Salvation Army. Leave a bar of glycerin soap out for the kids. Give your brother one of your mechanical pencils. Now, be honest: Did it hurt? If it's hard for you to part with your prize, you haven't spent enough time feeling divinely decadent. Buy yourself some more of your treat, whatever it is. Keep it all for yourself. Stuff it in your pillowcase. Sit on it for months, as though it's an egg you're trying to hatch. If you continue long enough, you will eventually begin to believe—really believe, deep down—that there is plenty of good stuff, and there always will be. When you can give away some of your divine-decadence item without experiencing any resentment or anxiety, you'll be ready for yet another exercise.

EXERCISE THREE: HOLD A GIVEAWAY

Giveaways are a central element of many cultures. People in these societies gain status not by having stuff but by giving stuff. While this philosophy has its own drawbacks and dysfunctions, most of us could stand a little more of it. In our culture, giving too often becomes a form of control—"I gave you life; you owe me everything"—or a way to feel self-consciously righteous. Giving for these reasons will make you more stingy, not less, and could very well keep you away from the life you were meant to live. A real giveaway, the kind that nails down your spot in the promised land, is willing and joyful. You give because it makes you happy. You don't have the slightest need to be repaid or to sit around admiring your own generosity. I must reiterate that *you can't feel this way about giving unless you're sure that there's plenty of good stuff for you.* It's impossible to force generosity out of a sense of deprivation. Don't even try it. But once you've experienced enough divine decadence to feel that the world may be generous after all, the following steps can make your Square Four experience even better:

1. Identify something you have in great abundance and don't mind sharing.
2. Find someone who needs what you have to share.
3. Figure out how much you can give away joyfully (do this by checking to see how your essential self responds to the prospect of giving various different amounts).
4. Give as much as you can *joyfully* afford. If possible, do this anonymously.
5. Dwell on the pleasure of seeing, or imagining, the good feelings you've created with your gift.

You'd be amazed how happy this exercise can make you. Weirdly enough, I also believe—really—that it's one of the best ways to increase your income. I remember reading this piece of advice in a financial-planning book and thinking that it was saccharine, bogus, and obviously untrue. See, I was raised in a religion that requires its members to give 10 percent of everything they earn to the church, and though I'd done this in my youth, I certainly never saw my income magically increase. But as I read the financial-planning book, it occurred to me that as a kid I'd always given under duress, often parted with more money than I wanted to give, and knew that my donation was going to a massive, faceless organization, however well-meaning. When I ran across the concept of a "giveaway" decades later, I decided to try it on my own terms. I calculated how much money I felt comfortable giving and identified someone whose life could literally be changed by this small amount. The actual anonymous donation of the cash left me feeling wonderful. And the next day, sure enough, I got an unexpected windfall check from a project I'd forgotten about long before. You could have knocked me down with a feather.

I don't know why this works, but it does. Whenever my financial affairs are looking worrisome, when greed and fear begin crooning their fetid whispers into my ear (this tends to happen right around April fifteenth), I hold a little giveaway to reverse the trend. As long as I give in a manner and amount that brings me joy, more money arrives in short order—money I had no good reason to expect. I've seen the same thing happen to my clients, over and over again, despite the fact that it makes no logical sense whatsoever. My current hypothesis is that there's a kind of cosmic Give-Receive valve connecting each of us to the universal ether. When the valve is closed, we neither give nor get. When it's open, money and love pour through our lives continuously. You can't open the valve to receive without being willing to give, and vice versa. Whatever you need, a giveaway is an always available way to start the flow of good things.

2. Be Overwhelmed by Joy.

One day our family dentist told me my son wasn't getting his back molars as clean as he should. Because Adam's Down's syndrome affects his motor control, it's quite difficult for him to reach all the molar surfaces with an ordinary toothbrush. Our dentist recommended an extremely whippy and expensive electric brush, which he happened to be selling out of his very own office—what a lucky coincidence! So I handed over mondo bucks for the toothbrush, took it home, taught Adam to use it, and sent him and his sisters to perform their ablutions. Seconds later I heard horrible sounds issuing from the bathroom, as if someone were in there plucking live chickens without anesthesia. Certain that Adam had electrocuted himself with the toothbrush, I rushed down the hall, almost knocking over my daughter Elizabeth as she emerged from the bathroom.

"What's the matter with Adam?" I asked her.

"There's nothing wrong with him, Mom," said Lizzie. "He's just overwhelmed by joy."

And so he was. Adam was standing by the sink in a kind of rapturous daze, running the multidirectional bristles over his teeth, whooping wildly, and grinning as though he were running for office. This is how he responds to almost any new experience. You can give Adam something like a lunchbox or new underwear, and he'll go out of his mind with delight. *"Oh my gosh! Look at this! Wow! Thank you!"*

The result of this is that Adam is spoiled rotten. Everyone gives him stuff, because it's such infectious fun to watch him receive. If you let yourself respond to your own good fortune like Adam does, people will want to give to you, too. You used to do this, back when you were really tiny, but in all likelihood it was knocked out of you before your own back molars even appeared. You learned to act abstemious, not needy. You learned never to show anyone how much you wanted something, or let people see how thrilled you were to get it. Most of us believe that overt demonstrations of either desire or fulfillment are deeply unwise, that they leave us frighteningly vulnerable in both personal and professional settings, that they attract sharks.

My observations suggest that this belief is composed mainly of road apples (which is a nice term for what bulls leave behind them). My least successful clients, the ones who just can't seem to get their lives together, tend to be the most obsessed with hiding their emotional reactions. On the other hand, when I interviewed highly successful people for this book, I was struck by how openly every one of them showed feelings of both gratitude and disappointment. Instead of minimizing their grief over losses, they'd say, "Oh, I was devastated when I didn't get that job. *Devastated.* I cried for three days." On the other hand, when something good came their way, they let themselves be overwhelmed by joy.

Like Adam, my successful subjects were constantly mentioning good things most of us take for granted. They'd interrupt an interview to say, "Look at that cloud! Is that beautiful? Hang on, I have to look at the clouds for a minute." Or: "Last night, I watched TV. It was fabulous. Oh, *Lord,* life is good!" Or: "Doesn't it feel wonderful to breathe? I just love breathing." I always ended up wanting to do things for these folks. People who express gratitude create pools of generosity in the world around them.

If you've really positioned your life by consulting your internal compasses and setting a path to your own North Star, you're going to experience a lot of good things. Celebrate them. Comment on them, frequently. Tell people about your reactions to both success and failure. Be both overwhelmed and open. You'll maximize your own happiness and lay the groundwork for it to continue indefinitely.

EXERCISE

List ten good things you have, right now. For example, at the moment I have: 1) healthy lungs, 2) many happy memories, 3) gum, 4) the ability to read, 5) a slight tan, 6) hope, 7) Diet Snapple, 8) plans to visit Jamaica, 9) a lovely view of North Phoenix, and 10) sweat glands. And that's just the beginning! Your turn:

1. _____

2. _____

3. _____

4. _____

5. _____

6. _____

7. _____

8. _____

9. _____

10. _____

Now take a second to focus on each of the things you listed. Congratulate yourself on every one. Dwell on your virtues and advantages. Gloat. If at all possible, push your own self-satisfaction to the point where you are overwhelmed by a grateful sort of joy. Express this feeling as often as possible. Far from turning people off, this will draw good friends and good fortune toward you.

3. Be Here Now.

Andrew Carnegie said, "Show me a contented man, and I'll show you a failure." In other words, the craving for more and the inability to be satisfied are fundamental ingredients of success. Huh? This is nonsense. It's like teaching medical students that only patients who are in severe pain can be considered healthy. Nevertheless, it's the way a lot of us have learned to think.

"I'm really worried that I may be losing my edge," said Gil, a particularly high-achieving client. "I don't seem to have any drive these days."

Gil had worked his way up from corporate greenhorn to the top of his profession. He was making half a million dollars a year, before bonuses. He was married to a terrific woman, and they'd just had a son. Gil had achieved all this by acting on enormous "drive." His problem wasn't that this had disappeared but that *it was being fulfilled.* The only thing Gil had lost was a sense of dissatisfaction, the conviction that he did not have enough. Andrew Carnegie might have advised him to get that discontent back, but I believe that it was time for Gil to stop hankering after more and enjoy what he was experiencing in the here and now. What good does it do to attain the promised land if all you do there is sit around fantasizing about being somewhere else? As they say in Vegas, you must be present to win.

There are all kinds of techniques in Asian religious practice for bringing your attention into the present moment, so that you don't miss out on life by perpetually leaning forward into hopes and fears, or backward toward past triumphs or misfortunes. One method is to sit still and focus on your breathing, a word, or some small object, like a candle flame. If you feel like trying this, I urge you to read up on meditation and give it a go. However, sitting still and focusing is extraordinarily difficult, and most of my clients never get around to doing it. Here are a couple of quicker, easier ways to be here now.

EXERCISE ONE: THE BEAUTY WAY

The Navajo Indians have a prayer-chant called "The Beauty Way," which I once learned from a Navajo friend. I'm sure there are many translations, and I'm also pretty positive that I changed it around a little in my head. Nevertheless, with apologies to the Navajo people, I'm going to teach you my version of the Beauty Way chant. It's very simple. It goes like this:

> *There is beauty before me, and there is beauty behind me.*
> *There is beauty to my left, and there is beauty to my right.*
> *There is beauty above me, and there is beauty below me.*
> *There is beauty around me, and there is beauty within me.*

I once read a commentary on the painter Degas that said, "He had a great talent for discovering beauty." Not creating beauty, or reproducing it, but discovering it. That was the first time I realized that an artist's real contribution isn't what he paints, but the way he sees. I've found that repeating the Beauty Way chant changes the way I see. It yanks me out of my perseverations and obsessions, revealing astonishing loveliness in the present moment—beauty I hadn't noticed, even though it was right there all along.

I often run through the Beauty Way chant when I'm out for a walk in the strangely gorgeous Sonoran Desert, and it's obvious why the people who inhabit this landscape would come up with such a prayer. But it actually works even better in less obviously beautiful circumstances. I recently repeated it to myself as I sat in an airplane at night. I hadn't thought of this as a particularly beautiful place—in fact, I'd been busily sending my mind other places, avoiding the tedium and claustrophobia of the trip. As I repeated the chant, I looked forward, backward, left, right, up and down, and was just knocked over by the beauty of sleeping passengers, the smell of food, the tiny lights in the black velvet landscape thirty thousand feet under my seat.

Shelley was right: Beauty is its own excuse for being. What the Andrew Carnegies of the world don't seem to realize is that the experience of beauty, the satisfaction it conveys, is its own very deep form of success. Repeat the Beauty Way chant right now, wherever you are. You'll begin to notice beauty, all kinds of beauty, everywhere—in birdsongs and battle cries, muscles and equations, angst and oatmeal. You will discover what it is to be present.

EXERCISE TWO: MINDFUL MUNCHING

This is based on a meditation practice called "mindfulness," in which you do ordinary things with extraordinary attention. First, fix a small serving of some food you really love—one grape will do, or a noodle, or (my favorite) a caramel-nut chocolate. Sit down at a time you know you won't be interrupted and eat this food very, very slowly. Try to focus on every sensation you experience: sight, smell, taste, sound, and texture. Notice how the food feels in your mouth, throat, and tummy. Play with it. Poke it with your fingers. Blow bubbles. Be fully present for the delight of this one experience. You will find that there is far more pleasure in it than you generally notice.

Now, once a day or so, bring this kind of mindfulness to another experience: hugging someone you love, petting the cat, getting dressed, picking your nose. Try to focus so intensely on actual sensations that your thoughts about your experience disappear and only the experience itself remains. Truly enjoy it, then let it go and enjoy the next moment. Andrew Carnegie would be thoroughly frustrated with you for doing this, but remember, he's dead. We can all hope that he's finally found contentment.

LATE SQUARE FOUR: CULTIVATING THE PROMISED LAND

So you've finally slowed down and begun to enjoy the abundant life of the promised land. This doesn't mean you have to stop doing anything, or become dull and redundant. Ideally, I'd like to see you spend your whole life in Square Four, a place where your true self can fully express and enjoy itself. But Square Four can last only if it allows for innovation and growth. If it doesn't, you'll find yourself back in Square One all too soon. Here are some ways to explore and enlarge your Square Four experience, so that it goes on as long as possible.

1. Add as Many Worthwhile Experiences as You Can.

A lot of people, as well as life-planning books, define the Good Life as acquiring a huge number of *things*. I prefer to think of it as having the fullest possible fund of interesting *experiences,* including the experience of wealth, if that's what turns you on. Experience enlarges you by weaving itself into the fabric of your identity; you are the sum of all you have experienced.

For this reason, when I have clients who've made it all the way to Square Four and seem to be well contented, I try to find out what new, unprecedented experiences appeal to them, what's tugging at their essential selves. You don't have to start a whole new change cycle to have such experiences; you just work them into a happy, prosperous, and comfortable Square Four. You grow everything you can in the soil of this promised land, here and now.

I used to ask people, "So, what do you want to do before you die?" After a while I noticed that this question made people wince and pull back, and I realized that it sounded like I was planning to slap blindfolds on them and march them out to the execution grounds. Now I phrase my questions more carefully, and I'd like to pose them to you, right now: What experiences would you like to have before you're finished with this particular go-round on planet Earth? Are there any interesting things you've never done that you would like to do?

People give the most delightfully unexpected answers to these questions. I asked four clients this morning, and here's what they said: Randy wants to learn Latin dancing. Kathy hopes to tour India. Orlando said he'd like to try hallucinogenic mushrooms. Jeanette has often toyed with the idea of spending some time in a cloistered convent. My reaction to all these revelations was: ! I never knew these people had such aspirations, but I find them all immensely interesting. Naturally, we immediately converted them into intentions, and I have no doubt that each of these clients will soon be making fascinating additions to their funds of experience.

2. Take Down All the "One Way" Signs.

I would like to assure any legal authorities who may be reading this book that the paragraph above is in no way meant to indicate that I encourage my clients to use hallucinogenic mushrooms. I know it's against the law, and I myself get a little nervous around psychoactive substances in general. But by the same token, I know several people who tell me they've had life-changing positive experiences through the use of psychedelic drugs, and while my true path doesn't take me in that direction, I have no basis for claiming that it's wrong for them.

It's very common for people who have reached Square Four to decide that they've discovered the One Way to happiness, and that everyone would benefit from living in exactly the same manner. If they feel better eating nothing but coleslaw, or joining a mosque, or being married, or jogging, then by God they're going to make sure everyone else does the same thing. These people are extremely principled, kind, and well-intentioned. Ignore them. You cannot find your own true path by locking on to someone else's North Star.

"One way" thinkers tend to get very confused when their North Stars lead them into unfamiliar territory. They're used to thinking that a certain set of actions and beliefs will assure them permanent happiness, when in fact security lies in adapting to constant change. What is right for you at one point in your life—and I mean your ideal life—will turn out to be dead wrong at another point. The promised land is no place for One Way signs, even for a single individual.

There's an old Chinese story about a monk who was traveling to meet an enlightened guru. At one point, the monk had to cross a wide river, so he built a raft out of bamboo and navigated to the other shore. The next part of his journey led into steep, mountainous terrain. But the monk had grown really attached to the bamboo raft. He'd worked hard building it, it had served him well, and it didn't seem prudent to abandon something so useful. The monk tried to drag his raft with him up the mountain and grew steadily more battered and weary in the attempt. Finally, he realized that unless he let go of his raft, he would never make it to the guru. What was essential for his journey at one point became a colossal hindrance later on. This can be true of anything in your life, from a relationship to a religion. In Buddhism, such things are called "golden chains," practices that are indeed sacred and precious but can still be wrong at this point on your journey, in this present moment.

If you are surgically attached to One Way thinking, you may not only knock other people off their true paths but also stop your own progress forward in the life you were meant to live. There may well be times when your internal compasses tell you to resist social pressure or to stop someone else from doing damage to you or others. If someone attacks you, go ahead and do whatever it takes to prevent them from fulfilling their intentions. But as long as other people aren't being dangerous or harmful, stop worrying about what they're doing and focus on finding your own way. This is what people learn in "codependency" treatment, after they've been severely hurt by other people's addiction, abusiveness, or crazy behavior: You cannot control anyone else's journey through life. Focus on your own. Compassion, honesty, self-scrutiny, and an open mind are the only "one way" to interact sanely and successfully with others. Of course, I could be wrong about this.

3. Expect Change.

It's almost universal for people in Square Four to resist change. Things are so nice, it's taken you so long to get here . . . no wonder you want everything to stay exactly as it is right now. Well, tough. Your life has changed since you started reading this sentence. You're a tiny bit older than you were when it began. Your hair and fingernails are longer, the time until your death a little shorter. Your mind contains the memory of a sentence you've never seen until now—wait, not now, I mean a moment ago, when you started reading. You and I and everything in our environment are continuously, permanently, relentlessly in transition.

We modern humans have to be even more accepting of this fact than folks who lived in earlier times. The pace of change in the world around us is accelerating geometrically. Consider the fact that until the invention of the steam engine, the fastest form of transportation was the sailing ship, a device that had been around for centuries. When the automobile was developed, doctors warned that human physiology probably couldn't stand speeds of more than thirteen miles an hour. Now the slowest among us drive faster than that in school zones, while those of us who happen to be fighter pilots routinely travel faster than sound. Within a few generations, we've also created and learned to transmit unimaginable amounts of information (there's more information in one edition of the *New York Times* than existed in all the world's literature in the thirteenth century), and we've proliferated to the point of destroying our own ecosystem. In short, things aren't just changing. They're changing very, very fast, and they're not going to slow down.

This is all the more reason why your Square Four, the life you put together in the outside world, must accommodate the reality of change. That doesn't mean you shouldn't be upset by things like aging, death, betrayal, decay, and the emergence of such social trends as tongue piercing. It simply means that your version of the promised land has space and time for resistance and grief. You don't cope with change by becoming indifferent to it. You learn to follow the flow, do-without-doing, fully experience surprise, tragedy, delight, and wonder as they come your way. In practical terms, this means not overburdening yourself with so much doing that you have no time to be. It means striking a balance between earning and enjoying, company and solitude, effort and rest. Here are some helpful hints for making your Square Four as resilient as possible.

EXERCISE ONE: SCOUT THE TERRAIN

There will come a time for each of us when we reach our final Square Four, a version of the promised land that will only be interrupted by the catalytic event of our death. But before that, we'll all get knocked into the change cycle several times, maybe *dozens* of times. As I sit here writing, I can look out my window and see a huge column of smoke billowing from a ridge about a mile away. It wasn't there when I sat down three hours ago; it started quite suddenly and grew frighteningly fast. The afternoon news report tells me that this great gray cloud contains all the physical matter that, two hours ago, was someone's house. There it goes, up into the desert sky, every floorboard and carpet, banister and door.

I've never had my own house burn down, but I've seen my carefully constructed life go up in smoke several times. I can guess what the owners of that house must be feeling. I hope with all my might that neither I nor you nor any other living thing will ever feel that way again. For that reason, I'd like you to build the practice of scouting into every Square Four. Without getting paranoid or fatalistic, be on the lookout for signs of change, either good or bad. Sometimes you can see catalytic events headed at you in time to divert them; installing smoke alarms and fire extinguishers may save your house from the flames. So stay watchful and alert. Here are some questions you should ask and answer on a regular basis.

1. Are your loved ones happy with the life you've got? People who assume their families are happy simply because they are often precipitate breakups, showdowns, and long-term resentment. You're not the only one in the promised land.
2. Is technology transforming areas of work and daily life that affect you? People who were working in slide-rule factories at the dawn of the computer age either got out fast or experienced an unwelcome shock.
3. Do you and your loved ones have regular medical and dental checkups? I know they're a bummer, but far less so than a major health crisis.
4. Are there any useful life skills you have yet to master? Plumbing, paperwork, investment strategies? I had one client who was charged with tax evasion

because he failed to report $200,000 of his annual income. "How was I sup-posed to keep track of *every little check?*" he fumed. By paying attention and fearing for his freedom, that's how. Once you're in Square Four, you'll have time to get around to learning all that stuff you've always known you should learn. Do it.

5. Are you harboring any emotional garbage? Often, Square Four allows people their first opportunity to deal with old emotional wounds, which pop up like submerged beach balls as soon as there is time and safety. If this happens to you, get a therapist, write your memoirs, or do whatever else it takes to process the feelings. Otherwise, you'll mess up Square Four.

6. Do you feel any restless stirrings from your essential self? Often, for no other reason than that it is time, you will feel an urge to try something new or change direction. Don't fight it.

7. Are new opportunities cropping up in your environment? Square Four makes an excellent launching ground. If something or somebody really spectacular comes along and you feel yourself drawn in that direction, go—even if it means moving on to a new Square One.

EXERCISE TWO:
REPEAT THE SQUARE FOUR MANTRA

The Square Four Mantra is:

"Everything is changing, and that's okay."

Say it to yourself often in Square Four. It may worry you, but it doesn't have to—after all, it's true whether you acknowledge it or not.

The phrase "This too shall pass" was supposedly designed by the wise adviser of an Indian prince. The prince had asked for something that would make him feel sad when he was happy, and happy when he was sad. To be aware of change is to remain conscious of both happi-ness and sadness, at all times. It means opening yourself to what Zorba called "the whole catastrophe," the array of wildly mixed emotions and experiences available to us. It means we don't have a moment without joy or a moment without the compassion that comes from suffering. Try to arrange your life so that you can't see one side or the other and you'll soon be shoved out of the promised land into Square One. The part of reality you've decided to ignore will creep up on you when you least expect it, and *boom!* There will go all your tidy plans for the future. And of course, that will be okay too.

EXERCISE THREE: BE LIKE WATER FLOWING

I recently gave a luncheon speech to a group of professional artists and writers, most of whom were in their seventies or older. I thought the event would be one long, dull endurance event, so I steeled myself to be politely attentive. When I sat down at the lunch table, the woman beside me immediately started talking about her dog, whom she'd inherited from another owner. "He called the other day and asked to talk to the dog," the woman said. "I told him he couldn't talk to her. She was on the other line." Things just got better from there. This party full of white-haired seniors was more vibrant and interesting than any of the self-consciously wild-and-crazy mixers I attended in college. Every artist at that luncheon had lived many years, but there wasn't an old person in the room.

If you leave a puddle of water standing for a few days, it will become poisonous and nasty, ridden with algae and bug larvae. On the other hand, you can get fresh, clean drinking water from a spring that has been running for a thousand years. People who refuse to change are stagnant and old by their twenties. People who actually *pursue* change are guaranteed to die young. They are like flowing water, forever refreshed and refreshing.

Studies show that children are born with high levels of "fluid intelligence," which makes them compulsively curious and great at acquiring new skills. As we age, we store an ever-increasing amount of "crystallized intelligence," or fixed information that enables us to function effectively in situations we've seen before. At a certain point (I heard one scientist speculate that the age was approximately twenty-three) most people have enough crystallized intelligence to make further learning unnecessary for survival. They stop using as much fluid intelligence, and their ability to learn declines. However, people who continue to confront unfamiliar situations and learn new things maintain higher levels of fluid intelligence, while their crystallized intelligence base also continues to grow.

To be like water flowing, you have to relax into every experience that comes your way. If you want to keep your good memory, creativity, and analytical edge, keep putting yourself into situations that flummox you. When Square Four starts to feel so comfortable it lacks a sense of challenge, take up something you can't do *at all,* like auto repair or the Finnish language. Build your own laser or log cabin. Write a novel and self-publish it on the Internet. List five things you'd like to know how to do and do one a year for five years. In the meantime, stay open to things that pop up on your radar screen before you've even considered trying them. Flow into every nook and cranny, every possibility that opens in your life. You'll be young for a hundred years.

AND FINALLY . . .

All of the advice in this book boils down to just one thing: You are designed with the ability to find the life you were meant to live. I can't do it for you. Neither can your mother, your lover, your religious leader, or anyone else. The instructions in this book are worth exactly nothing unless they help you free yourself from all instructions and come to trust yourself. I urge you to—please!—dismiss out of hand anything I've written that doesn't resonate with your sense of truth. No one but you has the ability to find your own North Star, and no one but you has the power to keep you from finding it. No one.

The journey through mortality will take you all over the place. You'll go through career phases, successes, and disappointments. You'll love and hate, rage and plead, suffer and enjoy. It's a long trip, and the terrain is spectacularly varied. The one thing that will never change is that always, in every single moment, your nature will be urging you to notice the still, bright point of light that leads you toward your destiny. The compasses inside you will always be pointing the right way, even if you forget to check them, even if you fail for a while to hold your course. You can begin again at any moment, and the instant you turn back toward true north, every mistake you've made and every minute you've spent following the wrong path will become the raw material of wisdom, compassion, and joy.

Lao-tzu said, "The master travels all day without ever leaving home." This is true two ways: If you are following your own North Star, your body can roam the world while you remain steadfastly centered in one spot; or you can have the wildest, most adventurous journey without moving at all. Dante's trip to Paradise was incredibly long and eventful, though it took place entirely in his mind and heart. The stars he saw as he emerged from the Inferno were within him, too. For you, as for him, your own North Star is not a place but a state of being. It is the state in which you are fully—and only—yourself. You may cover a million miles on the way, but ultimately you will come to see that all along, your own North Star has been, simply, you. You are the best destination you could possibly imagine or experience. Welcome home.

INDEX

dreaming and scheming phase of,
249–250, 286–314

failing to recognize, 257–259

hero's saga phase of, 250–252, 315–339

map of, 245

negotiating with metalearning,
261–262

pitfalls in, 260–261

Spencer, Diana, and, 252–253

Chaos, change cycle and, 257

Checklists. *See* Exercises

Cheerleaders, as fan club, 94

Chemicals, body imbalances and, 113

"Climbing back into your body" exercise,
112–115

Clinical depression, 183. *See also* Grief

Clothing, in dreaming and scheming
phase of change, 291

Coincidences. *See* Intuition

Communication
of painful events, 148

recognizing messages from body,
120–135

Companionship, pleasure in, 48–50

Company Men, 13

Compare and contrast exercise
evaluating your generalized other,
87–89

on feedback and self-perception,
83–87

on how individuals make you feel,
87–89

Compass, internal, xv

Compassion, for emotional wounds,
153–155

Confrontations
avoiding moralizing in, 202–203

describing consequences of inaction,
204–207

with people causing anger, 199–203

speaking of firsthand experience, 201

telling other person what you want,
203–204

using examples to support generalities,
200, 201

Connection Questions Quiz, 14–16

Contentment, experiencing, 354–357

Cool anger, 199–200

Creativity, in dreaming and scheming
phase of change, 290–291

Csikszentmihalyi, Mihaly, 57

Cues. *See* Body

Cultures. *See also* Generalized other
of organizations, 74–75

thresholds of change by, 280–281

Cycle of change. *See* Change cycle

Danger, avoiding, 66

Dante Alighieri, journey of, xiii, xiv, xvi

Death segment of death and rebirth phase
of change, 248–249, 263–285

letting go of old identity, 266–268

surviving the death segment, 265–273

threshold of, 273–281

type of catalytic event and, 268–273

De Becker, Gavin, 175–176

"Defrosting of dreams" exercise, 298–301

Depression, 183. *See also* Grief; "No"
(ways of saying)

Descartes, René, 109

Desire(s)
describing in confrontation, 203–204

vs. fear, 178–179

finding ways to achieve, 168–171

framing of, 165–168

hope and, 287

knowledge of, 110–111

Despair. *See* Emotional wounds

Destiny
intuition about, 231

sense of, 226–227

Diana, Princess. *See* Spencer, Diana

Dieting, body image and, 104–105

Disconnected self, 1–16

Discredit, of generalized other, 99–100

Divine Comedy, The (Dante Alighieri), xiii, xiv

Divine decadence, oversupplying oneself as, 349–350

"Doing without doing," 9–11

Do One Thing Different (O'Hanlon), 333

Dreaming and scheming phase of change, 249–250, 286–314. *See also* Dreams

  avoiding pain of failed dreams, 298–301

  changing appearance in, 291

  connecting with dreams exercise, 296–297

  creativity in, 290–291

  "defrosting of dreams" exercise in, 298–301

  dreamtime segment of, 292–294

  happiness in, 288–289

  imagination and, 294–295

  interview game exercise, 301–302

  laughter in, 288–289

  remodeling, redecorating, or renovating living space in, 291–292

  removing limitations and, 296–302

  scheming segment of, 307–314

  self-discovery in, 288–289

  symptoms of, 287–292

  transition to reality and, 302–306

Dreams. *See also* Change; Dreaming and scheming phase of change

  change cycle and, 257–258

  detailed schemes for, 321

  fulfilling, 250–254

  limiting of, 294–295

  of Spencer, Diana (Princess of Wales), 252–253

  of Winfrey, Oprah, 254–255

Dreamtime segment, of dreaming and scheming phase of change, 292–294

Eating disorders, 104

Education, generalized other and, 72–73

Eliot, T. S., 240

Emotion(s). *See also* Emotional wounds; Feelings

  anger as, 192–208

  experiencing joy as, 352–354

  fake, 174–175

  fear as, 173–182

  grief as, 182–192

  intuition and, 230–231

  joy as, 208–218

  use of four basic, 174–175

  using for change, 172–173

Emotional healing, 151–153

Emotional injuries. *See* Emotional wounds

Emotional intelligence, saying "yes" to essential self and, 48–50

Emotional wounds, 138–156

  accepting compassion for, 153–155

  aftermath of healing, 156–158

  dependence on, 158

  fear of removal, 143

  figuring out what hurt you, 144–146

  finding audience for, 146–150

  forgiving, 157–158

  grieving process and, 155–156

  healing of, 151–153

  removing, 143–156

  testing for, 141–142

  time for healing, 155–156

  treating, 142–156

  truth of event and, 150–153

Empathy, 49

Energy

  draining of, 21–23

  from saying "yes" to essential self, 41–43

Essential self, 2–4, 7. *See also* "No" (ways of saying)

  characteristics of, 4

Future
    anticipation of, 276–277
    intuition about, 231–234
Future vision, 287–288
    interview game and, 301

Generalized anxiety, 93–94
Generalized other, 60–62. *See also*
        Subconscious
    alternative voices as, 81–83
    conception of, 59–60
    creating omnipotent others, 81
    developing self-perceptions and, 75–76,
        77–79
    exchanging for new version, 61–62
    family as, 68–70
    generalized other and, 60–62
    groups as, 67–75
    identifying own conception of, 62–67
    ideological training and, 71–72
    media culture as, 70–71
    organizations as, 74–75
    peers as, 73–74
    pleasing, 75–76
    school experiences as, 72–73
    strategies for exchanging, 89–103
Gestures, identifying, 120–121
Gift of Fear, The (De Becker), 175–176
Giveaways, satisfaction through, 350–352
Goals. *See also* Hero's saga phase of
        change
    articulating unconscious, 233–234
    flow chart for meeting, 313–314
    meeting, 340–365
    process of meeting, 317–320
    rethinking, 330–332
    steps to meeting, 320–325
    visualizing, 303
    wildly improbable, 304–306
Goldberg, Natalie, 227

Grief, 174–175, 182–192. *See also*
        Grieving process
    authenticity of feelings, 183–184
    comforting activities for, 190
    dealing with, 182–192
    depression and, 183–184
    identifying and honoring loss,
        184–185
    losses and gains of, 190–192
    place for, 188–189
    for something irreplaceable, 187–190
    survival tools for, 188–190
    time for, 189–190
    using for change, 174–175
Grieving process. *See also* Grief
    for emotional wounds, 155–156
    lessening of, 293
    options for dealing with, 185–187
Group psychology, on perception of
        generalized other, 81–83
Groups
    family as generalized other, 68–70
    as generalized other, 67–75
    ideological training by, 71–72
    media culture as generalized other,
        70–71
    organizations as generalized other,
        74–75
    peers as generalized other, 73–74
    schools as generalized other, 72–73
Guilt, after opportunity catalyst, 271

Hair, changing in dreaming and scheming
        phase of change, 291
Happiness. *See also* Joy
    determining requirements for, 165–168
    in dreaming and scheming phase of
        change, 288–289
    "one way" to, 358–359
"Happy talk," 40–54

Index   *379*

"Yes" (getting to), 38–58. *See also* "No" (ways of saying)
   best-case scenarios for, 56–57
   emotional intelligence and, 48–50
   energy from, 41–43
   good mood from, 52–54
   "happy talk" and, 40–54
   health from, 43–45
   memory and, 46–47
   romantic attraction and, 50–52
   time and involvement in activities, 47–48